Mastering MySQL Database

From Basics to Expert Proficiency

Contents

Introduction

MySQL, an open-source relational database management system (RDBMS), is an indispensable tool for developers, database administrators, and organizations worldwide. This book, titled "Mastering MySQL Database: From Basics to Expert Proficiency," is devised to provide a thorough understanding of MySQL, equipping readers with the knowledge required to employ MySQL effectively across a range of applications.

The objective of this book is not merely to cover the theoretical aspects of MySQL but to delve into practical, real-world applications. This pragmatic approach ensures that you gain hands-on experience in crafting efficient, scalable, and secure databases. The book is thoughtfully structured into distinct chapters, each focusing on a core aspect of MySQL, facilitating a progressive and comprehensive learning experience.

Initially, we will begin with an "Introduction to MySQL," aiming to familiarize readers with the fundamental concepts, historical context, architectural overview, and key features of MySQL. This foundational chapter lays the groundwork for understanding the subsequent, more intricate topics.

Following the introduction, the chapter "Installing and Configuring MySQL" will guide you through the process of setting up MySQL on various operating systems, including Windows, Linux, and macOS. This chapter also covers essential post-installation configurations and basic administration tasks.

The subsequent chapters, "Basic SQL Queries" and "Advanced SQL Queries," delve into the core functionality of MySQL—querying and manipulating data. Beginning with fundamental operations such as SELECT, INSERT, UPDATE, and DELETE, these chapters progress into advanced querying techniques, including subqueries, joins, and window functions, ensuring a robust comprehension of SQL.

Understanding the principles of "Database Design and Normalization" is crucial for creating efficient and relationally sound databases. This chapter imparts essential knowledge on database schema design, defining relationships, and applying normalization rules to eliminate redundancy and improve data integrity.

Stored procedures and functions play a vital role in encapsulating business logic within the database. The chapter "Stored Procedures and Functions" explores creating, executing, and managing these programmable objects in MySQL, highlighting their importance in optimizing performance and ensuring consistency.

Performance often determines the success of database-driven applications. The "Indexes and Performance Tuning" chapter provides insights into the creation and management of indexes, query optimization strategies, and various performance tuning techniques, empowering you to enhance the efficiency of MySQL databases.

Transactional integrity and concurrent access control are paramount in multi-user database environments. The chapter "Transactions and Concurrency" addresses transactional principles, ACID properties, isolation levels, and concurrency control mechanisms, ensuring data consistency and reliability.

In an era where data breaches capture headlines, securing your MySQL database is non-negotiable. The chapter "Security and User Management" explores methods to create secure user accounts, manage privileges, and implement robust security measures to protect your data against unauthorized access and vulnerabilities.

Finally, no database management discussion is complete without addressing data preservation. The chapter "Backup and Recovery" covers essential strategies for creating reliable backups, restoring data, and planning for disaster recovery, ensuring the durability and availability of your data.

By the end of this book, you will have traversed the landscape of MySQL, equipped with the knowledge and skills necessary to design, implement, and manage robust database systems. Your journey through the pages of "Mastering MySQL Database: From Basics to Expert Proficiency" promises to elevate your proficiency and confidence in leveraging MySQL to its fullest potential.

In every chapter, practical examples, exercises, and best practices are provided to reinforce learning and enable you to apply the concepts in real-world scenarios. This approach ensures that you not only understand theoretical aspects but also gain pragmatic skills that you can translate into tangible outcomes in your professional or personal projects.

Chapter 1

Introduction to MySQL

This chapter provides an overview of MySQL, covering its definition, historical evolution, and the reasons for its widespread adoption. It explains the fundamental architecture and key features of MySQL, along with its various editions and licensing options. Basic terminology and concepts related to relational databases are introduced, culminating in practical introductions to using the MySQL Command Line Client and MySQL Workbench.

1.1 What is MySQL?

MySQL is an open-source relational database management system (RDBMS) that facilitates the structured storage, retrieval, and management of data using a combination of tables, schemas, and specific query languages such as SQL (Structured Query Language). It provides a multi-user environment that allows multiple people to access and manage databases concurrently, using a server-client architecture. The system adheres to the principles of the relational model proposed by E. F. Codd, offering a comprehensive and powerful means of maintaining and manipulating data.

MySQL is designed with a focus on robustness, efficiency, and ease of use. Written in C and C++, it is highly optimized for performance, accommodating a variety of storage engines to manage data persistence. Among its most celebrated features are its transaction processing capabilities, support for foreign keys, and the use of indexes to expedite data retrieval.

The server-client architecture of MySQL is primarily composed of the MySQL server, which handles all database instructions, and various client applications that interface with the server to perform database operations. The MySQL server runs as a background service that continues to operate irrespective of the client interfaces, managing all database creation, querying, updates, and deletions. The client applications range from command-line tools to graphical user interfaces (GUIs), all designed to facilitate interaction with the MySQL server.

One key aspect of understanding MySQL involves comprehending the basics of its operational model. A typical MySQL setup includes the following components:

- **MySQL Server:** The core database engine that runs on the server machine, processing requests and managing database files.
- **Client Applications:** Programs or interfaces through which users interact with the MySQL server. These applications can submit SQL queries, retrieve results, and interact with the database in a user-friendly manner.
- **Connector/Driver:** Middleware that facilitates communication between client applications and the MySQL server, enabling the transmission of SQL queries and the reception of results.
- **Storage Engines:** Modular components within MySQL that manage how data is stored and retrieved on the disk. Prominent examples include InnoDB and MyISAM, each offering different features like transaction support, foreign key constraints, and full-text indexing.

```
SELECT * FROM employees WHERE department = 'Sales';
```

To illustrate, the given SQL query retrieves all records from the employees table where the department column equals 'Sales'. The query is transmitted from a client application to the MySQL server, where it is parsed, executed, and results are returned to the client.

```
+-------------+------------+-----------+------------+
| employee_id | first_name | last_name| department|
+-------------+------------+-----------+------------+
| 1           | John       | Doe       | Sales      |
| 2           | Jane       | Smith     | Sales      |
+-------------+------------+-----------+------------+
```

In terms of usage, MySQL supports a variety of operating systems, including Linux, Windows, macOS, and various UNIX variants, making it versatile and adaptable to many environments.

It is worth noting that MySQL offers different editions catering to different needs. The Community Edition is available at no cost and is open-source, making it particularly suitable for individual developers and educational purposes. In contrast, the Enterprise Edition provides additional features such as advanced security measures, scalability tools, and round-the-clock technical support, making it more suitable for large organizations and mission-critical applications.

Moreover, MySQL is renowned for its compatibility with numerous programming languages and development frameworks, including but not limited to PHP, Java, Python, and .NET. This compatibility is largely facilitated by connectors/drivers that provide seamless database connectivity.

Thus, MySQL is not merely a database solution but a comprehensive platform supporting a broad spectrum of use cases, from simple web applications to sophisticated data-driven enterprise applications. By adhering to standards and continuously evolving through community contributions and professional enhancements, MySQL maintains a pivotal role in modern database management.

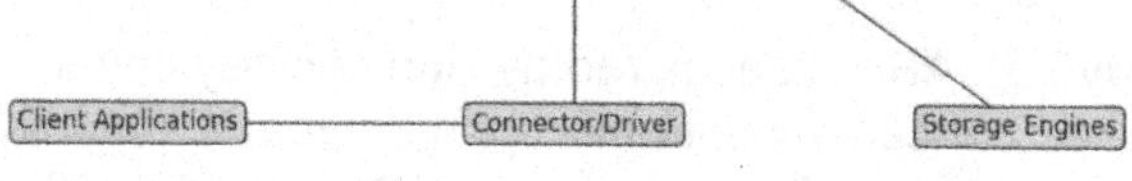

1.2 History of MySQL

MySQL, a powerful and widely-used relational database management system (RDBMS), has a rich history that reflects its evolution and impact on database technologies. Understanding this historical context can provide valuable insight into why MySQL has become a cornerstone in the realm of data management.

MySQL was initially conceived and developed by a Swedish company named MySQL AB. The company was founded by David Axmark, Allan Larsson, and Michael "Monty" Widenius in 1995. The trio had a vision to create a free, open-source database management system that was reliable, scalable, and efficient.

The first version of MySQL was released on May 23, 1995. This version was based on the mSQL (mini SQL) framework, but significant improvements were made to provide better performance and features. Monty Widenius and his team rewrote much of the original code, and the new system was named after Monty's daughter, My. Consequently, the name "MySQL" was chosen to symbolize both a personal connection and an SQL-based database system.

MySQL quickly gained popularity due to its open-source nature and its performance advantages over other databases available at the time. The willingness of the developers to listen to user feedback and incorporate suggestions into subsequent versions played a critical role in its early adoption.

By 2000, MySQL had established itself as a reliable database management system with a rapidly growing user base. The release of version 3.23 in January 2001 marked a significant milestone by including essential features such as support for InnoDB storage engine, full-text indexing, and replication. These enhancements ensured that MySQL could be used for a wider range of applications, from small personal projects to large enterprise environments.

In 2008, MySQL AB was acquired by Sun Microsystems, a move that initially raised concerns within the open-source community about the potential commercial influence over MySQL. However, Sun Microsystems assured users of their commitment to keeping MySQL open-source and continued its development under this philosophy. The acquisition also provided MySQL with more resources and a broader distribution channel, further accelerating its growth and adoption.

The landscape shifted again in 2010 when Oracle Corporation acquired

Sun Microsystems, including all its assets such as MySQL. This acquisition caused significant apprehension, given Oracle's competing RDBMS product line. Contestations revolved around the future of MySQL's open-source status and its development direction. Under Oracle's stewardship, MySQL has continued to evolve, although the open-source community has kept a close watch on these developments. Despite these concerns, Oracle has maintained MySQL's dual-licensing model, offering both an open-source version and a commercial enterprise version.

The open-source community also responded by developing forks of MySQL to ensure an open and independent path for its development. The most notable of these forks is MariaDB, created by Monty Widenius in response to the Oracle acquisition. MariaDB aims to maintain a high level of compatibility with MySQL while providing performance improvements and additional features.

Since then, MySQL has seen continuous development and numerous version releases. Each new version introduces enhancements, offering improved performance, better security, and new features. For instance, the release of MySQL 8.0 in 2018 was a significant leap forward, providing a host of new capabilities such as a transactional data dictionary, JSON improvements, and common table expressions (CTEs).

Throughout its evolution, MySQL has maintained a strong focus on maintaining backward compatibility, ensuring that applications developed for older versions can run on newer versions with minimal changes. This commitment has fostered a robust ecosystem of applications and tools that depend on MySQL, thereby cementing its role as a critical component in many technological stacks.

Understanding the history of MySQL provides a framework for appreciating the ongoing efforts by both corporate stakeholders and the open-source community to enhance and sustain its development. This collaboration ensures MySQL remains a relevant and reliable RDBMS choice for many users and applications around the world.

1.3 Why Use MySQL?

MySQL stands out as a preferred relational database management system (RDBMS) for developers, database administrators, and organizations across the globe for various compelling reasons. Its widespread adoption is driven by a combination of performance, reliability, scalability, and an extensive feature set that meets the needs of both beginners and experienced professionals. This section delineates the principal reasons that advocate the usage of MySQL.

Performance: MySQL is renowned for its high performance and efficiency even under substantial loads. It employs a multi-threaded architecture enabling concurrent query processing, which significantly improves response times for complex and large-scale database applications. Furthermore, MySQL supports several storage engines such as InnoDB and MyISAM, allowing users to optimize performance based on specific application requirements. Benchmark tests have consistently demonstrated MySQL's superior performance in transaction processing and read-heavy operations.

Reliability and Durability: Reliability is a critical factor for any database system, and MySQL delivers it through advanced features like ACID (Atomicity, Consistency, Isolation, Durability) compliance, transactions, and commit/rollback mechanisms. InnoDB, the default storage engine for MySQL, ensures data durability through its robust crash recovery capabilities and support for foreign key constraints. MySQL performs automatic data integrity checks, providing assurance that data remains uncorrupted and consistent.

Open Source and Cost-Effectiveness: MySQL is released under the GNU General Public License (GPL), making it free to download, use, and modify. This open-source nature allows developers and organizations to adapt the software according to their specific needs without incurring the high costs associated with proprietary database systems. MySQL's community edition is widely used in production environments where cost savings are crucial without compromising on quality and performance.

Scalability and Flexibility: MySQL exhibits exceptional scalability, essential for applications ranging from small-scale start-ups to large-scale enterprise operations. It can handle a wide range of data volumes, from a few gigabytes to several terabytes, without a notable drop in performance. MySQL's architecture supports vertical and horizontal scaling, providing flexibility to scale up or scale-out based on system demands. Additionally, its support for replication and sharding facilitates the distribution of data across multiple servers, further enhancing scalability.

Security: MySQL includes robust security features to safeguard data, with support for advanced encryption techniques, authentication protocols, and fine-grained privileges. Administrators can configure user permissions at granular levels, ensuring that only authorized users have access to sensitive data. MySQL's secure communication channels (SSL/TLS) protect data during transmission, mitigating risks associated with data breaches and unauthorized access.

Comprehensive Support and Active Community: MySQL benefits from an active and expansive community of developers, users, and contributors who continuously enhance and support the platform. This extensive community-driven support ensures that users can readily access a wealth of resources, including documentation, forums, tutorials, and troubleshooting guides. Moreover, Oracle Corporation provides professional support services, training, and consultancy for MySQL, ensuring that enterprise users have access to expert assistance when needed.

Compatibility and Integration: MySQL is highly compatible with various operating systems, including Linux, Windows, and macOS, and it supports numerous programming languages such as Java, PHP, Python, and C++. This compatibility simplifies integration with existing applications and systems, making MySQL a versatile choice for diverse development environments. Additionally, MySQL's support for standard SQL along with proprietary extensions enhances its utility in handling complex queries and interactions with other database systems.

Ease of Use: MySQL is designed with simplicity and user-friendliness in mind, providing tools like MySQL Workbench that offer intuitive graphical interfaces for database design, administration, and querying. The MySQL Command Line Client also caters to users who prefer scripting and direct interaction with the database server. Extensive documentation and community resources make it easier for newcomers to learn and utilize MySQL effectively.

Extensibility: MySQL supports plugins and custom storage engines, enabling users to extend its functionality beyond the default capabilities. This extensibility allows for the incorporation of specific functionalities tailored to unique application requirements. MySQL's dynamic loading of plugins means that new features can be added without necessitating a complete system restart, thereby enhancing the database's adaptability and uptime.

```
SELECT * FROM employees WHERE status = 'active';
```

```
+-------+----------+------------------+
| emp_id| emp_name | status           |
+-------+----------+------------------+
|     1 | Alice    | active           |
|     2 | Bob      | active           |
+-------+----------+------------------+
```

MySQL's array of strengths cement its status as a robust, versatile, and reliable RDBMS, making it an ideal choice for a wide range of database applications.

1.4 MySQL Architecture Overview

MySQL architecture consists of several components designed to optimize performance and maintain flexibility. These components collectively ensure data integrity, efficient queries, and concurrent access to the database. Central to understanding MySQL's architecture are the concepts of the *Storage Engine*, *Query Processing*, *Connections Management*, and the *Cache and Buffer Manager*.

Storage Engine Layer

The Storage Engine Layer is responsible for the mechanism of data storage and retrieval. It handles the reading and writing operations to the actual storage mediums. MySQL supports multiple storage engines, such as *InnoDB* and *MyISAM*, each tailored for specific workloads. Configuring the appropriate storage engine for database tables is crucial as it directly impacts performance, transactional capabilities, and data integrity features. For instance, InnoDB supports ACID-compliant transactions and row-level locking, making it suitable for high-concurrency applications. MyISAM, on the other hand, provides faster read operations but only supports table-level locking, which may become a bottleneck under high write loads.

Query Processing

Query Processing is at the core of the MySQL architecture. It involves parsing, optimizing, and executing SQL queries. When a query is issued, the MySQL server first parses the SQL statement to validate its syntax. This is followed by the optimization phase, where the query optimizer determines the most efficient way to execute the query. The optimizer evaluates various execution plans and selects one with the least cost in terms of I/O operations and CPU usage. The execution phase involves retrieving the requested data using the chosen execution plan and applying any necessary transformations stipulated by the SQL command.

Consider a scenario where an SQL query retrieves data from multiple tables using a join operation. The optimizer might choose to execute a nested-loop join or a hash join based on the table sizes, indexes, and data distribution statistics. The ability to choose the most efficient strategy significantly affects query performance.

Connections Management

Connections Management in MySQL handles client connections and query requests. The MySQL server creates a connection thread for each client connection. These threads manage the interaction between the client and the server. MySQL uses a thread-per-connection model by default, which provides each client with an isolated thread to handle requests. However, this model can lead to increased overhead under high concurrency because each thread consumes system resources.

The MySQL Thread Pool plugin addresses high-scalability needs by implementing a thread pool mechanism, which efficiently manages a limited number of threads to serve a large number of client connections. The thread pool dynamically allocates threads to handle client requests, thus optimizing resource utilization and improving overall performance on multi-core systems.

Cache and Buffer Manager

The Cache and Buffer Manager plays a vital role in enhancing the performance of MySQL databases. It includes components like the *Query Cache*, *InnoDB Buffer Pool*, and other memory structures designed to reduce disk I/O and accelerate query response times.

The Query Cache stores the results of SELECT queries along with their respective query strings. If an identical query is received, MySQL can circumvent query parsing and optimization phases by directly returning the cached result, assuming the underlying data has not changed. Note that modifications to tables referenced in cached queries invalidate the corresponding cache entries.

The InnoDB Buffer Pool is a critical component of the InnoDB storage engine, functioning as a cache for data and index pages. When data is read from disk, it is cached in the buffer pool. Subsequent reads from the same pages can access memory directly, significantly improving read performance. This buffer pool also caches modified data until it is flushed to disk, enhancing transactional write performance by consolidating multiple disk I/O operations.

Here's an example to illustrate the integration of these components. Suppose we have two tables, users and orders, stored with InnoDB:

```
CREATE TABLE users (
  id INT AUTO_INCREMENT PRIMARY KEY,
  username VARCHAR(255) NOT NULL,
```

```
    email VARCHAR(255) NOT NULL
) ENGINE = InnoDB;

CREATE TABLE orders (
    order_id INT AUTO_INCREMENT PRIMARY KEY,
    user_id INT,
    order_date DATE,
    amount DECIMAL(10, 2),
    FOREIGN KEY(user_id) REFERENCES users(id)
) ENGINE = InnoDB;
```

When a complex query is executed, such as:

```
SELECT u.username, COUNT(o.order_id) as total_orders
FROM users u
LEFT JOIN orders o ON u.id = o.user_id
GROUP BY u.id;
```

The query processing component will parse and optimize the query. The optimization phase determines the most efficient way to perform the join and grouping operations. If results from previous similar queries exist in the Query Cache, the server may directly return those results, avoiding the need for re-execution.

During query execution, data pages for the users and orders tables are read into the InnoDB Buffer Pool, reducing the need for disk access if the same data is queried again. The Connection Manager ensures each client's request is handled efficiently, whether using individual threads or via the Thread Pool.

The seamless integration of these architectural components allows MySQL to perform effectively across different use cases—from high-read environments typical in web applications to write-intensive transactional systems. Understanding this architecture enables database administrators to leverage MySQL's full capabilities, fine-tuning performance and reliability according to application requirements.

1.5 Key Features of MySQL

MySQL offers a wide array of features, encompassing performance optimization, security measures, scalability, and ease of use. These attributes have made it a predominant choice among relational database management systems (RDBMS). This section delves into the critical features that set MySQL apart from its counterparts.

Performance and Scalability: MySQL is renowned for its high-performance capabilities. Its architecture is optimized for speed, managing high volumes of data without compromising efficiency. MySQL employs a host of performance-enhancing mechanisms such as indexing, optimized storage engines, and query caching. Indexes are fundamental to database performance. An index in MySQL drastically reduces the amount of data that needs to be scanned when executing a query. The following example illustrates how to create an index on a table:

```
CREATE INDEX idx_user_name ON users (name);
```

In addition to indexing, MySQL supports multiple storage engines like InnoDB and MyISAM, each suitable for different use cases. InnoDB, the default storage engine, supports ACID-compliant transactions and foreign keys, enhancing performance for complex transactional applications. Below is the command to create a table employing InnoDB:

```
CREATE TABLE orders (
    order_id INT AUTO_INCREMENT,
    order_date DATE,
    customer_id INT,
    PRIMARY KEY (order_id)
) ENGINE=InnoDB;
```

Security: MySQL incorporates various security features including user authentication, privilege management, and SSL support. User authentication verifies the identity of users accessing the database, ensuring that only authorized entities can interact with the data. The example below demonstrates creating a user with specific privileges:

```
CREATE USER 'admin'@'localhost' IDENTIFIED BY 'password';
GRANT ALL PRIVILEGES ON database_name.* TO 'admin'@'localhost';
```

MySQL also supports SSL for encrypting data transmitted between the MySQL server and client, protecting sensitive information from being intercepted during transit.

Replication: MySQL's replication feature is extensively used for increasing data redundancy and improving data high availability. MySQL supports both master-slave and master-master replication. This feature allows data written to the master to be replicated to one or more slave servers, ensuring data consistency across the systems.

High Availability: MySQL ensures high availability through several mechanisms, including clustering and automated failover. MySQL Group Replication allows the creation of a fault-tolerant system where the service continues to run even if some of the nodes fail. In addition, MySQL's InnoDB Cluster offers an integrated, native high-availability solution, which provides automatic failover using InnoDB as its storage engine.

Support for Large Data Volumes: MySQL is designed to handle a large number of concurrent users and high transaction rates. This is particularly beneficial for applications like e-commerce sites or banking systems which have heavy read and write operations.

SQL Standards Compliance: MySQL adheres to standard SQL (Structured Query Language) ensuring compatibility and ease of use for individuals familiar with SQL. MySQL also extends SQL with unique functionalities such as JSON support, allowing for efficient handling of semi-structured data.

Extensibility: MySQL is highly extensible, supporting custom storage engines and plugins to enhance functionality tailored to specific use cases. The following command exemplifies adding a plugin to MySQL:

```
INSTALL PLUGIN my_plugin SONAME 'my_plugin.so';
```

User-Friendly Interface: MySQL offers various interfaces like the MySQL Command Line Client and graphical tools like MySQL Workbench, making database management straightforward. MySQL Workbench provides an intuitive visual environment for database design, SQL development, and server administration.

Community and Enterprise Editions: MySQL offers both Community and Enterprise editions. The Community edition is open-source and freely available, while the Enterprise edition includes additional features such as comprehensive support from Oracle, advanced security features, and performance tuning capabilities.

These features collectively establish MySQL as a versatile, powerful, and widely-adopted relational database management system, catering to a broad range of applications from simple data storage solutions to complex, mission-critical systems.

1.6 MySQL Editions and Licensing

MySQL, a powerful and widely used relational database management system (RDBMS), is available in several editions, each tailored to specific use cases, ranging from small-scale personal projects to large-scale enterprise solutions. Understanding the distinct editions and the associated licensing models is essential for selecting the appropriate version for your needs. This section provides a comprehensive overview of the MySQL Editions and the corresponding licensing options.

MySQL Editions are chiefly categorized into the following:

- **MySQL Community Edition**
- **MySQL Enterprise Edition**
- **MySQL Cluster CGE**
- **MySQL Embedded**

MySQL Community Edition is the freely available and open-source version, under the General Public License (GPL). This edition is ideal for developers, open-source enthusiasts, and small-scale applications. While it receives updates and bug fixes from the MySQL community, it lacks some of the advanced features and technical support offered in the commercial versions.

MySQL Enterprise Edition is a paid, commercial edition providing advanced features, management tools, and plugins that cater to enterprise customers. Some key features exclusive to this edition include:

- **MySQL Enterprise Security**: Enhances data protection with advanced encryption mechanisms and security policies.
- **MySQL Enterprise Scalability**: Supports advanced replication methods and utilities for performing large-scale deployments.
- **MySQL Enterprise High Availability**: Includes MySQL InnoDB Cluster for ensuring data availability and consistency across clustered databases.
- **MySQL Enterprise Backup**: Offers tools for performing efficient, consistent, online backups without interrupting database operations.
- **Technical Support**: Enterprise Edition provides access to 24/7 support from Oracle's technical team, which includes fast response times and extensive problem-solving capabilities.

MySQL Cluster CGE (Carrier Grade Edition) is designed for applications with high throughput and low latency requirements. It is particularly suitable for telecom and network environments. The Carrier

Grade Edition includes all features of the MySQL Enterprise Edition, with additional robust support for distributed, ACID-compliant processing, making it apt for real-time applications needing high availability.

MySQL Embedded is tailored for Independent Software Vendors (ISVs) who need to embed MySQL within their own products. This edition allows for seamless integration and requires a separate commercial license. It is optimized to be lightweight, easy to manage, and capable of running on various platforms and devices.

Licensing is an essential aspect when considering MySQL. The licensing options are broadly categorized into:

1. GPL (General Public License)

- The MySQL Community Edition is distributed under the GPL, allowing users to run, study, share, and modify the software.
- GPL mandates that any derivative work or distribution must also be released under the GPL license.
- Ideal for open-source projects where GPL license compatibility is required.

2. Commercial License

- MySQL Enterprise Edition, MySQL Cluster CGE, and MySQL Embedded typically require a commercial license.
- A commercial license grants the user the ability to integrate and distribute closed-source derivative works without the obligation to disclose the source.
- Commercial licenses come with Oracle's support services and are often preferred by enterprises needing reliable technical support and advanced features.

Choosing between the GPL and a commercial license depends largely on the intended use case. For independent, non-commercial projects, the Community Edition under GPL provides all the fundamental functionalities needed. However, for mission-critical applications demanding enterprise-level features, technical support, and proprietary rights, opting for a commercial license is more suitable.

Finally, consideration of licensing terms and compliance is crucial, as misuse or infringement can lead to legal repercussions. Ensuring proper license acquisition and adherence helps leverage MySQL's capabilities while respecting intellectual property laws.

Understanding the distinct features and licensing options of MySQL Editions ensures that users can make informed decisions that best align with their technical and commercial requirements, facilitating optimal database performance and compliance.

1.7 Basic MySQL Terminology

Understanding the terminology associated with MySQL is fundamental to effectively utilizing and mastering the database management system. This section elucidates key terminologies that frequently appear in MySQL documentation and usage.

Database Schema: A schema in MySQL refers to the structure of a database, encompassing tables, views, indexes, and other relevant elements. It defines how data is organized and how the relationships among data are managed. The SQL command used to create a schema is CREATE SCHEMA or CREATE DATABASE.

Table: A table is a collection of related data entries organized into rows and columns, with each table in a database having a unique name. The table creation syntax in SQL is straightforward:

```
CREATE TABLE table_name (
    column1 datatype constraints,
    column2 datatype constraints,
    ...
);
```

Column: Each table consists of columns, with each column representing a particular attribute of the data. Columns have data types (e.g., INT, VARCHAR, DATE) that define the nature of the data they can hold. Constraints like NOT NULL, UNIQUE, PRIMARY KEY, etc., can be applied to columns to enforce data integrity.

Row: A row, also known as a record or tuple, represents a single, implicitly structured data item in a table. The number of rows in a table grows as new data is inserted. Each column in the row contains data corresponding to that column's attribute.

Primary Key: A primary key is a column, or a set of columns, that uniquely identifies each row in a table. A table can have only one primary key, which ensures the uniqueness and existence of data entries.

The primary key is defined at the time of table creation:

```
CREATE TABLE table_name (
    id INT NOT NULL PRIMARY KEY,
    column1 datatype constraints,
    ...
);
```

Foreign Key: A foreign key is a column or set of columns in one table that uniquely identifies rows in another table. It establishes and enforces a link between the data in the two tables, ensuring referential integrity. A foreign key is defined as follows:

```
CREATE TABLE child_table (
    id INT NOT NULL,
    parent_id INT,
    FOREIGN KEY (parent_id) REFERENCES parent_table(id)
);
```

Index: An index is a data structure that improves the speed of data retrieval operations on a database table at the cost of additional storage space and additional time required for insert and update operations. Indexes are created on columns that are frequently searched against:

```
CREATE INDEX index_name
ON table_name (column_name);
```

View: A view is a virtual table composed of a SQL query's result set. Views encapsulate the complexity of a query and present simplified data to users. Views are created using:

```
CREATE VIEW view_name AS
SELECT column1, column2, ...
FROM table_name
WHERE condition;
```

Stored Procedure: A stored procedure is a precompiled collection of one or more SQL statements stored under a name and processed as a unit. Stored procedures can accept parameters and be executed on demand using:

```
CREATE PROCEDURE procedure_name (parameters)
BEGIN
    SQL statements;
END;
```

Trigger: A trigger is a special type of stored procedure that automatically runs when certain events occur in the database. Common events include INSERT, UPDATE, or DELETE. Triggers are defined by specifying the event and the associated SQL statements:

```
CREATE TRIGGER trigger_name
BEFORE INSERT ON table_name
FOR EACH ROW
BEGIN
    SQL statements;
END;
```

Transaction: A transaction is a sequence of one or more SQL statements that are executed as a single unit of work. Transactions are used to ensure data consistency and integrity by adhering to properties such as atomicity, consistency, isolation, and durability (ACID). Transactions start with the BEGIN statement and end with either COMMIT to save changes or ROLLBACK to discard them:

```
BEGIN;
-- SQL statements
COMMIT; -- Or ROLLBACK;
```

Normalization: Normalization is a process in database design aimed at organizing columns and tables to reduce data redundancy and improve data integrity. There are several normal forms, each with specific rules met sequentially from first normal form (1NF) to fifth normal form (5NF).

Join: A join is an SQL operation for combining columns from one or more tables based on their related columns. Common types of joins include INNER JOIN, LEFT JOIN, RIGHT JOIN, and FULL OUTER JOIN. For example:

```
SELECT A.column1, B.column2
FROM table1 A
INNER JOIN table2 B ON A.common_field = B.common_field;
```

Replication: Replication refers to the process of copying and maintaining database objects, such as tables, in multiple database instances. This enables distributed database systems, enhancing availability and reliability. MySQL supports several replication models, including master-slave and master-master replication.

Familiarity with this basic terminology is essential for anyone working with MySQL, as it provides a foundation for understanding more complex operations and configurations. Each term serves as a building block that, when combined, allows for sophisticated database design and querying capabilities. Additionally, the terms discussed here will frequently reappear throughout this book as we delve deeper into MySQL's functionalities and optimization techniques.

1.8 Understanding Relational Databases

Relational databases constitute a critical component of modern data management practices. The basis of these databases is the relational model, which organizes data into tables, or relations, each consisting of rows and columns. This section delves into the fundamental principles and terminology associated with relational databases, aiming to provide a solid foundation for comprehending more advanced topics in MySQL.

A **relation** (or table) in a relational database is a set of tuples (rows) that each conform to a specific structure determined by attributes (columns). Each row within the table represents a single record, while columns represent the data fields of the records. This tabular structure ensures that the data is organized in a clear, logical manner.

The **schema** of a relational database is the formal definition of the database's structure. It includes the tables, the fields within each table, and the relationships between fields and tables. A schema can be visualized as a blueprint that dictates how data is organized and how the various elements interrelate.

In relational databases, **primary keys** play a crucial role. A primary key is a field, or a combination of fields, that uniquely identifies a record within a table. The uniqueness of primary keys ensures that each record can be distinctly identified, which facilitates data retrieval, updates, and deletion.

```
CREATE TABLE Employees (
    employee_id INT PRIMARY KEY,
    first_name VARCHAR(50),
    last_name VARCHAR(50),
    position VARCHAR(50)
);
```

In the example above, employee_id serves as the primary key for the Employees table, ensuring that each employee can be uniquely identified.

Another essential concept in relational databases is the **foreign key**. A foreign key is a field (or collection of fields) in one table that uniquely identifies a row in another table. Foreign keys are used to enforce referential integrity, ensuring that relationships between tables remain consistent.

```
CREATE TABLE Departments (
    department_id INT PRIMARY KEY,
```

```
    department_name VARCHAR(50)
);

CREATE TABLE Employees (
    employee_id INT PRIMARY KEY,
    first_name VARCHAR(50),
    last_name VARCHAR(50),
    position VARCHAR(50),
    department_id INT,
    FOREIGN KEY (department_id) REFERENCES Departments(department_id)
);
```

In this example, the department_id in the Employees table is a foreign key that references the department_id in the Departments table. This relationship enforces that each employee is assigned to a valid department.

Relational databases also rely on the manipulation and retrieval of data through a structured query language, or **SQL**. SQL provides a standardized language to perform various operations such as querying, updating, and managing data within the database. This language includes a broad suite of commands and functions that enable complex data manipulations while maintaining the integrity and consistency of the database.

Key operations of SQL include:

- **SELECT** - Used to query and retrieve data from one or more tables.

```
SELECT first_name, last_name FROM Employees WHERE position = '
    Manager';
```

- **INSERT** - Adds new rows to a table.

```
INSERT INTO Employees (employee_id, first_name, last_name, position,
    department_id)
VALUES (101, 'Jane', 'Doe', 'Engineer', 1);
```

- **UPDATE** - Modifies existing rows in a table.

```
UPDATE Employees SET position = 'Senior Engineer' WHERE
    employee_id = 101;
```

- **DELETE** - Removes rows from a table.

```
DELETE FROM Employees WHERE employee_id = 101;
```

Normalization is a process that aims to organize the data in a database to reduce redundancy and improve data integrity. It involves decomposing tables into smaller, stable structures without duplicating data. The main goal of normalization is to ensure that each piece of data is stored only once. Normalization is often carried out in stages, called **normal forms**, each with specific rules and requirements. The most common normal forms are the first (1NF), second (2NF), and third (3NF):

- **First Normal Form (1NF)** - Ensures that each column contains atomic, indivisible values and each record is unique.
- **Second Normal Form (2NF)** - Achieved when the table is in 1NF, and all non-key attributes are fully functionally dependent on the primary key.
- **Third Normal Form (3NF)** - Achieved when the table is in 2NF and all the attributes are not dependent on non-key attributes.

Understanding these foundational principles is critical for effective database design and management. By comprehending the relational model, primary and foreign keys, SQL operations, and normalization techniques, one can efficiently organize, manipulate, and maintain data.

1.9 Getting Started with the MySQL Command Line Client

The MySQL Command Line Client is an essential tool for interacting with the MySQL database server. It allows for executing SQL commands and managing database tasks directly through the command line interface (CLI) without the need for a graphical user interface. This section will guide you through the steps necessary to get started with the MySQL Command Line Client, including installation, starting the client, basic commands, and some practical examples.

Installation

Before you can use the MySQL Command Line Client, you need to have MySQL installed on your system. The installation process may vary depending on your operating system. Below is an overview of the installation steps for different environments.

For Windows:

- Visit the MySQL website and download the MySQL Installer.

- Run the installer and choose the Custom setup type.
- Select MySQL Server and MySQL Command Line Client, then proceed with the installation.
- Once installed, you can open the Command Line Client from the Start Menu.

For macOS:

- Use Homebrew to install MySQL by executing the command:

```
brew install mysql
```

- Start the MySQL server:

```
brew services start mysql
```

- Access the Command Line Client by typing:

```
mysql -u root -p
```

For Linux:

- Use the package manager for your distribution to install MySQL:

Debian/Ubuntu:

```
sudo apt update
sudo apt install mysql-server
```

RHEL/CentOS:

```
sudo yum install mysql-server
```

- Start the MySQL server:

```
sudo systemctl start mysqld
```

- Access the Command Line Client:

```
mysql -u root -p
```

Starting the MySQL Command Line Client

To start the MySQL Command Line Client, open your terminal or command prompt and enter the following command:

```
mysql -u [username] -p
```

Replace [username] with your MySQL username (common default is root). You will be prompted to enter your password. Once authenticated, you will enter the MySQL shell, where you can begin executing commands.

Basic Commands

Here are some basic commands to get you started:

Displaying Databases: To list all available databases, use the command:

```
SHOW DATABASES;
```

Selecting a Database: To select a specific database to work on, use the USE command:

```
USE [database_name];
```

Displaying Tables: To show all tables within the selected database:

```
SHOW TABLES;
```

Describing a Table: To describe the structure of a table, use the DESCRIBE command:

```
DESCRIBE [table_name];
```

These commands form the foundation for interacting with MySQL via the command line. Below are more detailed examples and practical uses.

Practical Examples

Creating a Database:

```
CREATE DATABASE example_db;
```

Query OK, 1 row affected (0.01 sec)

Creating a Table:

```
CREATE TABLE example_table (
    id INT AUTO_INCREMENT PRIMARY KEY,
    name VARCHAR(100),
    age INT
);
```

Query OK, 0 rows affected (0.05 sec)

Inserting Data:

```
INSERT INTO example_table (name, age) VALUES ('Alice', 30), ('Bob', 25);
```

```
Query OK, 2 rows affected (0.02 sec)
Records: 2  Duplicates: 0  Warnings: 0
```

Querying Data:

```
SELECT * FROM example_table;
```

```
+----+-------+-----+
| id | name  | age |
+----+-------+-----+
|  1 | Alice |  30 |
|  2 | Bob   |  25 |
+----+-------+-----+
2 rows in set (0.00 sec)
```

Updating Data:

```
UPDATE example_table SET age = 31 WHERE name = 'Alice';
```

```
Query OK, 1 row affected (0.01 sec)
Rows matched: 1  Changed: 1  Warnings: 0
```

Deleting Data:

```
DELETE FROM example_table WHERE name = 'Bob';
```

```
Query OK, 1 row affected (0.01 sec)
```

These examples outline the basic operational commands in MySQL through the command line, giving you practical tools to start managing your databases effectively.

1.10 Exploring MySQL Workbench

MySQL Workbench is a unified visual tool for database architects, developers, and DBAs. It provides data modeling, SQL development, and comprehensive administration tools for server configuration, user administration, backup, and more. This section delves into the capabilities of MySQL Workbench, illustrating its functionality with practical examples.

- **Installation and Setup**:
  - MySQL Workbench can be downloaded from the MySQL official website and supports multiple operating systems including Windows, macOS, and various Linux distributions.

- Follow the installation wizard, ensuring that the MySQL server is running and accessible for initial configuration.

- **User Interface Overview**:

  - The main workbench screen is divided into several panels, including the Navigator, the Query Panel, and various administrative tools.
  - The Navigator provides access to database connections and management features such as database design, SQL development, and server administration.

Creating and Managing Connections

To utilize MySQL Workbench effectively, establishing connections to MySQL servers is fundamental. This process starts with the Connection Manager.

- **Creating a Connection**:

```
1. Open MySQL Workbench.
2. In the "MySQL Connections" section, click the '+' icon.
3. Enter connection details:
   a. Connection Name: Name your connection.
   b. Connection Method: Standard (TCP/IP).
   c. Hostname: Address of the server (localhost by default).
   d. Port: Default port 3306.
   e. Username: Your MySQL username.
4. Click "Test Connection" to ensure connectivity.
5. Save the connection.
```

Server connection established successfully.

- **Managing Existing Connections**:

  - Use the Navigator panel to manage and organize your connections.
  - Edit existing connections by right-clicking on the connection and selecting Edit Connection.
  - Secure connections can be set up using SSL/TLS options provided under connection settings.

Database Design and Modeling

Database modeling is a crucial aspect of database design, and MySQL Workbench offers an intuitive interface for creating and visualizing database schemas.

- **Creating an EER Model**:
  - Navigate to File > New Model to create a new EER (Enhanced Entity-Relationship) model.
  - Add tables by selecting the Add Table button and defining columns, data types, primary keys, and indexes.
  - Relationships between tables can be established using the relationship tools to create foreign key constraints.
  - Utilize diagramming tools to visually arrange and connect tables for better schema visualization.
- **Forward and Reverse Engineering**:
  - Forward Engineering generates SQL scripts from an EER model to create schemas directly on the server. Access this feature via Database > Forward Engineer.
  - Reverse Engineering allows extracting an EER model from an existing database schema by navigating to Database > Reverse Engineer.
- **Schema Synchronization**:
  - Compare and sync database schemas using Database > Synchronize Model. This ensures the live database and the model are consistent.

SQL Development and Querying

One of the core functionalities of MySQL Workbench is the SQL Editor, which aids in creating, editing, and running scripts.

- **Writing and Executing Queries**:

```
1. Open a connection to a database.
2. Navigate to the SQL Editor tab.
3. Write a SQL query in the editor.
   Example:
```

```
SELECT * FROM employees;
4. Execute the query by clicking the 'Execute SQL' button or pressing Ctrl+
   Enter.
```

```
+----+---------+----------------+
| ID | Name    | Position       |
+----+---------+----------------+
|  1 | John    | Manager        |
|  2 | Alice   | Developer      |
|  3 | Robert  | Analyst        |
+----+---------+----------------+
```

- **Managing Scripts and Results**:
  - Save SQL scripts using File > Save Script to preserve complex queries for future use.
  - Query results are displayed in a grid format, which can be exported to various formats such as CSV or JSON.

Administrative Tools

MySQL Workbench also provides a comprehensive set of administrative tools to manage the MySQL server's operational aspects.

- **User and Privilege Management**:
  - Navigate to Server > Users and Privileges to manage user accounts and their permissions.
  - Create new users, define roles, and assign specific privileges to control access to database resources.
- **Backup and Recovery**:
  - Schedule and perform database backups using the Data Export feature found under Server > Data Export.
  - Import data and restore databases using Server > Data Import.
- **Performance Monitoring and Tuning**:
  - Monitor server performance metrics via Server > Dashboard, where real-time statistics like query performance and server load are displayed.
  - Utilize Performance Reports to identify and troubleshoot performance bottlenecks.

This exploration of MySQL Workbench outlines its potential in database management and highlights how the tool can streamline various database activities. The features provided by Workbench not only simplify database design but also facilitate robust querying and efficient server administration, making it an indispensable tool for MySQL users.

[illegible]

Chapter 2

Installing and Configuring MySQL

This chapter guides you through the process of installing MySQL on different operating systems including Windows, Linux, and macOS. It covers essential steps such as downloading MySQL, performing post-installation setups, configuring MySQL files, and starting and stopping the MySQL server. Additionally, it provides details on using the MySQL Command Line Client and configuring MySQL Workbench, as well as instructions for upgrading and uninstalling MySQL.

2.1 System Requirements

A meticulous understanding of system requirements is crucial for the seamless installation and optimal performance of MySQL. This section will detail the minimum and recommended specifications necessary for the various operating systems that MySQL supports: Windows, Linux, and macOS. Ensuring your system meets these requirements can prevent potential installation issues and enhance MySQL's operational efficiency.

Hardware Requirements:

- **Processor:** MySQL requires an x86-64 architecture processor. While MySQL can run on a single-core processor, a multi-core processor is recommended for improved performance, especially for handling larger databases and multiple concurrent connections.

- **RAM:** A minimum of 1 GB of RAM is required for installing MySQL. However, for a production environment or large databases, it is advisable to have 4 GB or more. The more RAM available, the better the performance, particularly for complex queries and large datasets.
- **Disk Space:** MySQL requires at least 500 MB of free disk space for a minimal installation. Additional space is required for database storage and log files. For production servers, it is recommended to have at least 2 GB of free disk space.
- **Network:** A standard Ethernet network interface is required for networked configurations. Gigabit Ethernet is recommended for high-performance connections, especially in environments with heavy database traffic.

Software Requirements:

- **Operating System:**
  - **Windows:** MySQL supports Windows 7, Windows 8, Windows 10, and corresponding server versions including Windows Server 2012, 2016, and 2019. The 64-bit versions of these operating systems are recommended.
  - **Linux:** MySQL is compatible with various Linux distributions such as Ubuntu, Debian, Fedora, Red Hat Enterprise Linux (RHEL), CentOS, and Oracle Linux. It is recommended to use the latest stable release of these distributions. MySQL primarily supports 64-bit architectures.
  - **macOS:** MySQL runs on macOS 10.13 and later versions. For best performance, it is recommended to use the latest version of macOS.
- **Libraries and Utilities:**
  - **C Standard Library:** A compatible C++ Standard Library is required. For Linux, the GNU C Library (glibc) 2.12 or later is necessary.

  - **Perl:** Some MySQL scripts utilize Perl. Ensure Perl is installed, which it typically is by default on most Unix-like systems.
  - **SSL/TLS Libraries:** If you plan to use MySQL's secure connections, OpenSSL libraries must be installed.

- **Additional Software:**
  - **MySQL Workbench:** For users intending to utilize the MySQL Workbench, ensure your system can support its graphical requirements. The Workbench requires a GUI environment which includes a graphical desktop, and it is recommended to have a display resolution of at least 1280x1024.
  - **Java:** If your application stack requires connector solutions like Connector/J, ensure that a compatible version of the Java Runtime Environment (JRE) is installed.

Network Configuration:

- **Port Availability:** MySQL by default communicates over port 3306. Ensure this port is not blocked by firewall settings or used by other applications.
- **Hostname Resolution:** Networked installations of MySQL necessitate proper hostname resolution. Ensure DNS settings are correctly configured to avoid connectivity issues.

By adhering to these hardware and software specifications, you configure a robust foundation for installing and running MySQL efficiently. Misalignment with the requirements could result in suboptimal performance, operational hindrances, or installation failures, which are often difficult to troubleshoot post-installation.

2.2 Downloading MySQL

Downloading MySQL is a straightforward process that involves accessing the official MySQL website and selecting the appropriate version for your operating system. The steps are detailed below to ensure the correct software package is obtained. We will cover the download process for all major operating systems, including Windows, Linux, and macOS.

First, navigate to the official MySQL website at https://dev.mysql.com/downloads/mysql/. Here, you will find various MySQL software products and versions. It is advisable to download the latest stable release to benefit from the newest features and security updates.

- For Windows users, locate the section titled **MySQL Installer for Windows**. This installer is an integrated, easy-to-use package that includes several MySQL products.
- For Linux users, packages are typically distributed in the form of RPMs or DEBs, suitable for distribution-specific package managers such as YUM or APT.
- For macOS users, options include a DMG archive, which facilitates the installation process via a user-friendly graphical interface.

Step-by-Step Download Instructions for Windows:

- On the MySQL download page, under *MySQL Installer for Windows*, click the **Download** button.
- You will be redirected to a page offering two versions of the MySQL Installer - a **web** (online) installer and a **full** (offline) installer. The web installer is smaller, but requires an active internet connection to download the components during installation. The full installer is larger, around 400MB, but contains all components.
- Select the desired installer version by clicking the corresponding **Download** button. For users with reliable internet connections, the web installer is recommended.
- Upon selecting the installer, you may be prompted to log in or sign up for an Oracle Web account. This step can be bypassed by selecting *No thanks, just start my download*.

Step-by-Step Download Instructions for Linux:

- At the MySQL download page, locate the section for **Linux Generic** builds. Alternatively, you can select your specific Linux distribution from the dropdown menu for more tailored instructions.

- Choose between the TAR package or the RPM package based on your system's requirements.
  - TAR packages offer a generic build and are convenient if you wish to unpack and manually manage the MySQL components.
  - RPM packages integrate neatly with package managers like YUM or DNF for automated installation and dependency resolution.
- Click the **Download** button to proceed to the download page. Select the appropriate version and architecture (e.g., x86_64).
- As with Windows, you may bypass the Oracle Web account login by selecting *No thanks, just start my download* if you do not wish to create an account.

Step-by-Step Download Instructions for macOS:

- Navigate to the MySQL download page and locate the **macOS** section.
- Choose either the **DMG Archive** or **Package Installer**. The DMG Archive provides a graphical installer for ease of use.
- Click the **Download** button next to the desired installer.
- Similarly, bypass the Oracle Web account login by selecting *No thanks, just start my download*.

To validate the integrity and authenticity of the downloaded package, it is recommended to verify the MD5 checksum or GPG signature provided on the download page. The checksums ensure the package has not been tampered with or corrupted during the download process.

```
# Example command to verify MD5 checksum on Linux or macOS
md5sum mysql-installer-community-8.0.26.0.msi
# Compare the output with the provided checksum
```

This preliminary downloading phase is crucial as it sets the foundation for a smooth installation and configuration process. The downloaded installer will be used in subsequent sections to install MySQL on your operating system of choice. The next steps will detail specific installation procedures, ensuring a robust and performant MySQL environment.

2.3 Installing MySQL on Windows

To begin the installation of MySQL on a Windows operating system, one must first download the MySQL installer package from the official MySQL website. This section provides a step-by-step guide for downloading, installing, and verifying the MySQL installation on a Windows machine.

First, navigate to the [MySQL Community Downloads](https://dev.mysql.com/downloads/installer/) page. Here, you will find two installer options: the "web" installer and the "full" installer. The "web" installer is smaller, containing only the essential files, and will download the required components during installation. The "full" installer includes all the necessary files within the package and is useful if you need to install MySQL offline.

1. **Downloading the Installer:**
    - On the MySQL Community Downloads page, select the installer that suits your needs (e.g., mysql-installer-web-community-X.Y.Z.msi or mysql-installer-community-X.Y.Z.msi, where X.Y.Z represents the version numbers).
    - Click on the "Download" button. You may be prompted to log in or sign up for an Oracle Web Account; however, this step can be bypassed by clicking on the "No thanks, just start my download" link.
2. **Running the Installer:**
    - Navigate to the directory where the installer file was downloaded and double-click on the .msi file to launch the MySQL Installer.
    - Upon launching, you are presented with the MySQL Installer setup wizard. Click **Next** to proceed.
    - On the *Choosing a Setup Type* page, select the setup type that best matches your needs. The options include *Developer Default*, *Server only*, *Client only*, *Full*, and *Custom*. For a comprehensive installation, *Developer Default* is recommended as it includes the MySQL server, MySQL Workbench, and other development tools. Click **Next** to continue.
3. **Check Requirements:**

- The installer will check for any software requirements such as the Microsoft Visual C++ Redistributable. If any prerequisites are missing, the installer will provide guidance on how to resolve these issues. Ensure all requirements are met before proceeding.

4. **Installation:**

   - Click **Execute** to begin downloading (if using the web installer) and installing the MySQL products. This may take several minutes depending on the setup selected and your internet speed.
   - Once all products have been downloaded and installed, click **Next**.

5. **Product Configuration:**

   - The installer will now guide you through configuring the MySQL server. Click **Next** on the Product Configuration page to start the configuration process.
   - On the *Type and Networking* page, select the appropriate configuration for your server:
     - Select *Standalone MySQL Server* unless you are setting up a dedicated server as part of a multi-server system.
     - Ensure the *Config Type* is set to *Development Machine*, *Server Machine*, or *Dedicated Machine* depending on your use case, which adjusts memory allocation accordingly.
     - Leave the networking configuration as default, with the MySQL server running on port 3306 (this can be changed if necessary). Ensure the option *Open Windows Firewall for network access* is checked if you plan to access the server over a network.
     - Click **Next** to proceed.
   - On the *Authentication Method* page, select *Use Strong Password Encryption for Authentication (RECOMMENDED)*. Click **Next**.
   - On the *Accounts and Roles* page, set the root password for the MySQL server. It is essential to use a strong password. Optionally, you can create additional user accounts here. Click **Next**.

- On the *Windows Service* page, ensure the MySQL server is configured to run as a Windows service:
  - The service name can be left as the default *MySQLXX* (where *XX* represents the version number).
  - Ensure the option *Start the MySQL Server at System Startup* is checked.
  - Optionally, configure the server to log in as a specific Windows user if additional security is needed. Otherwise, select *Standard System Account*.
  - Click **Next**.
- On the *Apply Configuration* page, click **Execute** to apply the configuration settings. This will start the MySQL server as a service and apply all the specified configurations. Click **Finish** once complete.

6. **Complete Installation:**

   - The final screen of the installation wizard confirms that the installation and configuration have been completed successfully. Click **Finish** to exit the installer.

To verify the installation, open the MySQL Command Line Client from the Start menu. Upon execution, you will be prompted to enter the root password set during installation. Upon successful login, you can execute the following command to ensure the MySQL server is running correctly and check the installed version:

```
SELECT VERSION();
```

The output will display the MySQL server version, confirming that the installation was successful:

```
+-----------+
| version() |
+-----------+
| X.Y.Z     |
+-----------+
1 row in set (0.00 sec)
```

With MySQL installed and verified, the environment is now ready for further configuration and database management tasks, which will be covered in subsequent sections.

2.4 Installing MySQL on Linux

Installing MySQL on a Linux distribution such as Ubuntu or CentOS involves several distinct steps, each paramount to ensuring the database system operates correctly and efficiently. This comprehensive approach ensures that users can seamlessly integrate MySQL into their environments, benefiting from its powerful features.

Step 1: Update Package Repository

Before installing MySQL, update the package repository cache to ensure you have the most recent list of packages and dependencies. Use the following command:

```
sudo apt-get update # For Debian-based distributions like Ubuntu
sudo yum update # For RPM-based distributions like CentOS
```

Updating the package list helps prevent potential conflicts and ensures that the latest versions of required software are available.

Step 2: Install MySQL Server

Install the MySQL server package. For Debian-based distributions such as Ubuntu, execute:

```
sudo apt-get install mysql-server
```

For RPM-based distributions like CentOS, use the following command:

```
sudo yum install mysql-server
```

These commands will install the MySQL server along with its dependencies. During the installation process, you might be prompted to set a root password for MySQL. Ensure that a strong password is used to enhance security.

Step 3: Secure MySQL Installation

Post installation, it is crucial to run a security script provided by MySQL. This script removes insecure default settings and improves the security of your MySQL installation. Invoke it by running:

```
sudo mysql_secure_installation
```

The script will prompt you with several questions to enhance your server's security:

```
Enter current password for root (enter for none):
Set root password? [Y/n]
New password:
Re-enter new password:
Remove anonymous users? [Y/n]
Disallow root login remotely? [Y/n]
Remove test database and access to it? [Y/n]
Reload privilege tables now? [Y/n]
```

Answering 'yes' to these prompts enforces best practices in regards to security.

Step 4: Start MySQL Service

After installation, ensure that the MySQL service is running. Start the service using:

```
sudo systemctl start mysql # For Debian-based distributions like Ubuntu
sudo systemctl start mysqld # For RPM-based distributions like CentOS
```

To ensure MySQL starts at boot, enable the service with:

```
sudo systemctl enable mysql # For Debian-based distributions like Ubuntu
sudo systemctl enable mysqld # For RPM-based distributions like CentOS
```

Step 5: Verify MySQL Installation

To confirm that MySQL has been installed correctly, check its version:

```
mysql --version
```

You should see an output similar to:

```
mysql Ver 8.0.25-0ubuntu0.20.04.1 for Linux on x86_64 (MySQL Community Server - GPL)
```

This indicates that MySQL is properly installed. Additionally, you can log in to the MySQL server using the root credentials to double-check functionality:

```
mysql -u root -p
```

You will be prompted to enter the root password you set earlier. Successful login will bring you to the MySQL command prompt.

Step 6: Manage MySQL Service

Control MySQL service using systemd commands for operational tasks. To stop the MySQL service, utilize:

```
sudo systemctl stop mysql # For Debian-based distributions like Ubuntu
sudo systemctl stop mysqld # For RPM-based distributions like CentOS
```

To restart MySQL, use:

```
sudo systemctl restart mysql # For Debian-based distributions like Ubuntu
```

```
sudo systemctl restart mysqld # For RPM-based distributions like CentOS
```

These commands offer control over the MySQL service, allowing for maintenance, updates, or troubleshooting activities.

Ensuring MySQL is correctly installed and configured on your Linux system enables robust database management, integrating seamlessly with your operating system's service management utilities. Following structured steps mitigates installation errors and sets a foundation for reliable database operations.

2.5 Installing MySQL on macOS

To install MySQL on macOS, you need to follow a series of steps that include downloading the MySQL DMG archive, running the installer package, and configuring the installation. We will go through these steps in meticulous detail.

Step 1: Download the MySQL DMG Archive

1. Open your preferred web browser and go to the MySQL Community downloads page: https://dev.mysql.com/downloads/mysql/ 2. Select the macOS platform under the "Select Operating System" dropdown menu. 3. Click the "Download" button for the macOS 10.x DMG Archive. 4. You will be redirected to the MySQL login or sign up page, but you can bypass this by clicking the link "No thanks, just start my download."

Step 2: Run the Installer Package

Once the download is complete, you will have a DMG file that contains the MySQL installer package.

1. Open the DMG file by double-clicking it. 2. You will see a window with MySQL installer package files. The key file you need is called mysql-... .pkg. Double-click this file to start the installation. 3. The installer will guide you through the setup process. Click Continue to proceed with each step of the installation process.

Step 3: Installation Process

The installation wizard will ask you to select the type of MySQL installation to be performed. Choose Custom installation or Standard depending on your requirements. For most users, the Standard installation is sufficient.

4. The installation process also includes selecting the installation location. Typically, the default location is fine for most users. 5. Click Install to begin the installation. You may be prompted to enter your macOS administrator password to proceed.

Step 4: Configuring the MySQL Installation

1. Once the installation is complete, a MySQL_Preference_Pane will be placed in the System Preferences for easier management. 2. The MySQL Server needs to be initialized for the first use. During the configuration, the installer prompts you to set a password for the root user. Ensure you choose a strong password and optionally write it down for reference. 3. Choose the default authentication plugin that's compatible with most applications, typically Use Strong Password Encryption (RECOMMENDED).

Step 5: Starting MySQL Server on macOS

Post-installation, you can start the MySQL server from the System Preferences or the command line.

Using System Preferences:

1. Navigate to System Preferences from the Apple menu. 2. Click on the MySQL icon. 3. Click Start MySQL Server to start the server.

Using Terminal:

1. Open the Terminal application from Applications > Utilities. 2. Enter the following command to start the MySQL server:

```
sudo /usr/local/mysql/support-files/mysql.server start
```

3. You will be prompted to enter your administrator password.

To stop the server, use:

```
sudo /usr/local/mysql/support-files/mysql.server stop
```

You can verify the installation by logging into the MySQL command line client using the following command in the terminal:

```
mysql -u root -p
```

You will be prompted to enter the root password you configured during installation. On successful entry, you should see the MySQL command line client prompt:

```
Welcome to the MySQL monitor.  Commands end with ; or \g.
Your MySQL connection id is 11
Server version: 8.0.26 MySQL Community Server - GPL

Copyright (c) 2000, 2021, Oracle and/or its affiliates.

Oracle is a registered trademark of Oracle Corporation and/or its
affiliates. Other names may be trademarks of their respective
owners.

Type 'help;' or '\h' for help. Type '\c' to clear the current input statement.

mysql>
```

In case you encounter any issues with the MySQL server not starting, you can refer to the MySQL logs located at:

```
/usr/local/mysql/data/mysqld.err
```

The error log can provide more insights into what might be going wrong.

Automatic Start of MySQL Server

To configure the MySQL server to start automatically upon system boot, you can use the following:

```
sudo cp /usr/local/mysql/support-files/mysql.server /Library/StartupItems/
     MySQLCOM
sudo chmod +x /Library/StartupItems/MySQLCOM
```

Ensure the commands are executed as the system administrator.

The above steps enable you to successfully install and configure MySQL on a macOS system. The MySQL server should be up and running, allowing you to proceed with database management and other MySQL command line operations as needed.

2.6 Post-Installation Setup and Testing

Upon successful installation of MySQL, it is crucial to perform a post-installation setup to ensure that the system is configured correctly and is functioning as expected. This section encompasses the essential steps to verify the installation, secure the MySQL server, and conduct basic tests to validate its operation.

After installation, a default MySQL setup usually completes preliminary initialization, such as creating the necessary database directory structures, populating system tables, and setting security configurations. Post-installation setup involves additional configurations and security enhancements. Below are the detailed steps:

- Verify the MySQL Installation
- Secure the MySQL Installation
- Basic Connectivity and Operations Test

Verifying the MySQL Installation

To verify that MySQL is installed correctly, follow these steps:

1. **Checking the MySQL Service Status (Linux/macOS):** Ensure the MySQL service is running. Use the following command:

```
sudo systemctl status mysql
```

   If the service is active and running, the installation is verified. You can also check the service status using:

```
ps -ef | grep mysqld
```

2. **Checking the MySQL Service Status (Windows):** Open the Services control panel (services.msc) and locate the MySQL service. Ensure that it is started. Alternatively, you can check the service status using:

```
sc query MySQL
```

3. **Checking the MySQL Version:** Verify the MySQL version by connecting to the MySQL server using mysql command-line tool:

```
mysql -u root -p
```

   Once connected, execute the command:

```
SELECT VERSION();
```

   This command should return the MySQL server version.

```
+-----------+
| VERSION() |
+-----------+
| 8.0.23    |
+-----------+
```

Securing the MySQL Installation

MySQL provides a security script (mysql_secure_installation) that helps in securing the MySQL installation. This script enables you to:

- Set a root password.

- Remove anonymous user accounts.
- Disable root login remotely.
- Remove test databases.
- Reload privilege tables.

Execute the script as follows:

```
sudo mysql_secure_installation
```

Follow the prompts to secure your MySQL installation. A typical interaction is as follows:

```
Enter password for user root:
The 'validate_password' plugin is installed on the server.
The subsequent steps will run with the validating password plugin enabled.
...

Set root password? [Y/n] Y
New password:
Re-enter new password:
...

Remove anonymous users? [Y/n] Y
Success.

Disallow root login remotely? [Y/n] Y
Success.

Remove test database and access to it? [Y/n] Y
 - Dropping test database...
Success.
 - Removing privileges on test database...
Success.

Reload privilege tables now? [Y/n] Y
Success.

All done!
```

Basic Connectivity and Operations Test

Ensure that the MySQL server is responsive and operational by performing basic database operations.

1. **Connecting to MySQL:** Connect to the MySQL server from the command line:

   ```
   mysql -u root -p
   ```

2. **Creating a Test Database:**

   ```
   CREATE DATABASE testdb;
   ```

```
Query OK, 1 row affected (0.00 sec)
```

3. **Creating a Table:**

```
USE testdb;
CREATE TABLE users (
  id INT AUTO_INCREMENT PRIMARY KEY,
  name VARCHAR(100) NOT NULL,
  email VARCHAR(100) NOT NULL UNIQUE
);
```

```
Query OK, 0 rows affected (0.01 sec)
```

4. **Inserting Data:**

```
INSERT INTO users (name, email) VALUES ('Alice', 'alice@example.com');
```

```
Query OK, 1 row affected (0.01 sec)
```

5. **Querying Data:**

```
SELECT * FROM users;
```

```
+----+-------+-------------------+
| id | name  | email             |
+----+-------+-------------------+
|  1 | Alice | alice@example.com |
+----+-------+-------------------+
1 row in set (0.00 sec)
```

Completing these steps confirms a successful installation and basic configuration of MySQL, ensuring that it is ready for database management and operation.

2.7 MySQL Configuration Files

MySQL configuration files, also known as option files or my.cnf files, are critical for ensuring the correct operation and fine-tuning of the MySQL database server. These files contain configuration options that affect how the server runs, such as buffer sizes, memory allocation, maximum allowed connections, and more. Understanding the structure, syntax, and location of these files is essential for any database administrator or developer working with MySQL.

MySQL reads configuration options from files in a fixed order. The following list outlines the standard sequence in which MySQL examines these files (not all of these files will necessarily exist on every system):

- /etc/my.cnf – Global options.
- /etc/mysql/my.cnf – Global options (alternative).
- $MYSQL_HOME/my.cnf – Server-specific options ($MYSQL_-HOME refers to the MySQL installation directory).
- defaults-extra-file – Additional options, before ~/.my.cnf.
- ~/.my.cnf – User-specific options.

The syntax of MySQL configuration files is simple. They are structured in sections, each denoted by square brackets, e.g., [mysqld] for server options or [client] for client options. Within each section, configuration options are specified in the variable=value format.

For illustration, consider a typical my.cnf file structure:

```
[mysqld]
user=mysql
pid-file=/var/run/mysqld/mysqld.pid
socket=/var/run/mysqld/mysqld.sock
port=3306
basedir=/usr
datadir=/var/lib/mysql
tmpdir=/tmp
lc-messages-dir=/usr/share/mysql

[client]
port=3306
socket=/var/run/mysqld/mysqld.sock

[mysqld_safe]
log-error=/var/log/mysql/mysql_error.log
pid-file=/var/run/mysqld/mysqld.pid
```

[mysqld] section description: This section contains server-specific configurations. Key variables include:

- user - Specifies the system user under which the MySQL server should run.
- port - Defines the port number on which the MySQL server listens for incoming connections.
- datadir - Indicates the directory where MySQL database files are stored.
- socket - The Unix socket file path for local connections.
- basedir - The base directory of the MySQL installation.

[client] section description: This section is for configurations that affect MySQL client programs, such as mysql, mysqldump, etc. Key variables include:

- port - Specifies the port number for the MySQL client to connect to the server.
- socket - Defines the path to the MySQL Unix socket file.

[mysqld_safe] section description: This section pertains to the mysqld_-safe program, which is used to start the MySQL server with certain security features. Important variables include:

- log-error - Specifies the file where errors encountered during startup will be logged.
- pid-file - Indicates the path to the file containing the process ID of the MySQL server.

Common Configuration Considerations

Memory Allocation: MySQL's performance is heavily influenced by memory-related settings. Two key memory-related variables are:

```
[mysqld]
innodb_buffer_pool_size=1G
query_cache_size=64M
```

- innodb_buffer_pool_size - Determines the memory allocated to the InnoDB buffer pool used for caching data and indexes of InnoDB tables.
- query_cache_size - Sets the amount of memory allocated to the query cache, which stores the result of SELECT queries and can significantly improve performance if the same queries are executed frequently.

Connection Limits: MySQL connection parameters are critical for managing the number of simultaneous users and preventing resource exhaustion. Two important variables are:

```
[mysqld]
max_connections=500
wait_timeout=300
```

- max_connections - Specifies the maximum number of simultaneous client connections allowed.
- wait_timeout - Defines the timeout duration for idle connections before they are closed.

Logging: Logging configuration ensures that activities, errors, and general server operations are properly recorded. Common logging settings include:

```
[mysqld]
general_log_file=/var/log/mysql/mysql.log
general_log=1
slow_query_log_file=/var/log/mysql/mysql-slow.log
slow_query_log=1
long_query_time=2
```

- general_log_file - Sets the file to log general query logs.
- general_log - Enables or disables general query logging.
- slow_query_log_file - Specifies the file to log slow queries.
- slow_query_log - Enables or disables the slow query log.
- long_query_time - Defines the threshold time (in seconds) for a query to be considered slow.

Special Considerations for Different Systems

Windows-Specific Configurations: While the general organization of the my.cnf file is consistent across platforms, there are some Windows-specific settings to be aware of:

```
[mysqld]
basedir="C:/Program Files/MySQL/MySQL Server 8.0/"
datadir="C:/ProgramData/MySQL/MySQL Server 8.0/Data/"
```

Paths may contain backslashes or forward slashes, but using forward slashes is often recommended for consistency.

Linux-Specific Configurations: On Linux systems, file paths and permissions significantly impact how MySQL interacts with the underlying OS:

```
[mysqld]
user=mysql
pid-file=/var/run/mysqld/mysqld.pid
log_bin_trust_function_creators=1
```

Adjusting user permissions and ensuring that MySQL has the necessary rights to read and write in specified directories is crucial.

Editing and Testing Configuration Files

To apply changes made in the configuration file, the MySQL server must be restarted. This can be accomplished via the command line with the following commands, depending on your system:

```
# On Linux:
sudo systemctl restart mysql

# On Windows:
net stop MySQL && net start MySQL
```

After restarting MySQL, it is essential to verify that the server starts correctly and that no errors are logged. This can be achieved by reviewing the contents of the error log file as specified in the configuration settings. Additionally, testing connectivity and performing simple queries can help ensure that the changes have taken effect as expected.

Properly configuring MySQL through its my.cnf file is a fundamental task that helps to optimize performance, manage resources effectively, and ensure the stability and security of the database server. Each adjustment should be made with careful consideration of the environment and workload requirements to achieve optimal results.

2.8 Starting and Stopping the MySQL Server

To effectively manage a MySQL server, it is imperative to understand the process of starting and stopping the server across different operating systems. This section provides detailed instructions for initiating and halting the MySQL server on Windows, Linux, and macOS platforms.

Starting MySQL Server

Windows On Windows, the MySQL server can be started using the Command Prompt or via the Services utility. Both methods are valid; thus, users may choose based on their preference.

1. **Using Command Prompt:**

```
C:\> "C:\Program Files\MySQL\MySQL Server 8.0\bin\mysqld" --console
```

This command starts the MySQL server with output directed to the console, aiding in diagnostics.

2. **Using Services:**

   (a) Open the Services utility by typing services.msc in the Run dialog (Win + R).

   (b) Locate the MySQL service, right-click, and select Start.

Linux Linux distributions typically use systemd or init.d to manage services. The following commands start the MySQL server:

1. **Using systemd:**

```
sudo systemctl start mysql
```

2. **Using init.d:**

```
sudo /etc/init.d/mysql start
```

macOS On macOS, the MySQL server can be started using launchctl or the mysql.server script.

1. **Using launchctl:**

```
sudo launchctl load -F /Library/LaunchDaemons/com.oracle.oss.mysql.
    mysqld.plist
```

2. **Using mysql.server:**

```
sudo /usr/local/mysql/support-files/mysql.server start
```

Stopping MySQL Server

Windows The MySQL server can be stopped using the Command Prompt or via the Services utility.

1. **Using Command Prompt:**

```
C:\> "C:\Program Files\MySQL\MySQL Server 8.0\bin\mysqladmin" -u
    root -p shutdown
```

2. **Using Services:**
   (a) Open the Services utility by typing services.msc in the Run dialog (Win + R).
   (b) Locate the MySQL service, right-click, and select Stop.

Linux The process of stopping the MySQL server on Linux is straightforward and relies on systemd or init.d.

1. **Using systemd:**

```
sudo systemctl stop mysql
```

2. **Using init.d:**

```
sudo /etc/init.d/mysql stop
```

macOS On macOS, the MySQL server can be stopped using launchctl or the mysql.server script.

1. **Using launchctl:**

```
sudo launchctl unload -F /Library/LaunchDaemons/com.oracle.oss.mysql.
    mysqld.plist
```

2. **Using mysql.server:**

```
sudo /usr/local/mysql/support-files/mysql.server stop
```

Verification of Server Status

Once the actions to start or stop the MySQL server have been executed, verifying the server's status is crucial to ensure that it is functioning as expected.

Windows To check if the MySQL server is running, you can inspect the Services utility or use the Command Prompt.

- **Using Command Prompt:**

```
C:\> "C:\Program Files\MySQL\MySQL Server 8.0\bin\mysqladmin" -u
    root -p status
```

Linux On Linux, the status can be verified using:

1. **Using systemd:**

```
sudo systemctl status mysql
```

2. **Using init.d:**

```
sudo /etc/init.d/mysql status
```

macOS For macOS, the verification commands are:

1. **Using launchctl:**

```
sudo launchctl list | grep mysqld
```

2. **Using mysql.server:**

```
sudo /usr/local/mysql/support-files/mysql.server status
```

Successful execution of commands without errors indicates that the MySQL server is correctly started or stopped. Errors returned by these commands can be used diagnostically to troubleshoot issues in server management.

2.9 Using MySQL Command Line Client

The MySQL Command Line Client is an essential tool for database administrators and developers. It provides a powerful interface to interact with the MySQL server using SQL commands. This section elucidates the usage of the MySQL Command Line Client, including launching the client, logging in, executing SQL statements, and utilizing various client options for optimal performance and productivity.

To begin, ensure that the MySQL server is up and running. On Windows, the MySQL Command Line Client can be accessed through the Start Menu. On Linux and macOS, you can open a terminal and use the following command, assuming MySQL is properly installed and added to your system's PATH:

```
mysql -u root -p
```

The above command initiates the MySQL Command Line Client and prompts for the root user's password. Upon successful authentication, you will be presented with the MySQL prompt:

```
mysql>
```

At this prompt, you can execute SQL statements and commands. For instance, to view all available databases, use the SHOW DATABASES; statement:

```
SHOW DATABASES;
```

The output will display a list of databases on the MySQL server:

```
+--------------------+
| Database           |
+--------------------+
| information_schema |
| mysql              |
| performance_schema |
| sys                |
+--------------------+
```

To select a specific database for use, the USE command followed by the database name is used. For example, to use the mysql database:

```
USE mysql;
```

Upon successful execution, the prompt confirms the active database:

```
Database changed
```

SQL statements executed after this command will apply to the selected database. For example, to retrieve a list of tables within the mysql database:

```
SHOW TABLES;
```

The output might look like this:

```
+---------------------------+
| Tables_in_mysql           |
+---------------------------+
| columns_priv              |
| component                 |
| db                        |
| default_roles             |
...
+---------------------------+
```

You can execute various SQL queries to interact with the database, such as creating tables, inserting data, updating records, or retrieving information. For example, to create a new table named example_table:

```
CREATE TABLE example_table (
```

```
    id INT AUTO_INCREMENT PRIMARY KEY,
    name VARCHAR(100),
    created_at TIMESTAMP DEFAULT CURRENT_TIMESTAMP
);
```

To insert a record into example_table:

```
INSERT INTO example_table (name) VALUES ('Sample Name');
```

Querying the data from example_table can be achieved using:

```
SELECT * FROM example_table;
```

The output will display the records inserted into the table:

```
+----+-------------+---------------------+
| id | name        | created_at          |
+----+-------------+---------------------+
|  1 | Sample Name | 2023-01-01 12:00:00 |
+----+-------------+---------------------+
```

The Command Line Client also supports various options and commands to manage the MySQL server. For example, to check the version of the MySQL server, the following command can be used:

```
SELECT VERSION();
```

To quit the MySQL Command Line Client, simply use the QUIT; or EXIT; command:

```
QUIT;
```

This command terminates the session and returns to the operating system prompt.

Additionally, the MySQL Command Line Client supports several command-line options that can modify its behavior. Some of the frequently used options include:

- -h – Specifies the host name of the MySQL server.
- -u – Specifies the MySQL user name to log in as.
- -p – Prompts for the MySQL user's password.
- –port – Specifies the port number to connect to.
- –default-auth – Specifies the default authentication plugin.

For example, to connect to a MySQL server running on a remote host with a specific port:

```
mysql -h remote_host -u user_name -p --port=3306
```

The utility of the MySQL Command Line Client extends beyond simple queries and includes numerous features for advanced database management, making it an indispensable tool for database professionals. This section provides a foundation, and users are encouraged to explore further commands and options detailed in the official MySQL documentation.

2.10 Configuring MySQL Workbench

Configuring MySQL Workbench involves several steps to ensure that the tool is properly set up to manage and interact with MySQL databases. This section outlines the procedural steps needed to configure MySQL Workbench for optimal use, including setting up connections, customizing preferences, and understanding key features.

First, launch MySQL Workbench. Depending on your operating system, this can be done by searching for "MySQL Workbench" in the start menu or applications folder.

- **Launching MySQL Workbench:**

```
# On Windows:
Start Menu > All Programs > MySQL > MySQL Workbench

# On macOS:
Applications > MySQL Workbench

# On Linux:
Search for MySQL Workbench in your application launcher or run the
    command:
$ mysql-workbench
```

When MySQL Workbench opens, you will be greeted with the Home screen, displaying your existing MySQL connections, models, and other relevant tools.

Creating a New Connection: To begin configuring MySQL Workbench, the first step is to set up a connection to a MySQL server.

1. Click on the + icon next to *MySQL Connections* to create a new connection. 2. In the *Setup New Connection* dialog, enter a connection name in the *Connection Name* field. 3. For *Connection Method*, select

Standard (TCP/IP). 4. Enter the hostname or IP address of the MySQL server in the *Hostname* field, typically localhost for local instances. 5. Specify the port number, defaulting to 3306 if unchanged. 6. Input the MySQL username in the *Username* field. 7. Click *Store in Vault...* to save your password securely.

The dialog should look similar to the following:

```
Connection Name: Localhost Connection
Connection Method: Standard (TCP/IP)
Hostname: localhost
Port: 3306
Username: root
```

Click *Test Connection* to validate the credentials and server details. If the connection is successful, you will see a confirmation dialog. Save the connection by clicking *OK*.

Customizing MySQL Workbench Preferences: MySQL Workbench offers various preferences that can be customized to tailor the environment to your needs.

- Go to Edit > Preferences on Windows/Linux or MySQL Workbench > Preferences on macOS.
- Key sections include:
  - *General*: Modify appearance settings like theme, language, and diagram options.
  - *SQL Editor*: Configure editor settings, such as syntax color, auto-complete, and tab spacing.
  - *Query*: Set preferences for query execution, including default limit, confirm data changes, and logging options.
  - *Database*: Manage database-specific settings, such as default storage engine and MySQL time zone.

Understanding Key Features: Once configured, familiarizing yourself with key features of MySQL Workbench enhances productivity.

- **SQL Development:** Accessing the SQL Editor allows users to create, edit, and run SQL queries. The editor supports syntax highlighting, auto-complete, and result set viewing:

```
SELECT * FROM `database_name`.`table_name`;
```

- **Data Modeling:** The Database Modeling interface helps in designing and visualizing database schemas. Supports creating EER diagrams, forward and reverse engineering, and schema synchronization.

- **Database Administration:** Provides tools for server administration tasks such as managing users and privileges, monitoring server health, performing backups and restores.

Executing Queries: To run SQL queries, select your MySQL connection from the Workbench Home screen or the File > Open Connection menu:

1. In the SQL Editor window, type your query. 2. Execute the query by clicking the *Execute* button or pressing Ctrl+Enter (Windows/Linux) or Cmd+Enter (macOS). 3. View output in the result pane:

```
+------------+-------------+
| column1    | column2     |
+------------+-------------+
| value1     | value2      |
+------------+-------------+
```

MySQL Workbench is equipped with features to streamline database management, providing a robust platform for database development, design, and administration. Following these steps ensures the tool is configured correctly, enhancing efficiency and productivity in managing MySQL databases.

2.11 Upgrading MySQL

Upgrading MySQL is a critical task that ensures your database system benefits from the latest features, performance improvements, and security patches. The process of upgrading MySQL involves preparing the system, backing up existing data, performing the upgrade, and verifying the success of the operation. This section covers the steps involved in upgrading MySQL across different operating systems: Windows, Linux, and macOS.

Step 1: Preparing for the Upgrade

Before starting the upgrade process, assess the database system's state and requirements to prevent data loss. It is crucial to review the MySQL release notes to identify any changes that may impact the existing database configuration or applications.

- Verify the current MySQL version and the available upgrade version.
- Review the MySQL release notes for any critical changes.
- Identify deprecated features or configurations that might affect your system.
- Plan the upgrade during a maintenance window to minimize operational impact.

Step 2: Backing Up Your Data

Data integrity is paramount; thus, backing up the existing databases is non-negotiable. Use tools such as mysqldump or the MySQL Enterprise Backup to create a complete backup.

```
mysqldump --all-databases --routines --triggers --events --user=[username] --password >
    alldatabases-backup.sql
```

Ensure the backup is stored safely and verify its integrity by performing a restoration test if possible.

Step 3: Performing the Upgrade

Depending on the operating system, the steps to upgrade MySQL differ slightly. Detailed below are the upgrade processes for Windows, Linux, and macOS.

Upgrading MySQL on Windows

- **Stop the MySQL Server**: Use the Services management console or the Task Manager to stop the MySQL server:

  ```
  net stop mysql
  ```

- **Backup the MySQL Directory**: Ensure you have a complete backup of the current MySQL installation directory, including data, my.cnf, and any custom configuration files.

  ```
  xcopy C:\Program Files\MySQL\MySQL Server 5.7\* C:\Backup\MySQL-
      Backups\MySQL\ /s /e /c /d /i /h /r /y
  ```

- **Download and Install the New Version**: Download the latest MySQL installer and execute it, following the prompts to upgrade the installation.

- **Run MySQL Upgrader**: Execute the mysql_upgrade tool to upgrade the system tables and reorganize data structures where necessary:

```
mysql_upgrade --user=[username] --password
```

- **Restart the MySQL Server**:

```
net start mysql
```

Upgrading MySQL on Linux

- **Stop the MySQL Server**:

```
sudo systemctl stop mysql
```

- **Backup the MySQL Data Directory**:

```
sudo cp -r /var/lib/mysql /var/backups/
```

- **Upgrade MySQL Packages**: Update the package repository and upgrade MySQL using the package manager:

```
sudo apt-get update
sudo apt-get install mysql-server
```

- **Run MySQL Upgrader**:

```
sudo mysql_upgrade --user=[username] --password
```

- **Restart the MySQL Server**:

```
sudo systemctl start mysql
```

Upgrading MySQL on macOS

- **Stop the MySQL Server**:

```
sudo launchctl unload -F /Library/LaunchDaemons/com.oracle.oss.mysql.
    mysqld.plist
```

- **Backup the MySQL Data Directory**:

```
sudo cp -r /usr/local/mysql/data /usr/local/mysql-backups
```

- **Download and Install the New Version**: Download the latest version of MySQL from the official website and follow the installation prompts.
- **Run MySQL Upgrader**:

```
mysql_upgrade --user=[username] --password
```

- **Restart the MySQL Server**:

```
sudo launchctl load -F /Library/LaunchDaemons/com.oracle.oss.mysql.
    mysqld.plist
```

Step 4: Verifying the Upgrade

Post-upgrade verification is essential. Check the MySQL server's operational status by connecting and running basic queries. Ensure that no errors are present in the error logs and that all databases and their schemas are intact.

```
mysql> SELECT version();
+-----------+
| version() |
+-----------+
| x.x.xx    |
+-----------+
1 row in set (0.00 sec)
```

```
SHOW DATABASES;
```

Troubleshooting Upgrade Issues

In case of any issues during the upgrade, review MySQL logs located typically at:

- /var/log/mysql/error.log (Linux)
- C:
  ProgramData
  MySQL
  MySQL Server x.x
  data
  mysql-error.log (Windows)
- /usr/local/mysql/data/mysqld.err (macOS)

Solving any discrepancies or errors that appear in these logs will ensure a smooth transition to the upgraded MySQL version.

2.12 Uninstalling MySQL

Uninstalling MySQL involves several steps to ensure that all components and dependencies are thoroughly removed from your system. This process varies slightly depending on the operating system, but fundamentally it encompasses stopping the MySQL service, removing MySQL programs, and deleting configuration files and directories.

Uninstalling MySQL on Windows

To uninstall MySQL on a Windows system, follow these steps:

1. First, ensure that the MySQL server and any related services are stopped. Open a command prompt with administrative privileges and execute the following commands:

```
net stop MySQL
```

2. Open the Control Panel and navigate to Programs and Features (or Add or Remove Programs on older versions of Windows). Locate MySQL Server X.Y in the list of installed programs, where X.Y represents the version number.

3. Select MySQL Server and click Uninstall/Change. Follow the prompts to complete the uninstallation process.

4. After the uninstallation, manually delete any remaining MySQL files and directories. Common locations include:

- C:\Program Files\MySQL\
- C:\ProgramData\MySQL\
- C:\Users\<username>\AppData\Roaming\MySQL\

5. Optionally, clean the Windows registry of MySQL entries. This step requires caution. Open the Registry Editor by typing regedit in the Start menu search. Navigate to the following paths and remove any MySQL-related keys:

- HKEY_LOCAL_MACHINE\SOFTWARE\MySQL AB
- HKEY_CURRENT_USER\SOFTWARE\MySQL AB

Uninstalling MySQL on Linux

On Linux systems, MySQL is typically uninstalled using the package manager of the specific distribution. Below are the steps for common distributions.

Ubuntu/Debian: 1. Stop the MySQL service:

```
sudo systemctl stop mysql
```

2. Uninstall MySQL packages:

```
sudo apt-get remove --purge mysql-server mysql-client mysql-common
```

3. Remove MySQL configuration and data files:

```
sudo rm -rf /etc/mysql /var/lib/mysql
sudo apt-get autoremove
sudo apt-get autoclean
```

CentOS/RHEL: 1. Stop the MySQL service:

```
sudo systemctl stop mysqld
```

2. Uninstall MySQL packages:

```
sudo yum remove mysql-server mysql
```

3. Remove MySQL configuration and data files:

```
sudo rm -rf /etc/my.cnf /var/lib/mysql
```

Uninstalling MySQL on macOS

On macOS, MySQL can be uninstalled by following these steps:

1. Stop the MySQL server. Open the terminal and execute:

```
sudo /usr/local/mysql/support-files/mysql.server stop
```

2. Remove MySQL directories and files:

```
sudo rm -rf /usr/local/mysql*
sudo rm -rf /Library/StartupItems/MySQLCOM
sudo rm -rf /Library/PreferencePanes/My*
sudo rm -rf /Library/LaunchDaemons/com.oracle.oss.mysql.*
sudo rm -rf ~/Library/PreferencePanes/My*
```

3. Additionally, remove MySQL's command-line tools links:

```
sudo rm -rf /usr/local/bin/mysql*
```

4. Optionally, remove configuration files if they were customized:

```
sudo rm -rf /etc/my.cnf
```

```
sudo rm -rf /etc/mysql/
```

After completion, verify that MySQL has been entirely removed from your system by checking the expected directories and ensuring no related processes are running. Each of these steps eliminates the various MySQL artifacts, returning the system to its state prior to installation.

Chapter 3

Basic SQL Queries

This chapter introduces the fundamental SQL commands used to query and manipulate data in MySQL. Topics include selecting data with the SELECT statement, filtering data using the WHERE clause, sorting results with ORDER BY, and limiting the number of results with LIMIT. It also covers the use of DISTINCT to remove duplicates, joining tables with JOIN operations, grouping data with GROUP BY, and filtering groups with the HAVING clause. Additional topics include using aliases for columns and tables, and basic date, time, and string functions.

3.1 Introduction to SQL

Structured Query Language (SQL) is the standard language for interacting with relational databases. It encompasses a wide range of operations for querying, updating, and managing data. SQL is declarative, meaning that the user specifies what data to retrieve or what changes to make, leaving the database management system (DBMS) to determine how to accomplish these tasks efficiently.

The SQL language is broadly divided into several categories:

- **Data Query Language (DQL)**: Primarily comprises the SELECT statement, used to query the database.
- **Data Definition Language (DDL)**: Involves commands like CRE-

ATE, ALTER, and DROP to define and modify the structure of the database objects.

- **Data Manipulation Language (DML)**: Consists of INSERT, UPDATE, and DELETE statements, which are used to manipulate the data within tables.
- **Data Control Language (DCL)**: Comprises GRANT and REVOKE statements, which manage access permissions.
- **Transaction Control Language (TCL)**: Includes COMMIT, ROLLBACK, and SAVEPOINT commands to manage transaction boundaries and control transactional consistency.

SQL syntax is composed of a combination of keywords, operators, and clauses. Commands should be executed by the DBMS in a specific sequence to produce the desired results. Unlike procedural programming languages, SQL does not follow the typical flow of control (e.g., loops, conditionals), but rather relies on a set-based logic which is essential for efficiently querying large datasets.

Basic SQL Commands

The core of SQL consists of a few basic commands which can be combined to perform complex queries. Below is an outline of each category's fundamental commands:

Data Query Language (DQL):

- SELECT: Retrieves data from one or more tables.

Data Definition Language (DDL):

- CREATE TABLE: Creates a new table.

```
CREATE TABLE tablename (
    column1 datatype constraints,
    column2 datatype constraints,
    ...
    columnN datatype constraints
);
```

- ALTER TABLE: Modifies an existing table.

```
ALTER TABLE tablename
ADD column datatype constraints;
```

- DROP TABLE: Deletes an existing table.

```
DROP TABLE tablename;
```

Data Manipulation Language (DML):

- INSERT INTO: Adds new rows to a table.

```
INSERT INTO tablename (column1, column2, ..., columnN)
VALUES (value1, value2, ..., valueN);
```

- UPDATE: Modifies existing data in a table.

```
UPDATE tablename
SET column1 = value1, column2 = value2, ...
WHERE condition;
```

- DELETE FROM: Removes rows from a table.

```
DELETE FROM tablename
WHERE condition;
```

Data Control Language (DCL):

- GRANT: Gives rights to users.

```
GRANT SELECT, INSERT ON tablename TO 'username';
```

- REVOKE: Takes back rights from users.

```
REVOKE SELECT, INSERT ON tablename FROM 'username';
```

Transaction Control Language (TCL):

- COMMIT: Saves the changes made during the current transaction.

```
COMMIT;
```

- ROLLBACK: Reverts the changes made during the current transaction.

```
ROLLBACK;
```

- SAVEPOINT: Sets a savepoint within the transaction for partial rollback.

```
SAVEPOINT savepoint_name;
```

Example Session

To provide further clarity, consider a simple demonstration of a SQL session involving the creation and manipulation of a table:

- Create a table called students:

```
CREATE TABLE students (
    student_id INT PRIMARY KEY,
    first_name VARCHAR(50),
    last_name VARCHAR(50),
    enrollment_date DATE
);
```

- Insert data into the students table:

```
INSERT INTO students (student_id, first_name, last_name, enrollment_date)
VALUES (1, 'Alice', 'Johnson', '2023-08-21'),
       (2, 'Bob', 'Smith', '2023-08-22');
```

- Update a record in the students table:

```
UPDATE students
SET first_name = 'Robert'
WHERE student_id = 2;
```

- Select all records from the students table:

```
SELECT * FROM students;
```

Output:

```
+------------+------------+-----------+---------------+
| student_id | first_name | last_name | enrollment_date|
+------------+------------+-----------+---------------+
|     1      | Alice      | Johnson   | 2023-08-21    |
|     2      | Robert     | Smith     | 2023-08-22    |
+------------+------------+-----------+---------------+
```

SQL's versatility and power come from its ability to handle a multitude of operations through a relatively straightforward set of commands. By mastering these fundamental constructs, one can effectively interact with MySQL databases to perform a wide range of data operations.

3.2 Selecting Data with SELECT Statement

The SELECT statement is one of the most fundamental and frequently used commands in SQL. It is employed to retrieve data from one or more tables within a database. The general syntax of the SELECT statement is:

```
SELECT column1, column2, ...
FROM table_name;
```

You specify the columns you wish to retrieve after the SELECT keyword and the table name from which data is to be fetched after the FROM keyword. Here is an example where we select the columns first_name and last_name from a table named employees:

```
SELECT first_name, last_name
FROM employees;
```

If you aim to select all columns from a table, you can use the asterisk (*) wildcard character. For instance, to select all columns from the employees table, you would write:

```
SELECT *
FROM employees;
```

Column Aliases Column aliases are used to temporarily rename columns in the output of the SELECT statement. This is useful for improving the readability of query results or when combining columns. The syntax for using an alias is:

```
SELECT column_name AS alias_name
FROM table_name;
\end{lstisting}

For example, if we want to alias the \texttt{first\_name} column as \texttt{
    FirstName} and \texttt{last\_name} as \texttt{LastName}, the query would be:

\begin{lstlisting}
SELECT first_name AS FirstName, last_name AS LastName
FROM employees;
```

Selecting Distinct Values To eliminate duplicate rows from the results of a query, the DISTINCT keyword is used. The syntax is:

```
SELECT DISTINCT column1, column2, ...
FROM table_name;
```

For example, to get a unique list of job titles from the employees table, you would use:

```
SELECT DISTINCT job_title
FROM employees;
```

Using Expressions in SELECT The SELECT statement is not limited to retrieving existing columns; it can also include expressions. Ex-

pressions can perform arithmetic operations or concatenate strings. For example, to add a calculated field showing the annual salary (assuming the salary column contains monthly salaries) and display the full name of employees, we can write:

```
SELECT first_name, last_name, salary * 12 AS annual_salary
FROM employees;
```

Here, the column salary * 12 is aliased as annual_salary.

Concatenating Columns Columns can be concatenated using the CONCAT() function. For instance, to concatenate the first_name and last_name columns into a single fullname column, use:

```
SELECT CONCAT(first_name, ' ', last_name) AS fullname
FROM employees;
```

The function CONCAT() combines first_name and last_name with a space in between.

Using Functions in SELECT SQL supports an extensive set of built-in functions that can be used within the SELECT statement. Functions such as COUNT(), SUM(), AVG(), MIN(), and MAX() perform calculations on table data. For example, to count the number of employees:

```
SELECT COUNT(*) AS total_employees
FROM employees;
```

Or, to find the average salary of all employees:

```
SELECT AVG(salary) AS average_salary
FROM employees;
```

The SELECT statement serves as the cornerstone for querying databases, and its applications extend to numerous complex operations essential for data analysis and manipulation within MySQL.

3.3 Filtering Data with WHERE Clause

The WHERE clause is a critical component of SQL queries that controls which rows are returned by a SELECT statement. It is used to filter records based on specific conditions, making it possible to hone in on precisely the data you need. The WHERE clause is powerful and flexible, capable of handling a variety of comparison operators and logical expressions.

Basic Syntax

The WHERE clause is used in the following general form of a SELECT statement:

```
SELECT column1, column2, ...
FROM table_name
WHERE condition;
```

In this structure, condition represents the criteria that must be met for rows to be included in the result set. Conditions typically involve comparisons between column values and constants or expressions. Each row is evaluated individually, and only those rows for which condition is true are returned.

Comparison Operators

The WHERE clause supports several comparison operators:

- **'=':** Equal to
- **'<>' or** !=**:** Not equal to
- **'<':** Less than
- **'<=':** Less than or equal to
- **'>':** Greater than
- **'>=':** Greater than or equal to

For example, to find all employees with a salary greater than 50,000:

```
SELECT first_name, last_name, salary
FROM employees
WHERE salary > 50000;
```

Logical Operators

Multiple conditions can be combined using logical operators:

- **AND:** All conditions must be true
- **OR:** At least one condition must be true
- **NOT:** Reverses the truth value of the condition

To find employees with a salary between 40,000 and 60,000:

```
SELECT first_name, last_name, salary
FROM employees
WHERE salary >= 40000 AND salary <= 60000;
```

To find employees either in the 'Sales' department or 'Marketing' department:

```
SELECT first_name, last_name, department
FROM employees
WHERE department = 'Sales' OR department = 'Marketing';
```

Pattern Matching with LIKE and Wildcards

The LIKE operator is used to search for a specified pattern in a column. It is often combined with wildcard characters:

- **%:** Represents zero, one, or multiple characters
- **_:** Represents a single character

To find all employees whose name starts with 'J':

```
SELECT first_name, last_name
FROM employees
WHERE first_name LIKE 'J%';
```

To locate employees with 'a' as the second character in their last name:

```
SELECT first_name, last_name
FROM employees
WHERE last_name LIKE '_a%';
```

Range and Set Membership with BETWEEN and IN

The BETWEEN operator is used to filter the result set within a specific range. It is inclusive of the boundary values:

```
SELECT first_name, last_name, salary
FROM employees
WHERE salary BETWEEN 40000 AND 60000;
```

The IN operator allows checking a column against multiple values:

```
SELECT first_name, last_name, country
FROM customers
WHERE country IN ('USA', 'Canada', 'UK');
```

Checking for NULL with IS NULL and IS NOT NULL

To check whether a column contains NULL values or not, IS NULL and IS NOT NULL operators are used. For instance, to find all customers with no specified phone number:

```
SELECT first_name, last_name
FROM customers
WHERE phone_number IS NULL;
```

To find employees who have a specified commission percentage:

```
SELECT first_name, last_name, commission_pct
FROM employees
WHERE commission_pct IS NOT NULL;
```

Complex Conditions and Operator Precedence

Complex conditions can combine multiple operators. Parentheses can be used to explicitly define the precedence:

```
SELECT first_name, last_name, salary, department
FROM employees
WHERE (department = 'Sales' OR department = 'Marketing')
AND salary > 50000;
```

This query ensures the condition for department is evaluated first due to the parentheses, then combined with the salary condition using 'AND'. Utilizing the WHERE clause effectively enables precise control over the rows returned by a SQL query, ensuring that the results meet specific criteria and are relevant to the analysis task.

3.4 Sorting Data with ORDER BY Clause

The ORDER BY clause is an essential tool in SQL for arranging query results in a specified order. By default, SQL queries return results in an arbitrary order, typically determined by the order in which rows were inserted into the table. To introduce structure into our data retrieval process, SQL provides the ORDER BY clause, which allows the user to sort the data either in ascending or descending order based on one or more columns.

To utilize the ORDER BY clause, its syntax is straightforward:

```
SELECT column1, column2, ...
FROM table_name
ORDER BY column1 [ASC|DESC], column2 [ASC|DESC], ...;
```

In this syntax:

- column1, column2, ... are the names of the columns by which you want to sort the data.
- The ASC keyword sorts the data in ascending order, while DESC sorts it in descending order. If neither is specified, the default is ASC.

Example 1: Sorting in Ascending Order

Consider a table named students with the following structure:

```
CREATE TABLE students (
    id INT,
    name VARCHAR(100),
    age INT,
    grade FLOAT
);
```

Suppose we want to retrieve the names and ages of all students sorted by their ages in ascending order. The appropriate query would be:

```
SELECT name, age
FROM students
ORDER BY age ASC;
```

The output of this query would appear as follows:

```
+-------+-----+
| name  | age |
+-------+-----+
| Alice | 18  |
| Bob   | 20  |
| Carol | 22  |
| Dave  | 25  |
+-------+-----+
```

Example 2: Sorting in Descending Order

To sort the same list of students by age in descending order, the query would be:

```
SELECT name, age
FROM students
ORDER BY age DESC;
```

Here, the query would output:

```
+-------+-----+
| name  | age |
+-------+-----+
| Dave  | 25  |
| Carol | 22  |
| Bob   | 20  |
| Alice | 18  |
+-------+-----+
```

Example 3: Sorting by Multiple Columns

The ORDER BY clause also allows sorting by multiple columns. If students share the same age, we may wish to further sort them by their names in alphabetical order. The query would then be:

```
SELECT name, age
FROM students
ORDER BY age ASC, name ASC;
```

Let's assume the table contains the following additional data:

```
+----+-------+-----+-------+
| id | name  | age | grade |
+----+-------+-----+-------+
|  1 | Alice | 20  |  3.5  |
|  2 | Bob   | 20  |  3.7  |
|  3 | Carol | 22  |  2.8  |
|  4 | Dave  | 18  |  3.0  |
|  5 | Eve   | 20  |  3.9  |
+----+-------+-----+-------+
```

The result set that sorts first by age and then by name would show:

```
+-------+-----+
| name  | age |
+-------+-----+
| Dave  | 18  |
| Alice | 20  |
| Bob   | 20  |
| Eve   | 20  |
| Carol | 22  |
+-------+-----+
```

In situations where sorting is required based on columns not part of the SELECT statement, this can be seamlessly achieved. For instance, sorting students by their grades, but only displaying their names and ages, would require the following query:

```
SELECT name, age
FROM students
ORDER BY grade DESC;
```

This flexibility allows for robust query design, where data can be sorted based on various criteria without always displaying the sorting columns.

For real-world applications, the ORDER BY clause serves as a powerful mechanism to organize and analyze data. Whether dealing with large datasets or simple query results, having data in a specific order enhances readability and aids in making informed decisions based on the dataset.

3.5 Limiting Results with LIMIT

In querying large datasets, it is often beneficial to constrain the number of results returned to improve performance and manageability. The LIMIT clause in MySQL serves this precise purpose by specifying the number of records to fetch from a result set. This is particularly useful for paginating results and optimizing response times in applications.

The syntax for the LIMIT clause is straightforward, typically appended to a SELECT statement:

```
SELECT column1, column2, ...
FROM table_name
LIMIT number_of_records;
```

To demonstrate the utility of the LIMIT clause, consider a table named employees with the following schema:

```
CREATE TABLE employees (
    employee_id INT PRIMARY KEY,
    first_name VARCHAR(50),
    last_name VARCHAR(50),
    salary DECIMAL(10,2)
);
```

Suppose this table contains a substantial number of records, and you are only interested in examining the first 10 entries. You can specify:

```
SELECT employee_id, first_name, last_name, salary
FROM employees
LIMIT 10;
```

Executing this query retrieves the top 10 rows from the employees table:

```
+-------------+------------+-----------+--------+
| employee_id | first_name | last_name | salary |
+-------------+------------+-----------+--------+
|           1 | Alice      | Smith     | 80000  |
|           2 | Bob        | Johnson   | 75000  |
|           3 | Carol      | Williams  | 68000  |
|           4 | Dave       | Brown     | 65000  |
|           5 | Eve        | Jones     | 62000  |
|           6 | Frank      | Miller    | 60000  |
|           7 | Grace      | Davis     | 58000  |
|           8 | Henry      | Garcia    | 55000  |
|           9 | Irene      | Martinez  | 53000  |
|          10 | Jack       | Anderson  | 51000  |
+-------------+------------+-----------+--------+
```

For scenarios requiring the selection of records starting from a specific offset, the LIMIT clause can be paired with OFFSET:

```
SELECT column1, column2, ...
FROM table_name
LIMIT number_of_records OFFSET offset_value;
```

Here number_of_records defines the number of rows to fetch, and offset_value specifies the starting point. Utilizing the same employees table, to retrieve employees 11 through 20, the query would be:

```
SELECT employee_id, first_name, last_name, salary
FROM employees
LIMIT 10 OFFSET 10;
```

This query results in:

```
+-------------+------------+-----------+--------+
| employee_id | first_name | last_name | salary |
+-------------+------------+-----------+--------+
|          11 | Karen      | Thompson  | 49500  |
|          12 | Leo        | White     | 48000  |
|          13 | Mark       | Harris    | 46500  |
|          14 | Nancy      | Clark     | 45000  |
|          15 | Oscar      | Lewis     | 43500  |
|          16 | Paul       | Robinson  | 42000  |
|          17 | Quinn      | Walker    | 40500  |
|          18 | Rachel     | Perez     | 39000  |
|          19 | Steve      | Hall      | 37500  |
|          20 | Tina       | Young     | 36000  |
+-------------+------------+-----------+--------+
```

An alternative and often more common form of the LIMIT clause involves a comma-separated pair indicating both the offset and the number of records:

```
SELECT column1, column2, ...
FROM table_name
LIMIT offset_value, number_of_records;
```

Using our example, the above query can be rewritten as:

```
SELECT employee_id, first_name, last_name, salary
FROM employees
LIMIT 10, 10;
```

The operation of this query aligns precisely with the previous LIMIT and OFFSET specification.

In practice, the LIMIT clause aids remarkably in queries executed within web applications where paginated results are standard. For instance, displaying search results or user lists, providing interfaces for users to navigate seamlessly through data.

When combined with the ORDER BY clause, LIMIT assists in retrieving the top records based on specific criteria. Consider sorting employees by salary in descending order, revealing the highest salaries:

```
SELECT employee_id, first_name, last_name, salary
FROM employees
ORDER BY salary DESC
LIMIT 5;
```

The result depicts the top five highest-paid employees:

```
+-------------+------------+-----------+--------+
| employee_id | first_name | last_name | salary |
+-------------+------------+-----------+--------+
|           1 | Alice      | Smith     | 80000  |
|           2 | Bob        | Johnson   | 75000  |
|           3 | Carol      | Williams  | 68000  |
|           4 | Dave       | Brown     | 65000  |
|           5 | Eve        | Jones     | 62000  |
+-------------+------------+-----------+--------+
```

Efficient use of the LIMIT clause allows developers and database administrators to manage and navigate large volumes of data effectively, enhancing query performance and user experience.

3.6 Using DISTINCT to Remove Duplicates

The DISTINCT keyword in SQL is utilized to return unique values by eliminating duplicates from the result set. Its primary purpose is to ensure that each value returned is distinct and appears only once, which is particularly useful in large datasets with redundant entries. This section explores the application of DISTINCT in various scenarios, discussing its behavior and potential impacts on query performance.

To apply the DISTINCT keyword, it must be placed directly after the SELECT clause, followed by the columns from which duplicates need to be removed. When used correctly, DISTINCT processes the result set and filters out any duplicate entries.

```
SELECT DISTINCT column1, column2, ...
FROM table_name;
```

The example below demonstrates a simple query without the DISTINCT keyword, followed by the same query using DISTINCT to eliminate duplicate entries.

```
-- Query without DISTINCT
SELECT city
FROM customers;
```

The result set of the above query might include several identical entries if multiple customers reside in the same city.

```
city
-----
New York
Los Angeles
New York
Chicago
Los Angeles
```

To remove these duplicates:

```
-- Query with DISTINCT
SELECT DISTINCT city
FROM customers;
```

The adjusted query ensures each city is listed only once:

```
city
-----
New York
Los Angeles
Chicago
```

When employing DISTINCT, it is crucial to ensure the selected columns collectively define what constitutes a duplicate. Consider the following scenario where multiple columns are involved:

```
-- Using DISTINCT with multiple columns
SELECT DISTINCT city, state
FROM customers;
```

Here, the combination of city and state values must be unique:

```
city       state
------------
New York    NY
Los Angeles CA
Chicago     IL
New York    NY
```

This query would eliminate rows only if both city and state pairs are identical across multiple records.

The DISTINCT keyword can be used in conjunction with other SQL elements to refine the result set further:

- DISTINCT **with** ORDER BY: Ensures that the distinct values are sorted as desired.
- DISTINCT **with** LIMIT: Retrieves a limited number of unique records.
- DISTINCT **with** COUNT: Counts the number of unique entries.

Examples:

```
-- DISTINCT with ORDER BY
SELECT DISTINCT city
FROM customers
ORDER BY city ASC;
```

This retrieves unique city names sorted alphabetically.

```
-- DISTINCT with LIMIT
SELECT DISTINCT city
FROM customers
LIMIT 5;
```

This returns up to five distinct city names.

```
-- COUNT with DISTINCT
SELECT COUNT(DISTINCT city)
FROM customers;
```

This query counts the number of unique cities within the customers table.

In practice, the use of DISTINCT may have performance implications, especially in large datasets with complex queries. The SQL engine must evaluate each row and determine the uniqueness across potentially vast amounts of data. Indexing pertinent columns can optimize performance but requires careful database schema planning.

Analyzing situations where DISTINCT provides substantial value ensures efficient and effective database querying. It is an indispensable tool for deduplication and attaining precise, relevant datasets, making it a foundational concept in SQL.

3.7 Joining Tables with JOIN

In relational database management, it is common to distribute data across multiple tables to maintain normalization and eliminate redundancy. However, there are many instances where data from these related tables needs to be combined to fulfill specific queries. This is where SQL JOIN operations become essential. The JOIN clause is used to merge rows from two or more tables based on a related column between them. There are several types of joins, the most commonly used being INNER JOIN, LEFT JOIN, RIGHT JOIN, and FULL JOIN.

INNER JOIN: This join returns only the rows where there is a match in both joined tables. It eliminates rows that do not have corresponding matches in the other table.

Consider the following tables:

- employees:

id	name	department_id
1	Alice	100
2	Bob	101
3	Charlie	102

- departments:

department_id	department_name
100	HR
101	Engineering

To join these tables and get a list of employees along with their department names, the following query can be used:

```
SELECT employees.name, departments.department_name
FROM employees
INNER JOIN departments
ON employees.department_id = departments.department_id;
```

The result of this query would be:

```
name     | department_name
---------|-----------------
Alice    | HR
Bob      | Engineering
```

LEFT JOIN: This join returns all rows from the left table (the first table), and the matched rows from the right table (the second table). If there is no match, the result is NULL on the side of the right table.

Using the same employees and departments tables, the LEFT JOIN operation can be performed as follows:

```
SELECT employees.name, departments.department_name
FROM employees
LEFT JOIN departments
ON employees.department_id = departments.department_id;
```

The result of this query would be:

```
name     | department_name
---------|-----------------
Alice    | HR
Bob      | Engineering
Charlie  | NULL
```

RIGHT JOIN: This join returns all rows from the right table, and the matched rows from the left table. If there is no match, the result is NULL on the side of the left table.

Using the same data, a RIGHT JOIN can be written as:

```
SELECT employees.name, departments.department_name
FROM employees
RIGHT JOIN departments
ON employees.department_id = departments.department_id;
```

The result of this query would produce:

```
name     | department_name
--------|-----------------
Alice    | HR
Bob      | Engineering
NULL     | Marketing
```

FULL JOIN: This join returns all rows when there is a match in one of the tables. If there is no match, the result is NULL from the left or right table, as appropriate.

Assume that the departments table is updated to include a new department with no employees:

department_id	department_name
100	HR
101	Engineering
103	Marketing

To join these with all possible matches, including non-matches, the FULL OUTER JOIN can be written:

```
SELECT employees.name, departments.department_name
FROM employees
FULL OUTER JOIN departments
ON employees.department_id = departments.department_id;
```

However, note that MySQL does not support the FULL OUTER JOIN by default. As an alternative, a UNION of LEFT JOIN and RIGHT JOIN can be used:

```
SELECT employees.name, departments.department_name
FROM employees
LEFT JOIN departments
ON employees.department_id = departments.department_id
UNION
SELECT employees.name, departments.department_name
FROM employees
RIGHT JOIN departments
ON employees.department_id = departments.department_id;
```

The union of these results would be:

```
name    | department_name
--------|-----------------
Alice   | HR
Bob     | Engineering
Charlie | NULL
NULL    | Marketing
```

These types of joins enable complex queries to be efficiently executed, providing flexibility in data retrieval across multiple tables. Each join type offers unique functionalities suited for different requirements, enhancing the relational database's robustness.

3.8 Grouping Data with GROUP BY

The GROUP BY clause in SQL is a powerful tool used to aggregate data across multiple records and group the results based on one or more columns. When combined with aggregate functions such as SUM, AVG, COUNT, MAX, and MIN, it enables the summarization and analysis of data in an efficient and meaningful way.

Consider a fundamental table, sales, which records transactions:

```
CREATE TABLE sales (
    id INT AUTO_INCREMENT PRIMARY KEY,
    product_id INT,
    customer_id INT,
    sale_date DATE,
    amount DECIMAL(10, 2)
);
```

Assuming this table is populated with data, the GROUP BY clause can be utilized to calculate total sales for each product. The following SQL query demonstrates this:

```
SELECT product_id, SUM(amount) AS total_sales
FROM sales
GROUP BY product_id;
```

The output will look like this:

```
+------------+-------------+
| product_id | total_sales |
+------------+-------------+
| 1          | 15000.00    |
| 2          | 22000.00    |
| 3          | 18500.00    |
+------------+-------------+
```

In this example, the GROUP BY clause groups records by product_id, and the SUM function calculates the total sales amount for each grouped product.

The GROUP BY clause can also be used with multiple columns. For instance, to calculate total sales for each product by each customer, the query would be:

```
SELECT product_id, customer_id, SUM(amount) AS total_sales
FROM sales
GROUP BY product_id, customer_id;
```

The output will provide a detailed breakdown of sales by product and customer:

```
+------------+-------------+-------------+
| product_id | customer_id | total_sales |
+------------+-------------+-------------+
| 1          | 101         | 5000.00     |
| 1          | 102         | 10000.00    |
| 2          | 103         | 22000.00    |
| 3          | 101         | 7500.00     |
| 3          | 104         | 11000.00    |
+------------+-------------+-------------+
```

When using the GROUP BY clause, the SELECT statement can only include the columns listed in the GROUP BY clause or aggregate functions. Any attempt to include columns that are not aggregated or not listed in the GROUP BY clause will result in an SQL error.

For clarity, consider the effect of attempting to include a non-aggregated column that is not part of the GROUP BY clause:

```
SELECT product_id, customer_id, sale_date, SUM(amount) AS total_sales
FROM sales
GROUP BY product_id, customer_id;
```

This query will raise an error such as:

```
SQL Error [1055] [42000]: Expression #3 of SELECT list is not in GROUP BY clause and contains nonaggregated column 'sales.sale_date' which is not functionally dependent on columns in GROUP BY clause; this is incompatible with sql_mode=only_full_group_by
```

To avoid this error, ensure that all non-aggregated columns in the SELECT clause are included in the GROUP BY clause.

A common use case for the GROUP BY clause involves calculating statistics over groups of records. For example, to find the average sales amount for each customer, the following query can be executed:

```
SELECT customer_id, AVG(amount) AS average_sales
FROM sales
GROUP BY customer_id;
```

The output will display the average sales amount per customer:

```
+-------------+---------------+
| customer_id | average_sales |
+-------------+---------------+
| 101         | 6250.00       |
| 102         | 10000.00      |
| 103         | 22000.00      |
| 104         | 11000.00      |
+-------------+---------------+
```

The GROUP BY clause can be employed in combination with the HAVING clause to filter groups based on aggregate functions. For example, to find customers whose total sales exceed $15,000, the query can be written as:

```
SELECT customer_id, SUM(amount) AS total_sales
FROM sales
GROUP BY customer_id
HAVING total_sales > 15000;
```

The result will show customers meeting the specified condition:

```
+-------------+-------------+
| customer_id | total_sales |
+-------------+-------------+
| 102         | 21000.00    |
| 103         | 22500.00    |
+-------------+-------------+
```

In practice, using GROUP BY in conjunction with aggregate functions enables extensive analysis of datasets, facilitating the extraction of meaningful insights. The examples provided illustrate core usage patterns, forming a basis for more complex data manipulation and reporting tasks.

3.9 Filtering Groups with HAVING Clause

The HAVING clause in SQL is used to filter records that work on summarized or grouped data. It is used in combination with the GROUP BY clause and differs from the WHERE clause which filters rows before grouping. The HAVING clause was added to SQL because the WHERE keyword could not be used with aggregate functions.

To illustrate the use of the HAVING clause, consider the following example where we have a table named sales, which contains columns for sale_id, product_id, quantity, and sale_amount. Suppose we want to find products that have a total sales quantity greater than 100. Here is how you might write such a query using the HAVING clause:

```
SELECT product_id, SUM(quantity) AS total_quantity
FROM sales
GROUP BY product_id
```

```
HAVING SUM(quantity) > 100;
```

In this example, product_id is grouped by, and the sum of quantities is calculated for each group. The HAVING clause then filters out groups where the total quantity is less than or equal to 100.

Practical Examples

1. Count employees in each department and show only those departments where the number of employees is greater than 10.

```
SELECT department_id, COUNT(employee_id) AS num_employees
FROM employees
GROUP BY department_id
HAVING COUNT(employee_id) > 10;
```

2. Find the average salary of employees in each department and display the departments where the average salary exceeds $5000.

```
SELECT department_id, AVG(salary) AS average_salary
FROM employees
GROUP BY department_id
HAVING AVG(salary) > 5000;
```

Combining HAVING with Other Clauses

The HAVING clause can be used in conjunction with other SQL clauses to create more complex queries. Consider this example which lists products with total sales amounts greater than $5000, but only for categories matched with the products table:

```
SELECT p.category_id, SUM(s.sale_amount) AS total_sales
FROM sales s
JOIN products p ON s.product_id = p.product_id
GROUP BY p.category_id
HAVING SUM(s.sale_amount) > 5000;
```

Differences Between WHERE and HAVING Clauses

While both WHERE and HAVING clauses are used to filter records, they are used in different stages of the query process:

- WHERE filters rows before any groupings are made. - HAVING filters groups after the GROUP BY clause has been applied.

For example, to filter the sales table for sales made in 2021, then group the results by product_id and filter groups where total sales exceed $2000, you would write:

```
SELECT product_id, SUM(sale_amount) AS total_sales
FROM sales
WHERE YEAR(sale_date) = 2021
GROUP BY product_id
```

```
HAVING SUM(sale_amount) > 2000;
```

Here, the WHERE clause filters the rows to include only sales from the year 2021. Then, the GROUP BY clause groups rows by product_id, and finally, the HAVING clause filters out groups where the total sales amount is less than $2000.

Avoiding Common Errors

- **Using HAVING without GROUP BY:** Although possible, using HAVING without GROUP BY is unusual and often a sign of a logical error. Always ensure your query's logic makes sense.
- **Misuse of Aggregate Functions:** Ensure that the aggregate functions in the HAVING clause match those in the SELECT statement to avoid confusion and errors.
- **Performance Considerations:** Be mindful of performance implications when using the HAVING clause, especially with large datasets, as it involves summary processing.

By understanding the mechanics and use cases of the HAVING clause, you can effectively filter groups of data, enabling more nuanced and powerful data analysis in MySQL.

3.10 Using Aliases for Columns and Tables

In SQL, aliases are temporary names assigned to columns or tables for the duration of a query. They make the SQL statements more readable and the column names more comprehensible, especially when dealing with complex queries or when the original names are not intuitive. The syntax for creating an alias is straightforward, involving the AS keyword. Although the AS keyword is optional in many SQL environments, using it enhances clarity.

Column Aliases

A column alias is used to create a temporary name for a column in the result set. This can be particularly useful when the column name is either unclear or cumbersome. The following example demonstrates a basic use of a column alias:

```
SELECT first_name AS fname, last_name AS lname
FROM employees;
```

In this query, the columns first_name and last_name are renamed to fname and lname respectively in the output. The result set would look like this:

```
+--------+--------+
| fname  | lname  |
+--------+--------+
| John   | Doe    |
| Jane   | Smith  |
+--------+--------+
```

Column aliases are also useful when performing calculations or using built-in functions where the default column name might be non-descriptive. Consider the following example that calculates the total price from a unit price and quantity:

```
SELECT product_name, unit_price, quantity,
       (unit_price * quantity) AS total_price
FROM order_details;
```

The alias total_price makes the output column label explicit and meaningful. A typical output can be:

```
+--------------+------------+----------+-------------+
| product_name | unit_price | quantity | total_price |
+--------------+------------+----------+-------------+
| Widget       | 10.00      | 4        | 40.00       |
| Gizmo        | 20.00      | 2        | 40.00       |
+--------------+------------+----------+-------------+
```

Table Aliases

Table aliases provide temporary names for tables, which can simplify query syntax and make it more understandable, especially when working with multiple tables or complex joins. Table aliases are defined in the FROM clause.

The basic syntax for creating table aliases is:

```
SELECT t1.column1, t2.column2
FROM table1 AS t1
JOIN table2 AS t2
ON t1.common_column = t2.common_column;
```

Here, table1 is aliased as t1, and table2 as t2. These aliases can now be used to refer to the tables within the query, streamlining the reference to columns from each table.

Consider an example where aliases improve readability in a join operation:

```
SELECT e.first_name, e.last_name, d.department_name
FROM employees AS e
JOIN departments AS d
ON e.department_id = d.department_id;
```

This becomes more readable as compared to using full table names, particularly in larger queries or when the same table is referenced multiple times. The output might look like:

```
+------------+-----------+----------------+
| first_name | last_name | department_name|
+------------+-----------+----------------+
| John       | Doe       | Sales          |
| Jane       | Smith     | Engineering    |
+------------+-----------+----------------+
```

Complex Queries with Aliases

Table aliases are particularly advantageous in scenarios involving self-joins, where the same table is joined with itself. Without aliases, such queries can become cumbersome and hard to read.

```
SELECT a.employee_id, a.first_name AS mentor, b.first_name AS mentee
FROM employees AS a
JOIN employees AS b
ON a.employee_id = b.mentor_id;
```

In this example, the employees table is used twice: once as a and once as b, distinguishing the roles of mentor and mentee within the same data set.

Aliased Subqueries

Aliases are also useful when working with subqueries. An aliased subquery can simplify outer queries, particularly when the subquery serves as a virtual table.

```
SELECT e.first_name, e.last_name, sub.department_total
FROM employees AS e
JOIN
    (SELECT department_id, COUNT(*) AS department_total
     FROM employees
     GROUP BY department_id) AS sub
ON e.department_id = sub.department_id;
```

Here, the subquery alias sub represents the result of the subquery, allowing its use in the main query without redundancy. The combined result might look as follows:

```
+------------+-----------+------------------+
| first_name | last_name | department_total |
+------------+-----------+------------------+
| John       | Doe       | 10               |
| Jane       | Smith     | 15               |
+------------+-----------+------------------+
```

Understanding and using aliases effectively can clarify and simplify SQL queries, facilitating better maintenance and comprehension, especially in complex database interactions.

3.11 Basic Date and Time Functions

Date and time functions are integral to managing and manipulating temporal data within MySQL databases. These functions provide a wide array of capabilities to extract, process, and format date and time values. Familiarity with these functions is essential for tasks requiring temporal data analysis and reporting.

Date and Time Retrieval Functions

A fundamental aspect of working with temporal data is the ability to retrieve the current date and time. The NOW() function returns the current date and time:

```
SELECT NOW();
```

The output is in the format 'YYYY-MM-DD HH:MM:SS':

```
+---------------------+
| NOW()               |
+---------------------+
| 2023-10-01 15:45:36 |
+---------------------+
```

To retrieve only the current date, the CURDATE() function is used:

```
SELECT CURDATE();
```

The output is in the format 'YYYY-MM-DD':

```
+------------+
| CURDATE()  |
+------------+
| 2023-10-01 |
+------------+
```

Similarly, CURTIME() returns the current time:

```
SELECT CURTIME();
```

The result is displayed in the format 'HH:MM:SS':

```
+----------+
| CURTIME()|
+----------+
| 15:45:36 |
+----------+
```

Date and Time Extraction Functions

To handle date and time values efficiently, it is often necessary to extract specific components from a complete date-time value.

The YEAR() function extracts the year:

```
SELECT YEAR('2023-10-01');
```

The result will be:

```
+-------------------+
| YEAR('2023-10-01')|
+-------------------+
| 2023              |
+-------------------+
```

Similarly, the MONTH() and DAY() functions extract the month and day components respectively:

```
SELECT MONTH('2023-10-01'), DAY('2023-10-01');
```

The output will be:

```
+-------------------+------------------+
| MONTH('2023-10-01')| DAY('2023-10-01')|
+-------------------+------------------+
| 10                | 1                |
+-------------------+------------------+
```

These functions can be used for hours, minutes, and seconds as well:

```
SELECT HOUR('15:45:36'), MINUTE('15:45:36'), SECOND('15:45:36');
```

The corresponding output would be:

```
+------------------+--------------------+--------------------+
| HOUR('15:45:36') | MINUTE('15:45:36') | SECOND('15:45:36') |
+------------------+--------------------+--------------------+
| 15               | 45                 | 36                 |
+------------------+--------------------+--------------------+
```

Date and Time Arithmetic

MySQL provides functions to perform arithmetic operations on date and time values. To add or subtract intervals, such as days, months, or years, functions like DATE_ADD() and DATE_SUB() are utilized.

For example, to add 10 days to a date:

```
SELECT DATE_ADD('2023-10-01', INTERVAL 10 DAY);
```

The result will reflect the new date:

```
+--------------------------------------+
| DATE_ADD('2023-10-01', INTERVAL 10 DAY)|
+--------------------------------------+
| 2023-10-11                           |
+--------------------------------------+
```

To subtract 2 months:

```
SELECT DATE_SUB('2023-10-01', INTERVAL 2 MONTH);
```

The output would be:

```
+---------------------------------------+
| DATE_SUB('2023-10-01', INTERVAL 2 MONTH)|
+---------------------------------------+
| 2023-08-01                            |
+---------------------------------------+
```

These functions support various interval units such as SECOND, MINUTE, HOUR, DAY, WEEK, MONTH, and YEAR.

Date and Time Formatting

Formatting is key to presenting date and time values in a readable and user-defined format. The DATE_FORMAT() function allows customization of the display format.

For instance, to format a date as 'Day, Month Year':

```
SELECT DATE_FORMAT('2023-10-01', '%W, %M %Y');
```

Resulting in:

```
+-------------------------------------------+
| DATE_FORMAT('2023-10-01', '%W, %M %Y')    |
+-------------------------------------------+
| Sunday, October 2023                      |
+-------------------------------------------+
```

Common format specifiers include:

- %Y: full year
- %y: two-digit year
- %M: full month name
- %m: two-digit month
- %d: day of the month
- %H: two-digit hour (24-hour format)
- %i: minutes
- %s: seconds

These formatting capabilities are vital for generating human-readable reports and custom date-time displays.

Handling Temporal Data Types

MySQL supports several temporal data types: DATE, TIME, DATETIME , TIMESTAMP, and YEAR. Each is designed to store distinct temporal information:

- **DATE:** Stores date values in 'YYYY-MM-DD' format.
- **TIME:** Stores time values in 'HH:MM:SS' format.
- **DATETIME:** Stores date and time values in 'YYYY-MM-DD HH:MM:SS' format.
- **TIMESTAMP:** Similar to DATETIME but with automatic time zone conversion.
- **YEAR:** Stores year values in either 2-digit or 4-digit format.

When defining a table schema, these data types ensure appropriate storage and manipulation of temporal data.

```
CREATE TABLE events (
    event_id INT AUTO_INCREMENT PRIMARY KEY,
    event_name VARCHAR(100),
    event_date DATE,
    event_time TIME,
    created_at TIMESTAMP DEFAULT CURRENT_TIMESTAMP
);
```

The above schema defines a table to hold event data with fields for the event date, time, and creation timestamp.

Mastering these functions equips you with robust tools to manage complex temporal datasets, facilitating sophisticated data analysis and ensuring precision in data operations.

3.12 String Functions and Operations

String functions in SQL serve a vital role in retrieving and manipulating text data stored in database tables. MySQL offers a wide range of functions designed to handle strings effectively, from basic operations such as concatenation and finding substring lengths to more complex functions like pattern matching and replacing segments of text. This section will cover the most commonly used string functions in MySQL, providing necessary syntax and examples.

MySQL provides several functions for handling strings. Some of the most commonly used ones include:

- **CONCAT()**
- **LENGTH()**

- **SUBSTRING()**
- **REPLACE()**
- **UPPER() and LOWER()**
- **TRIM()**
- **LPAD() and RPAD()**

CONCAT() is used to concatenate two or more strings into a single string. The syntax for the CONCAT() function is as follows:

```
SELECT CONCAT(string1, string2, ..., stringN);
```

Example:

```
SELECT CONCAT('Hello', ' ', 'World') AS greeting;
```

Output:

```
+-----------+
| greeting |
+-----------+
| Hello World |
+-----------+
```

LENGTH() returns the length of a string in bytes. The syntax for the LENGTH() function is:

```
SELECT LENGTH(string);
```

Example:

```
SELECT LENGTH('Database') AS length;
```

Output:

```
+--------+
| length |
+--------+
| 8      |
+--------+
```

SUBSTRING() extracts a substring from a longer string starting at a specified position. The syntax is:

```
SELECT SUBSTRING(string, position, length);
```

Example:

```
SELECT SUBSTRING('Hello World', 7, 5) AS substring;
```

Output:

```
+-----------+
| substring |
+-----------+
| World     |
+-----------+
```

REPLACE() replaces all occurrences of a substring with another substring. The syntax is:

```
SELECT REPLACE(string, substring_to_replace, replacement_substring);
```

Example:

```
SELECT REPLACE('Hello World', 'World', 'MySQL') AS updated_string;
```

Output:

```
+----------------+
| updated_string |
+----------------+
| Hello MySQL    |
+----------------+
```

UPPER() and **LOWER()** functions convert a string to uppercase or lowercase, respectively. The syntax for these functions is:

```
SELECT UPPER(string);
SELECT LOWER(string);
```

Examples:

```
SELECT UPPER('hello') AS upper_string;
SELECT LOWER('WORLD') AS lower_string;
```

Output:

```
+--------------+
| upper_string |
+--------------+
| HELLO        |
+--------------+
+--------------+
| lower_string |
+--------------+
| world        |
+--------------+
```

TRIM() removes leading and trailing spaces from a string. The syntax for the TRIM() function is:

```
SELECT TRIM(string);
```

Example:

```
SELECT TRIM(' Hello World ') AS trimmed_string;
```

Output:

```
+----------------+
| trimmed_string |
+----------------+
| Hello World    |
+----------------+
```

LPAD() and **RPAD()** functions pad a string to a certain length with another string. The syntax for these functions is as follows:

```
SELECT LPAD(string, length, pad_string);
SELECT RPAD(string, length, pad_string);
```

Examples:

```
SELECT LPAD('MySQL', 10, '*') AS lpad_string;
SELECT RPAD('MySQL', 10, '*') AS rpad_string;
```

Output:

```
+-------------+
| lpad_string |
+-------------+
| *****MySQL  |
+-------------+
+-------------+
| rpad_string |
+-------------+
| MySQL*****  |
+-------------+
```

These functions lay a solid foundation for handling and manipulating string data in MySQL. Understanding the application and integration of these functions into queries can significantly enhance data retrieval and transformation capabilities.

Chapter 4

Advanced SQL Queries

This chapter delves into more complex SQL querying techniques in MySQL. It covers subqueries and nested queries, the use of Common Table Expressions (CTEs), and window functions. Advanced join techniques, the use of UNION, INTERSECT, and EXCEPT, as well as sophisticated GROUP BY methods are discussed. The chapter also addresses handling NULL values, working with temporary tables, and the implementation of views and materialized views. Additional sections include dynamic SQL, error handling in queries, and recursive queries.

4.1 Subqueries and Nested Queries

Subqueries and nested queries are pivotal for constructing complex SQL queries. A subquery or inner query is a query nested within another SQL query, whereas the outer query is a standard SQL query. Subqueries can be placed in various clauses such as SELECT, FROM, WHERE, and HAVING, and are typically utilized to streamline complex operations and enhance the readability of the SQL code.

A subquery can return a scalar (single value), a row of values, or a table (set of rows), depending on its use case. It is essential to understand the basic types of subqueries: single-row subqueries, multi-row subqueries, and correlated subqueries.

Single-Row Subqueries: These return only one row and are often used with comparison operators such as =, <, >, <=, >=, and <>. For example:

```
SELECT employee_id, first_name, last_name
FROM employees
WHERE salary > (SELECT AVG(salary)
                FROM employees
                WHERE department_id = 30);
```

This query retrieves the employee details where the salary is greater than the average salary of employees in department 30. The subquery calculates the average salary, and the outer query filters employees based on this average.

Multi-Row Subqueries: These return multiple rows and are used with operators like IN, ANY, ALL, and EXISTS. For instance:

```
SELECT employee_id, first_name, last_name
FROM employees
WHERE department_id IN (SELECT department_id
                        FROM departments
                        WHERE location_id = 1700);
```

Here, the subquery returns a list of department IDs based in location 1700, and the outer query retrieves employees working in those departments.

Correlated Subqueries: Unlike other subqueries, a correlated subquery depends on the outer query for its values. It is executed repeatedly, once for each row selected by the outer query. An example:

```
SELECT e1.employee_id, e1.first_name, e1.last_name
FROM employees e1
WHERE EXISTS (SELECT 1
              FROM employees e2
              WHERE e2.manager_id = e1.employee_id);
```

This query fetches employee details for those employees who are managers (i.e., their employee IDs exist as manager IDs in the employees table).

Using Subqueries in SELECT: Subqueries in the SELECT clause generally perform calculations or fetch additional data that is incorporated into the result set of the outer query.

```
SELECT employee_id, first_name, last_name,
      (SELECT department_name
       FROM departments
       WHERE department_id = employees.department_id) AS department
FROM employees;
```

In this example, for each employee, the subquery retrieves the department name and includes it in the final result set.

Subqueries in FROM Clause: Sometimes referred to as inline views or derived tables, subqueries in the FROM clause act as temporary tables that the outer query uses to retrieve data. Example:

```
SELECT employee_id, first_name, last_name, avg_salary
FROM employees,
    (SELECT department_id, AVG(salary) AS avg_salary
     FROM employees
     GROUP BY department_id) dept_avg
WHERE employees.department_id = dept_avg.department_id;
```

The subquery calculates the average salary per department, and the outer query joins this result with the employees table to include the average salary for each employee's department.

Subqueries in WHERE and HAVING Clauses: Subqueries are frequently used in WHERE and HAVING clauses to filter results based on complex conditions. For example:

```
SELECT employee_id, first_name, last_name
FROM employees
WHERE department_id = 10
  AND salary > (SELECT MAX(salary)
                FROM employees
                WHERE department_id = 20);
```

This query retrieves details of employees in department 10 whose salaries are higher than the highest salary in department 20.

Subqueries with EXISTS and NOT EXISTS: The EXISTS and NOT EXISTS operators are used to check if subqueries return any records. They are efficient as SQL optimizers often optimize these queries differently. Example:

```
SELECT first_name, last_name
FROM employees e1
WHERE EXISTS (SELECT 1
              FROM dependents d
              WHERE d.employee_id = e1.employee_id);
```

This query lists employees who have at least one dependent. The subquery verifies the existence of their dependents, returning true if found.

It is crucial to ensure subqueries are well-indexed, especially correlated subqueries, as performance might degrade due to repeated execution. Using EXPLAIN and execution plans to review and optimize subquery performance is recommended diligently.

Through understanding and mastering these advanced query techniques with subqueries and nested queries, one can efficiently tackle a wide array of database querying needs, refining both the complexity and efficiency of database operations.

4.2 Common Table Expressions (CTEs)

Common Table Expressions (CTEs) provide a versatile method for organizing complex queries, promoting readability and maintainability by allowing the developer to break down complicated SQL statements into more manageable subqueries. CTEs can also be recursive, facilitating operations that require iterative processing.

A CTE is typically defined using the WITH clause, followed by the CTE name and the query that constitutes the CTE. This named result set can then be referenced within another query, much like a temporary result set. The syntax for a simple, non-recursive CTE is as follows:

```
WITH cte_name AS (
    SELECT column1, column2, ...
    FROM table_name
    WHERE condition
)
SELECT column1, column2, ...
FROM cte_name
WHERE condition;
```

To illustrate the practical application of CTEs, consider the following example where we wish to find the average salary by department and include departments with above-average payrolls. First, we construct our CTE to compute the average salary:

```
WITH AvgDeptSalaries AS (
    SELECT department_id, AVG(salary) AS avg_salary
    FROM employees
    GROUP BY department_id
)
SELECT department_id, avg_salary
FROM AvgDeptSalaries
WHERE avg_salary > (
    SELECT AVG(salary)
    FROM employees
);
```

In this example, the AvgDeptSalaries CTE calculates the average salary per department. The outer query then filters departments with an average salary above the company's overall average salary. This demonstrates the utility of CTEs in breaking down complex query logic into simpler, more comprehensible steps.

CTEs can also be recursive, enabling hierarchical data processing tasks, such as traversing organizational charts or processing bill-of-material structures. A recursive CTE includes an anchor member, which initializes the recursion, and a recursive member, which refers back to the CTE itself. The syntax for a recursive CTE is:

```
WITH RECURSIVE cte_name AS (
    -- Anchor member
    SELECT column1, column2, ...
    FROM table_name
    WHERE condition
    UNION ALL
    -- Recursive member
    SELECT column1, column2, ...
    FROM table_name
    INNER JOIN cte_name ON table_name.column = cte_name.column
)
SELECT column1, column2, ...
FROM cte_name;
```

To elucidate the concept with an example, we consider an employee hierarchy where each employee reports to a manager. The following recursive CTE helps us retrieve all subordinates of a particular manager:

```
WITH RECURSIVE EmployeeHierarchy AS (
    -- Anchor member: starting at the given manager
    SELECT employee_id, manager_id, name
    FROM employees
    WHERE manager_id IS NULL
    UNION ALL
    -- Recursive member: find employees reporting to the current level
    SELECT e.employee_id, e.manager_id, e.name
    FROM employees e
    INNER JOIN EmployeeHierarchy eh ON e.manager_id = eh.employee_id
)
SELECT employee_id, manager_id, name
FROM EmployeeHierarchy;
```

Here, EmployeeHierarchy starts by selecting the top-level managers (where manager_id is NULL). The recursion then continues to find employees reporting to these managers and iteratively applies this logic to lower levels of the hierarchy.

CTEs are advantageous for numerous reasons:

- **Improved Readability:** By segmenting a large query into smaller parts, CTEs make query logic easier to understand and maintain.
- **Elimination of Subqueries:** CTEs can often replace subqueries, reducing the complexity of the query and enhancing the ability to debug and optimize individual components.
- **Support for Recursion:** Recursive CTEs are invaluable for

traversing hierarchical data structures, which are common in organizational data and graph-related queries.

- **Logical Abstraction:** CTEs allow for logical abstraction and reuse within a query, acting similarly to temporary tables but confined to the duration of the query.

Consider another example where multiple CTEs are used sequentially. Suppose we want to determine the departments with the highest total salaries for employees hired within the last year:

```
WITH RecentHires AS (
    SELECT employee_id, department_id, salary, hire_date
    FROM employees
    WHERE hire_date >= DATE_SUB(CURDATE(), INTERVAL 1 YEAR)
),
DeptSalaries AS (
    SELECT department_id, SUM(salary) AS total_salary
    FROM RecentHires
    GROUP BY department_id
)
SELECT department_id, total_salary
FROM DeptSalaries
ORDER BY total_salary DESC
LIMIT 5;
```

In this case, the RecentHires CTE selects all employees hired within the last year, while the DeptSalaries CTE aggregates the total salaries for these recent hires by department. The final query then retrieves the top five departments with the highest total salaries.

CTEs significantly enhance the power and flexibility of SQL, particularly in MySQL. By promoting clean, modular query design, they empower developers to tackle complex data retrieval tasks systematically and efficiently, fostering clearer and more maintainable codebases.

4.3 Window Functions

Window functions are a set of SQL functionalities that enable the execution of calculations across a set of table rows related to the current row. This capability allows complex analyses to be performed over specific partitions or windows of data, enabling sophisticated querying techniques that go beyond standard group-based aggregations.

Unlike aggregate functions that return single result rows based on sets of rows, window functions perform calculations across a set of table rows while retaining the underlying row identities. This section focuses on the foundational concepts, syntax, and practical usage of window functions in MySQL, considering their relevance to advanced querying techniques.

Basic Syntax and Components

A window function in SQL comprises an OVER() clause, which determines the window or set of rows the function will apply to. The OVER() clause can contain the following components:

- PARTITION BY: This divides the result set into partitions to which the function applies.
- ORDER BY: This orders the rows within each partition.
- ROWS or RANGE: Specifies the frame for the window, defining which rows qualify relative to the current row.

The general syntax is as follows:

```
window_function() OVER (
    [PARTITION BY expression1, expression2, ...]
    [ORDER BY expression3, expression4, ...]
    [ROWS|RANGE between_frame_definition]
)
```

Important window functions in MySQL include ROW_NUMBER(), RANK(), DENSE_RANK(), LAG(), LEAD(), and various aggregate functions used as window functions.

ROW_NUMBER() Function

The ROW_NUMBER() function assigns a unique sequential integer to rows within a partition. Each partition starts numbering from 1, and numbering continues in the order specified by the ORDER BY clause.

Example:

```
SELECT employee_id, first_name, department_id,
       ROW_NUMBER() OVER (PARTITION BY department_id ORDER BY salary
              DESC) AS row_num
FROM employees;
```

The output assigns a row number to each employee, partitioned by department_id and ordered by salary within each partition:

```
employee_id | first_name | department_id | row_num
--------------------------------------------------
          1 | John       |            30 |       1
          4 | Lara       |            30 |       2
          5 | Peter      |            20 |       1
          6 | Alice      |            20 |       2
```

RANK() and DENSE_RANK() Functions

The RANK() function provides a rank number to each row within a partition, generating the same rank for rows with identical values. Gaps can exist between rank numbers. Conversely, DENSE_RANK() operates similarly but ensures no gaps exist between rank numbers.

Example:

```
SELECT employee_id, first_name, department_id, salary,
       RANK() OVER (PARTITION BY department_id ORDER BY salary DESC) AS
            rank,
       DENSE_RANK() OVER (PARTITION BY department_id ORDER BY salary
            DESC) AS dense_rank
FROM employees;
```

Output illustrating both ranking methods:

```
employee_id | first_name | department_id | salary | rank | dense_rank
---------------------------------------------------------------------
          1 | John       |            30 | 80000  |   1  |         1
          4 | Lara       |            30 | 75000  |   2  |         2
          5 | Peter      |            20 | 60000  |   1  |         1
          6 | Alice      |            20 | 60000  |   1  |         1
```

LAG() and LEAD() Functions

These functions access data from preceding (LAG) or succeeding (LEAD) rows at a specific offset. They are instrumental for tasks requiring comparison between current and prior or subsequent entries within the same partition.

Example:

```
SELECT employee_id, first_name, department_id, salary,
       LAG(salary, 1, 0) OVER (PARTITION BY department_id ORDER BY salary)
            AS prev_salary,
       LEAD(salary, 1, 0) OVER (PARTITION BY department_id ORDER BY salary)
            AS next_salary
FROM employees;
```

The result compares each employee's salary with the previous and next employee's salary:

```
employee_id | first_name | department_id | salary | prev_salary | next_salary
----------------------------------------------------------------------------
          1 | John       |            30 | 80000  |           0 |       75000
          4 | Lara       |            30 | 75000  |       80000 |           0
          5 | Peter      |            20 | 60000  |           0 |       60000
          6 | Alice      |            20 | 60000  |       60000 |           0
```

Aggregate Functions as Window Functions

Common aggregate functions like SUM(), AVG(), and COUNT() can also be employed as window functions to perform cumulative or moving calculations.

```
SELECT employee_id, department_id, salary,
       SUM(salary) OVER (PARTITION BY department_id ORDER BY salary ROWS
            BETWEEN UNBOUNDED PRECEDING AND CURRENT ROW) AS
           cumulative_salary
FROM employees;
```

The output calculates the cumulative salary within each department:

```
employee_id | department_id | salary | cumulative_salary
--------------------------------------------------------
          1 |            30 | 80000  |             80000
          4 |            30 | 75000  |            155000
          5 |            20 | 60000  |             60000
          6 |            20 | 60000  |            120000
```

This section has examined significant window functions, elucidating their syntax and practical applications in MySQL. These functions provide extensive capabilities for sophisticated data analysis and manipulation, invaluable in advanced SQL querying contexts.

4.4 Advanced JOIN Techniques

In relational databases, JOIN operations are essential for combining rows from two or more tables based on related columns. Advanced JOIN techniques extend the basic functionality to accommodate complex queries and enhance data retrieval efficiency.

1. Self-JOINs

A self-JOIN is a regular join but the table is joined with itself. This technique is useful in hierarchical data, where you may need to relate rows within the same table based on a hierarchical relationship.

```
SELECT A.employee_id, A.employee_name, B.manager_id, B.manager_name
FROM employees A
JOIN employees B ON A.manager_id = B.employee_id;
```

In this query, the employees table is joined with itself to find the manager names along with the employee details.

2. CROSS JOIN

A CROSS JOIN produces the Cartesian product of the two tables involved. Each row of the first table is paired with all rows in the second table.

```
SELECT A.product_id, B.customer_id
FROM products A
CROSS JOIN customers B;
```

This will return every possible combination of product_id and customer_id, which could be useful for generating all possible pairs for certain operations.

3. OUTER JOINS

OUTER JOINS can be classified into LEFT JOIN, RIGHT JOIN, and FULL JOIN. These joins return all rows from one table and the matched rows from the other table. If there is no match, NULL values are returned for columns of the table without a match.

Left Outer Join

```
SELECT A.customer_id, A.customer_name, B.order_id
FROM customers A
LEFT OUTER JOIN orders B ON A.customer_id = B.customer_id;
```

This retrieves all customers and their orders, including customers who have not placed any orders.

Right Outer Join

```
SELECT A.customer_id, A.customer_name, B.order_id
FROM customers A
RIGHT OUTER JOIN orders B ON A.customer_id = B.customer_id;
```

This retrieves all orders and their corresponding customers, including orders that haven't been placed by any customer, which is often unusual but may be useful in certain audits.

Full Outer Join MySQL does not support the FULL OUTER JOIN clause directly. However, it can be simulated using UNION:

```
SELECT A.customer_id, A.customer_name, B.order_id
FROM customers A
LEFT JOIN orders B ON A.customer_id = B.customer_id
UNION
SELECT A.customer_id, A.customer_name, B.order_id
FROM customers A
RIGHT JOIN orders B ON A.customer_id = B.customer_id;
```

This query ensures that all records from either customers or orders are included, with matching rows aligned side-by-side.

4. Using UNION, INTERSECT, and EXCEPT with JOINs

UNION, INTERSECT, and EXCEPT operators can be used in conjunction with JOIN operations to achieve more complex querying.

Union

```
SELECT customer_id, customer_name
FROM customers
```

```
WHERE region = 'North'
UNION
SELECT customer_id, customer_name
FROM customers
WHERE region = 'South';
```

Combining this with a JOIN:

```
SELECT A.customer_id, A.customer_name, B.order_id
FROM (
  SELECT customer_id, customer_name
  FROM customers
  WHERE region = 'North'
  UNION
  SELECT customer_id, customer_name
  FROM customers
  WHERE region = 'South'
) A
LEFT JOIN orders B ON A.customer_id = B.customer_id;
```

This combines customers from the North and South regions, then joins their orders.

5. Advanced JOIN Conditions

Join conditions can use more than primary key relations and can include complex expressions.

```
SELECT E1.employee_id, E1.employee_name, E2.employee_name AS manager_name
FROM employees E1
JOIN employees E2
ON E1.manager_id = E2.employee_id
AND E1.hire_date > E2.hire_date;
```

In this scenario, we retrieve employees along with their managers, but only if the employee was hired after the manager.

6. Anti-JOIN

An Anti-JOIN retrieves rows from the left table that do not have corresponding rows in the right table. It is useful in finding records with no related entries.

```
SELECT C.customer_id, C.customer_name
FROM customers C
LEFT JOIN orders O ON C.customer_id = O.customer_id
WHERE O.order_id IS NULL;
```

This identifies customers who have never placed an order.

7. Using EXISTS with JOINs

The EXISTS keyword can be used to test for the presence of rows in a subquery, which is often more performant in correlated subqueries.

```
SELECT C.customer_id, C.customer_name
FROM customers C
WHERE EXISTS (
  SELECT 1
  FROM orders O
  WHERE O.customer_id = C.customer_id
  AND O.order_date > '2023-01-01'
);
```

This returns customers who have placed orders after January 1, 2023.

These advanced JOIN techniques provide tools for handling a variety of complex querying scenarios, enhancing relational database querying capabilities significantly.

4.5 Using UNION, INTERSECT, and EXCEPT

The SQL set operations UNION, INTERSECT, and EXCEPT provide advanced functionality for combining result sets from multiple SELECT statements. These operations allow for sophisticated data manipulation and retrieval techniques essential for complex query requirements. Mastering these operations contributes significantly to one's expertise in SQL.

UNION combines the results of two or more SELECT statements into a single result set. By default, it removes duplicate rows unless the ALL keyword is specified. The basic syntax is:

```
SELECT column1, column2, ...
FROM table1
UNION [ALL]
SELECT column1, column2, ...
FROM table2;
```

Consider the following example:

```
SELECT first_name, last_name
FROM employees
WHERE department = 'Sales'
UNION
SELECT first_name, last_name
FROM employees
WHERE department = 'Marketing';
```

This query retrieves a list of first and last names of employees from both the Sales and Marketing departments, excluding duplicates. To include duplicates, use UNION ALL:

```
SELECT first_name, last_name
FROM employees
```

```
WHERE department = 'Sales'
UNION ALL
SELECT first_name, last_name
FROM employees
WHERE department = 'Marketing';
```

The **INTERSECT** operation returns the intersection of two result sets, that is, only the rows that appear in both result sets. MySQL does not natively support INTERSECT; it can be emulated using a subquery with an INNER JOIN:

```
SELECT first_name, last_name
FROM employees
WHERE department = 'Sales'
INTERSECT
SELECT first_name, last_name
FROM employees
WHERE department = 'Marketing';
```

To emulate this in MySQL:

```
SELECT first_name, last_name
FROM employees e1
WHERE e1.department = 'Sales'
AND EXISTS (
    SELECT 1
    FROM employees e2
    WHERE e2.department = 'Marketing'
    AND e1.first_name = e2.first_name
    AND e1.last_name = e2.last_name
);
```

The EXISTS clause checks for the existence of rows in the subquery that match the condition.

The **EXCEPT** operation, which MySQL also does not support natively, returns rows from the first result set that do not appear in the second result set. This can be emulated using a subquery with LEFT JOIN and IS NULL:

```
SELECT first_name, last_name
FROM employees
WHERE department = 'Sales'
EXCEPT
SELECT first_name, last_name
FROM employees
WHERE department = 'Marketing';
```

To achieve this in MySQL:

```
SELECT first_name, last_name
FROM employees e1
WHERE e1.department = 'Sales'
AND NOT EXISTS (
    SELECT 1
```

```
    FROM employees e2
    WHERE e2.department = 'Marketing'
    AND e1.first_name = e2.first_name
    AND e1.last_name = e2.last_name
);
```

This query filters out the employees from the Sales department who are also in the Marketing department.

In summary, understanding and effectively using UNION, INTERSECT, and EXCEPT enhances SQL data retrieval capabilities, facilitating the execution of intricate queries that require merging and comparing data from multiple sources.

4.6 Advanced GROUP BY Techniques

Advanced grouping techniques in SQL can help in summarizing and analyzing data more effectively. The GROUP BY clause is typically used to aggregate data and is often employed with aggregate functions like COUNT(), SUM(), AVG(), MAX(), and MIN(). Advanced GROUP BY techniques can leverage multiple columns, rollup operations, cube operations, grouping sets, and complex expressions to gain deeper insights.

Consider the following dataset of sales transactions:

```
CREATE TABLE Sales (
    TransactionID INT PRIMARY KEY,
    ProductID INT,
    CustomerID INT,
    Quantity INT,
    Price DECIMAL(10, 2),
    TransactionDate DATE
);

INSERT INTO Sales (TransactionID, ProductID, CustomerID, Quantity, Price,
      TransactionDate) VALUES
(1, 101, 1, 2, 300.00, '2023-01-01'),
(2, 102, 2, 1, 150.00, '2023-01-03'),
(3, 101, 1, 1, 300.00, '2023-01-07'),
(4, 103, 3, 4, 200.00, '2023-01-10'),
(5, 101, 4, 1, 300.00, '2023-01-12');
```

Multiple Columns in GROUP BY

A basic example of grouping by multiple columns is shown below, which groups the total sales by ProductID and CustomerID:

```
SELECT ProductID, CustomerID, SUM(Quantity * Price) AS TotalSales
FROM Sales
GROUP BY ProductID, CustomerID;
```

This query results in:

```
ProductID | CustomerID | TotalSales
-----------+------------+------------
      101 |          1 |     900.00
      102 |          2 |     150.00
      103 |          3 |     800.00
      101 |          4 |     300.00
```

ROLLUP

The ROLLUP operator provides a way to add subtotals and a grand total to the results. The following example demonstrates its usage:

```
SELECT ProductID, CustomerID, SUM(Quantity * Price) AS TotalSales
FROM Sales
GROUP BY ROLLUP(ProductID, CustomerID);
```

This produces:

```
ProductID | CustomerID | TotalSales
-----------+------------+------------
      101 |          1 |     900.00
      101 |          4 |     300.00
      101 |       NULL |    1200.00
      102 |          2 |     150.00
      102 |       NULL |     150.00
      103 |          3 |     800.00
      103 |       NULL |     800.00
     NULL |       NULL |    2150.00
```

The ROLLUP adds an extra row for each subtotal at each level of aggregation and a final row for the grand total.

CUBE

The CUBE operator generates a result set that shows aggregates for all combinations of values in the columns specified. Here is the CUBE operation:

```
SELECT ProductID, CustomerID, SUM(Quantity * Price) AS TotalSales
FROM Sales
GROUP BY CUBE(ProductID, CustomerID);
```

This results in:

```
ProductID | CustomerID | TotalSales
-----------+------------+------------
       101 |          1 |     900.00
       101 |          4 |     300.00
       101 |       NULL |    1200.00
       102 |          2 |     150.00
       102 |       NULL |     150.00
       103 |          3 |     800.00
       103 |       NULL |     800.00
      NULL |          1 |     900.00
      NULL |          2 |     150.00
      NULL |          3 |     800.00
      NULL |          4 |     300.00
      NULL |       NULL |    2150.00
```

The CUBE operation results in a superset of ROLLUP with more aggregation combinations.

GROUPING SETS

A more flexible aggregation can be achieved with GROUPING SETS, which allows specifying multiple groupings in a single query:

```
SELECT ProductID, CustomerID, SUM(Quantity * Price) AS TotalSales
FROM Sales
GROUP BY GROUPING SETS (
    (ProductID),
    (CustomerID),
    (ProductID, CustomerID),
    ()
);
```

This produces:

```
ProductID | CustomerID | TotalSales
-----------+------------+------------
       101 |       NULL |    1200.00
       102 |       NULL |     150.00
       103 |       NULL |     800.00
      NULL |          1 |     900.00
      NULL |          2 |     150.00
      NULL |          3 |     800.00
      NULL |          4 |     300.00
       101 |          1 |     900.00
       101 |          4 |     300.00
       102 |          2 |     150.00
       103 |          3 |     800.00
      NULL |       NULL |    2150.00
```

The GROUPING SETS operation is customizable and a powerful tool for tailored aggregation.

Complex Expressions in GROUP BY

The GROUP BY clause is not restricted to column names; you can use complex expressions as well. For example, grouping by year and month of the transaction date:

```
SELECT YEAR(TransactionDate) AS Year, MONTH(TransactionDate) AS Month,
```

```
    SUM(Quantity * Price) AS TotalSales
FROM Sales
GROUP BY YEAR(TransactionDate), MONTH(TransactionDate);
```

This provides a clear summary per month:

```
 Year | Month | TotalSales
------+-------+------------
 2023 |     1 |    2150.00
```

Advanced GROUP BY techniques provide versatile tools for data aggregation and are essential for complex data analysis in MySQL.

4.7 Handling NULL Values

In SQL, a NULL value represents missing or unknown data. Handling NULL values correctly is crucial due to their distinct behavior in operations and comparisons. This section explores various techniques to manage NULL values effectively in MySQL.

1. Detection of NULL Values

To detect NULL values, the IS NULL and IS NOT NULL operators are utilized. Consider the following table employees with some missing data:

```
CREATE TABLE employees (
    id INT AUTO_INCREMENT PRIMARY KEY,
    name VARCHAR(50),
    department VARCHAR(50),
    salary DECIMAL(10, 2)
);

INSERT INTO employees (name, department, salary) VALUES
('Alice', 'HR', 50000),
('Bob', NULL, 60000),
('Charlie', 'Engineering', NULL),
('Diana', 'HR', 65000);
```

To find employees with missing department information:

```
SELECT name FROM employees WHERE department IS NULL;
```

```
name
Bob
```

Similarly, to find employees with known salary information:

```
SELECT name FROM employees WHERE salary IS NOT NULL;
```

name
Alice
Bob
Diana

2. Dealing with NULL in Comparisons

A comparison involving NULL will always yield NULL. For example:

```
SELECT name FROM employees WHERE department = NULL;
```

This query returns an empty result set because no comparison with NULL yields TRUE. The appropriate way is to use IS NULL as shown above.

3. Using IFNULL, COALESCE, and NULLIF

The IFNULL function replaces NULL with a specified value. For instance, to replace NULL salaries with 0:

```
SELECT name, IFNULL(salary, 0) AS salary FROM employees;
```

name	salary
Alice	50000.00
Bob	60000.00
Charlie	0.00
Diana	65000.00

The COALESCE function returns the first non-NULL value among its arguments:

```
SELECT name, COALESCE(salary, 0) AS salary FROM employees;
```

The NULLIF function returns NULL if the two arguments are equal, otherwise, it returns the first argument. This is useful for avoiding division by zero errors:

```
SELECT name, salary / NULLIF(salary, 0) AS salary_ratio FROM employees;
```

4. Implications in Aggregate Functions

Aggregate functions such as SUM, AVG, MAX, MIN, and COUNT handle NULL values differently. COUNT excludes NULL values unless COUNT(*) is used.

Example:

```
SELECT SUM(salary) AS total_salary, AVG(salary) AS average_salary FROM
    employees;
```

total_salary	average_salary
175000.00	58333.33

Here, SUM and AVG ignore the NULL value for Charlie.

5. Sorting and NULL

When sorting, NULL values are considered lower than all non-NULL values by default. If a different sorting order is required, the IS NULL clause can be used.

Example for sorting salaries with NULL last:

```
SELECT name, salary FROM employees ORDER BY salary IS NULL, salary;
```

```
name    salary
Alice   50000.00
Bob     60000.00
Diana   65000.00
Charlie NULL
```

6. Conditional Logic and NULL

The CASE statement can manage NULL values effectively:

```
SELECT name,
    CASE
        WHEN salary IS NULL THEN 'Unknown'
        ELSE salary
    END AS salary_status
FROM employees;
```

```
name    salary_status
Alice   50000.00
Bob     60000.00
Charlie Unknown
Diana   65000.00
```

Inserting, updating, and filtering NULL values in a dataset is fundamental in SQL operations. Proper handling of NULL values ensures data integrity and accurate query results.

4.8 Temporary Tables

Temporary tables are a powerful feature in MySQL that allows you to store transient data within your session's context. These tables exist only for the duration of a database session, leading to efficient and resource-conservative data manipulation. Temporary tables are useful for breaking down complex queries into simpler steps, performing intermediate calculations, or storing results that do not need to persist.

A temporary table is created using the CREATE TEMPORARY TABLE statement. The syntax is similar to that of creating a regular table, with the addition of the TEMPORARY keyword.

```
CREATE TEMPORARY TABLE temp_table_name (
```

```
    column1 datatype [constraint],
    column2 datatype [constraint],
    ...
);
```

For instance, consider a scenario where you need to perform several transformations on a dataset before arriving at the final result. This can be managed by storing intermediate results in temporary tables. Let's create a temporary table to store these intermediate results:

```
CREATE TEMPORARY TABLE temp_sales_summary (
    product_id INT,
    total_sales DECIMAL(10, 2)
);
```

You can insert data into the temporary table as you would with a normal table. This often involves using INSERT INTO ... SELECT statements:

```
INSERT INTO temp_sales_summary (product_id, total_sales)
SELECT product_id, SUM(sales_amount)
FROM sales
GROUP BY product_id;
```

Temporary tables can also leverage indexes. Creating an index on a temporary table follows the same process as with a regular table:

```
CREATE INDEX idx_product_id ON temp_sales_summary(product_id);
```

Using temporary tables, complex data transformations can be simplified and made more readable. Consider a more detailed example involving multiple transformations:

1. Extract the total sales per product. 2. Filter products with low sales. 3. Store the final results for further processing.

```
-- Step 1: Calculate total sales per product
CREATE TEMPORARY TABLE temp_product_sales AS
SELECT
    product_id,
    SUM(sales_amount) AS total_sales
FROM
    sales
GROUP BY
    product_id;

-- Step 2: Filter products with sales above a threshold
CREATE TEMPORARY TABLE temp_filtered_sales AS
SELECT
    product_id,
    total_sales
FROM
    temp_product_sales
WHERE
```

```
    total_sales > 1000;

-- Step 3: Use results in further processing
SELECT
    product_id,
    total_sales
FROM
    temp_filtered_sales;
```

Upon closing the database session, any temporary tables created within that session are automatically dropped. However, it's good practice to manually drop temporary tables once they are no longer needed to free up resources. Dropping a temporary table is straightforward:

```
DROP TEMPORARY TABLE IF EXISTS temp_table_name;
```

Temporary tables do have some constraints. They are specific to the connection that creates them and are not accessible by other connections. This property ensures work carried out in a temporary table does not interfere with other database operations. Furthermore, a temporary table can have the same name as a regular table; MySQL will prioritize the temporary table for any operations performed by the session that created it.

In addition to the basic uses, temporary tables are instrumental in optimizing the performance of complex queries by storing intermediate computation results. They minimize data redundancy and provide a clean slate for operations that are session-specific and do not require persistent storage. Arrays of applications include data transformation stages in ETL processes, simplifying multi-step analyses, and reducing the complexity of dynamic SQL operations through temporary data storage. This makes temporary tables a versatile and invaluable tool for advanced query optimization and data handling techniques.

4.9 Views and Materialized Views

A view in MySQL is a virtual table based on the result set of an SQL query. Unlike a regular table, a view does not hold data; it dynamically retrieves data from the underlying tables whenever the view is referenced. Views can encapsulate complex SQL logic, simplify query usage, and provide an additional layer of security. In contrast, a materialized view stores the result set of a query physically, offering faster access times at the expense of storage space and periodic refresh requirements.

To create a view in MySQL, utilize the CREATE VIEW statement followed by the view name and the defining query. Consider the following example, which creates a view to display customer order summaries:

```
CREATE VIEW customer_order_summary AS
SELECT c.customer_id, c.customer_name,
       COUNT(o.order_id) AS total_orders,
       SUM(o.order_amount) AS total_amount
FROM customers c
JOIN orders o ON c.customer_id = o.customer_id
GROUP BY c.customer_id, c.customer_name;
```

```
Query OK, 0 rows affected (0.03 sec)
```

The view named customer_order_summary consolidates order data for each customer, showing the number of orders and the corresponding total amount. This view can now be queried as if it were a table:

```
SELECT * FROM customer_order_summary
WHERE total_amount > 1000;
```

Views can also be updated under certain conditions. However, complex views involving joins, aggregations, or subqueries may not support direct updates. If updates are permissible, they propagate to the underlying base tables. The following example shows an update on a simple view:

```
CREATE VIEW customer_details AS
SELECT customer_id, customer_name
FROM customers;

UPDATE customer_details
SET customer_name = 'John Doe'
WHERE customer_id = 1;
```

```
Query OK, 1 row affected (0.05 sec)
Rows matched: 1  Changed: 1  Warnings: 0
```

The update reflects in the customers table. To modify a view definition, use the CREATE OR REPLACE VIEW statement:

```
CREATE OR REPLACE VIEW customer_order_summary AS
SELECT c.customer_id, c.customer_name,
       COUNT(o.order_id) AS total_orders,
       SUM(o.order_amount) AS total_amount,
       AVG(o.order_amount) AS average_amount
FROM customers c
JOIN orders o ON c.customer_id = o.customer_id
GROUP BY c.customer_id, c.customer_name;
```

```
Query OK, 0 rows affected (0.04 sec)
```

This modification adds a new column, average_amount, to the customer_order_summary view. To delete a view, utilize the DROP VIEW statement:

```
DROP VIEW customer_order_summary;
```

```
Query OK, 0 rows affected (0.02 sec)
```

Materialized views are not natively supported in MySQL, but similar functionalities can be achieved through a combination of physical tables and scheduled data refreshes. One approach involves creating a table to store the materialized data, populating it using an INSERT INTO ... SELECT statement, and setting up a scheduled task to refresh the data.

For instance, to simulate a materialized view for the customer_order_summary, first create a physical table:

```
CREATE TABLE materialized_customer_order_summary AS
SELECT c.customer_id, c.customer_name,
       COUNT(o.order_id) AS total_orders,
       SUM(o.order_amount) AS total_amount,
       AVG(o.order_amount) AS average_amount
FROM customers c
JOIN orders o ON c.customer_id = o.customer_id
GROUP BY c.customer_id, c.customer_name;
```

```
Query OK, 3 rows affected (0.09 sec)
Records: 3  Duplicates: 0  Warnings: 0
```

To refresh the materialized view, truncate the table and repopulate it periodically:

```
TRUNCATE TABLE materialized_customer_order_summary;

INSERT INTO materialized_customer_order_summary
SELECT c.customer_id, c.customer_name,
       COUNT(o.order_id) AS total_orders,
       SUM(o.order_amount) AS total_amount,
       AVG(o.order_amount) AS average_amount
FROM customers c
JOIN orders o ON c.customer_id = o.customer_id
GROUP BY c.customer_id, c.customer_name;
```

```
Query OK, 0 rows affected (0.02 sec)

Query OK, 3 rows affected (0.08 sec)
Records: 3  Duplicates: 0  Warnings: 0
```

Utilize MySQL events to automate this refresh process. First, enable the event scheduler if it is not already activated:

```
SET GLOBAL event_scheduler = ON;
```

Then, create an event to refresh the materialized view at regular intervals:

```
CREATE EVENT refresh_materialized_customer_order_summary
ON SCHEDULE EVERY 1 DAY
DO
BEGIN
    TRUNCATE TABLE materialized_customer_order_summary;
    INSERT INTO materialized_customer_order_summary
    SELECT c.customer_id, c.customer_name,
           COUNT(o.order_id) AS total_orders,
           SUM(o.order_amount) AS total_amount,
           AVG(o.order_amount) AS average_amount
    FROM customers c
    JOIN orders o ON c.customer_id = o.customer_id
    GROUP BY c.customer_id, c.customer_name;
END;
```

```
Query OK, 0 rows affected (0.06 sec)
```

Use views and materialized views strategically to optimize query performance, maintain data abstraction, and manage security constraints effectively.

4.10 Dynamic SQL

Dynamic SQL is a powerful functionality in MySQL that allows the construction and execution of SQL queries at runtime as opposed to being predefined. This approach is particularly useful when the structure or exact nature of the query cannot be determined until the actual execution time. The flexibility afforded by dynamic SQL is indispensable in scenarios where the queries depend on the user input or other runtime parameters.

To understand dynamic SQL, the **PREPARE** and **EXECUTE** statements are paramount. These statements enable us to construct and run SQL statements dynamically. The **PREPARE** statement is used to prepare an SQL statement for execution. The **EXECUTE** statement is then employed to execute the prepared statement. Furthermore, the **DEALLOCATE PREPARE** statement is used to release the prepared statement once it is no longer needed.

```
PREPARE stmt FROM 'SELECT * FROM employees WHERE employee_id = ?';
SET @emp_id = 1001;
EXECUTE stmt USING @emp_id;
DEALLOCATE PREPARE stmt;
```

In this example, the **PREPARE stmt FROM** command is used to prepare a SQL statement that selects records from the employees table where the employee_id matches a specific value. The *?* acts as a placeholder for the variable. Then, an actual value is assigned to @emp_id, which is substituted in the query using the **EXECUTE stmt USING** command. Finally, the prepared statement is deallocated using **DEALLOCATE PREPARE stmt**.

Dynamic SQL is not limited to SELECT statements. It can be employed for a variety of SQL operations such as INSERT, UPDATE, and DELETE. The following example demonstrates how dynamic SQL can be used to insert data into a table dynamically.

```
PREPARE stmt FROM 'INSERT INTO employees (employee_id, first_name,
    last_name) VALUES (?, ?, ?)';
SET @emp_id = 1002;
SET @fname = 'John';
SET @lname = 'Doe';
EXECUTE stmt USING @emp_id, @fname, @lname;
DEALLOCATE PREPARE stmt;
```

In this script, the **PREPARE stmt FROM** command prepares an INSERT statement with three placeholders. The variables @emp_id, @fname, and @lname are then set with appropriate values. These values are used in the prepared INSERT statement which is executed by **EXECUTE stmt USING**.

Dynamic SQL also enables the execution of DDL (Data Definition Language) statements. This capability is useful when the structure of tables needs to be modified based on runtime conditions. For example, creating tables dynamically can be achieved as follows:

```
SET @table_name = 'new_employees';
SET @sql_query = CONCAT('CREATE TABLE ', @table_name, ' (id INT, name
    VARCHAR(100))');
PREPARE stmt FROM @sql_query;
EXECUTE stmt;
DEALLOCATE PREPARE stmt;
```

In this scenario, we use the **CONCAT** function to dynamically construct a CREATE TABLE statement by concatenating the table name with the rest of the statement. The command is then prepared and executed dynamically, thus creating a new table.

It is important to consider handling errors and ensuring the security of dynamic SQL. The flexibility of dynamic SQL comes with the risk of SQL injection if user inputs are not properly sanitized. Utilizing parameterized queries as demonstrated in the examples mitigates this risk. Error handling in dynamic SQL involves checking for errors post-execution of the prepared statement, which can be done using standard MySQL error-handling mechanisms.

Another common use of dynamic SQL involves constructing queries based on user input that includes dynamic conditions. For example, filtering records based on various optional parameters inputted by the user.

```
SET @base_query = 'SELECT * FROM employees WHERE 1=1';
IF @department_id IS NOT NULL THEN
    SET @base_query = CONCAT(@base_query, ' AND department_id = ',
        @department_id);
END IF;
IF @salary IS NOT NULL THEN
    SET @base_query = CONCAT(@base_query, ' AND salary > ', @salary);
END IF;
PREPARE stmt FROM @base_query;
EXECUTE stmt;
DEALLOCATE PREPARE stmt;
```

Here, the @base_query variable is initially set to retrieve all records from the employees table. Conditional checks are then performed to dynamically append additional WHERE clauses based on user-provided input. This approach exemplifies the dynamic construction of queries where optional filters are only included if the respective variables contain data.

Dynamic SQL is a robust feature to address complex querying needs where static SQL falls short. Mastery of dynamic SQL significantly extends your ability to handle diverse database operations efficiently.

4.11 Error Handling in SQL

Error handling in SQL is a critical aspect for maintaining robust database operations and ensuring data integrity. By proactively managing potential errors, database administrators and developers can prevent unexpected behavior and data corruption. MySQL provides various mechanisms to handle errors efficiently. This section explores the primary methods available for detecting and managing errors in SQL queries.

When executing SQL statements, MySQL can encounter various types of errors such as syntax errors, constraint violations, type mismatches, and runtime exceptions. The primary methods for handling these errors are using structured error handling constructs such as the TRY...CATCH blocks, leveraging SQLSTATE values, and using functions like IFNULL() and COALESCE() to manage NULL values and prevent errors.

TRY...CATCH Blocks:

MySQL does not provide native support for TRY...CATCH blocks as found in procedural programming languages like Python or Java. However, error handling can be implemented using MySQL stored procedures and the GET _ DIAGNOSTICS statement.

Consider the following stored procedure for dividing two numbers and handling the potential division by zero error:

```
DELIMITER //
CREATE PROCEDURE DivideNumbers(IN num1 INT, IN num2 INT, OUT result
    DECIMAL(10,2), OUT error VARCHAR(255))
BEGIN
  DECLARE CONTINUE HANDLER FOR SQLEXCEPTION
  BEGIN
    GET DIAGNOSTICS CONDITION 1
    error = MESSAGE_TEXT;
    SET result = NULL;
  END;

  IF num2 = 0 THEN
    SIGNAL SQLSTATE '45000' SET MESSAGE_TEXT = 'Division by zero error';

  ELSE
    SET result = num1 / num2;
    SET error = NULL;
  END IF;
END //
DELIMITER ;
```

Executing the stored procedure with valid and invalid inputs:

```
CALL DivideNumbers(10, 2, @result, @error);
SELECT @result, @error;

CALL DivideNumbers(10, 0, @result, @error);
SELECT @result, @error;
```

The output of these calls will be:

```
result | error
-----------------
5.00   | NULL
NULL    | Division by zero error
```

Using SQLSTATE Values:

Each error in MySQL is associated with a standard SQLSTATE value, which can be used to identify specific error conditions. The SQLSTATE is a five-character string where the first two characters indicate the error class, and the last three characters indicate the subclass.

For example:

- '23000' indicates an integrity constraint violation. - '22001' indicates a data exception: string data, right truncation.

Handling specific errors using SQLSTATE values:

```
DELIMITER //
CREATE PROCEDURE InsertWithCheck(IN value VARCHAR(10))
BEGIN
    DECLARE EXIT HANDLER FOR SQLEXCEPTION
    BEGIN
        DECLARE sqlstate CHAR(5);
        GET DIAGNOSTICS CONDITION 1 sqlstate = RETURNED_SQLSTATE;

        IF sqlstate = '23000' THEN
            SIGNAL SQLSTATE '45000' SET MESSAGE_TEXT = 'Integrity
                constraint violation';
        ELSE
            SIGNAL SQLSTATE '45000' SET MESSAGE_TEXT = 'A general SQL
                exception occurred';
        END IF;
    END;

    INSERT INTO example_table (example_column) VALUES (value);
END //
DELIMITER ;
```

Handling NULL Values:

NULL values can often lead to unexpected results and errors if not handled properly. MySQL provides functions like IFNULL() and COALESCE() to manage NULL values effectively.

```
SELECT IFNULL(column_name, 'default_value') AS result
FROM example_table;

SELECT COALESCE(column1, column2, 'default_value') AS result
FROM example_table;
```

The IFNULL() function returns the first non-NULL value from its two arguments, while the COALESCE() function returns the first non-NULL value from a list of arguments.

Output when column1 is NULL, and column2 is 'data':

```
result
------
data
```

Using Condition Handlers:

Using condition handlers in stored procedures helps manage errors more gracefully. A condition handler can be set to handle not only standard error conditions but also specific conditions such as NOT FOUND and SQLEXCEPTION.

Creating a condition handler for NOT FOUND condition:

```
DELIMITER //
```

```
CREATE PROCEDURE FindRecord(IN record_id INT, OUT result VARCHAR(255))
BEGIN
    DECLARE CONTINUE HANDLER FOR NOT FOUND
    BEGIN
        SET result = 'Record not found';
    END;

    SELECT column_name INTO result
    FROM example_table
    WHERE id = record_id;
END //
DELIMITER ;
```

Calling the procedure with an non-existing record_id will result in:

```
result
------
Record not found
```

Understanding and utilizing these error handling mechanisms effectively ensures that SQL operations are robust, predictable, and maintain data integrity within the MySQL database. Implementing advanced error handling techniques allows for sophisticated management of exceptions, resulting in reliable and stable database applications.

4.12 Recursive Queries

In the context of SQL, recursive queries are essential for performing repeated operations on data until a certain condition is met, which makes them particularly useful for dealing with hierarchical or graph-structured data. MySQL supports recursive queries through Common Table Expressions (CTEs).

A recursive query typically consists of two main parts: the base case and the recursive case. The base case is the initial query that sets the starting point. The recursive case is a query that references the cte_name, progressively adding its results to those of the base case until a termination condition is achieved.

The syntax for a recursive CTE in MySQL is as follows:

```
WITH RECURSIVE cte_name AS (
    -- Base case
    initial_query
    UNION
    -- Recursive case
    recursive_query
)
SELECT * FROM cte_name;
```

To illustrate the use of recursive queries, consider a classic example involving an organizational hierarchy, where each employee reports to a manager. The goal is to list all employees under a specific manager at any level in the hierarchy.

Assume we have a table employees with the following structure:

```
+-------------+--------------+------------+
| employee_id | employee_name| manager_id |
+-------------+--------------+------------+
| 1           | Alice        | NULL       |
| 2           | Bob          | 1          |
| 3           | Carol        | 1          |
| 4           | David        | 2          |
| 5           | Eve          | 2          |
| 6           | Frank        | 3          |
+-------------+--------------+------------+
```

In this table:

- Alice is the top-level manager with no superior.
- Bob and Carol report to Alice.
- David and Eve report to Bob.
- Frank reports to Carol.

To list all employees reporting to Alice (employee_id = 1), including indirect reports, we can construct a recursive query as follows:

```
WITH RECURSIVE employee_hierarchy AS (
    -- Base case: Select the top-level manager
    SELECT employee_id, employee_name, manager_id
    FROM employees
    WHERE employee_id = 1

    UNION ALL

    -- Recursive case: Select employees reporting to those already selected
    SELECT e.employee_id, e.employee_name, e.manager_id
    FROM employees e
    INNER JOIN employee_hierarchy eh
    ON e.manager_id = eh.employee_id
)
SELECT * FROM employee_hierarchy;
```

The base case initializes the CTE with Alice's record. The recursive case joins the employees table with the CTE on the condition that the manager_id of the employees matches the employee_id present in the CTE. This process continues until no more employees can be fetched.

The output of this query would include all employees under Alice:

employee_id	employee_name	manager_id
1	Alice	NULL
2	Bob	1
3	Carol	1
4	David	2
5	Eve	2
6	Frank	3

Let's consider a more complex example involving parent-child relationships stored in a Categories table that hierarchically organizes product categories:

category_id	name	parent_id
1	Electronics	NULL
2	Televisions	1
3	LCD TVs	2
4	Plasma TVs	2
5	Computers	1
6	Laptops	5
7	Desktops	5

To retrieve all subcategories under Electronics (category_id = 1), a recursive query would be structured as follows:

```
WITH RECURSIVE category_hierarchy AS (
    -- Base case: Select top-level category
    SELECT category_id, name, parent_id
    FROM Categories
    WHERE parent_id IS NULL

    UNION ALL

    -- Recursive case: Select subcategories
    SELECT c.category_id, c.name, c.parent_id
    FROM Categories c
    INNER JOIN category_hierarchy ch
    ON c.parent_id = ch.category_id
)
SELECT * FROM category_hierarchy;
```

The base case retrieves the primary categories (those without a parent). The recursive case iteratively joins the Categories table with the CTE to accumulate subcategories linked to the categories already included, continuing until no further subcategories are found.

The depth and efficiency of recursive queries depend on MySQL's limits and performance optimization which can be influenced by factors like max_recursion_depth.

Through recursive CTEs, complex hierarchical queries can be simplified, making recursive queries a powerful tool for tasks involving hierarchies and recursive relationships in relational databases.

Chapter 5

Database Design and Normalization

This chapter provides a comprehensive introduction to database design principles and normalization techniques. It covers the basics of defining entities and attributes, establishing primary and foreign keys, and understanding relationships between tables. The chapter explains the process of normalization, including First Normal Form (1NF), Second Normal Form (2NF), Third Normal Form (3NF), and Boyce-Codd Normal Form (BCNF). Additionally, it discusses the pros and cons of denormalization.

5.1 Introduction to Database Design

Database design is an essential facet of creating a robust and efficient database system. It involves the careful planning and structuring of data to ensure that it can be stored, retrieved, and manipulated effectively. Effective database design results in a logical, consistent, and usable data structure that minimizes redundancy and optimizes performance.

The primary objective of database design is to create an accurate representation of the data requirements of a system. This involves identifying the various entities within the system, understanding the attributes associated with these entities, and determining the relationships that exist between them. The logical design of a database can be envisioned as a conceptual model that guides the creation of a physical database schema.

Entities and Attributes: Entities represent real-world objects or concepts within the database. Each entity is defined by its attributes, which provide the necessary details about the entity. For instance, in a student database, *Student* would be an entity, with attributes such as *StudentID*, *Name*, *DateOfBirth*, and *Major*. Effective identification and definition of entities and attributes are critical initial steps in database design.

Primary Keys and Foreign Keys: A primary key is a unique identifier for each record in a database table. It ensures that each entry can be uniquely identified. For example, *StudentID* could serve as the primary key in a *Student* table. Foreign keys, on the other hand, establish a link between tables, enforcing referential integrity within the database. A foreign key in one table points to a primary key in another, creating relationships between entities.

Relationships Between Tables: Relationships are the connections between entities, reflecting how data in one table relates to data in another. These can be one-to-one, one-to-many, or many-to-many. For instance, a *Student* may enroll in multiple *Courses*, creating a one-to-many relationship between the *Student* and *Course* tables.

During database design, various stages are followed to ensure the structural integrity and efficiency of the database. These stages include conceptual, logical, and physical design phases:

Conceptual Design: This high-level phase focuses on identifying the entities, attributes, and relationships without concerning the technical implementation details. It typically results in an Entity-Relationship (ER) diagram that visually represents the data model. An example of an ER diagram is illustrated below:

```
[Student] --< enrolls in >-- [Course]
   |                          |
   | StudentID (PK)           | CourseID (PK)
   | Name                     | CourseName
   | DateOfBirth              | CreditHours
   | Major                    |
```

Logical Design: In the logical design phase, the conceptual model is translated into a logical structure that can be implemented using a database management system (DBMS). This involves defining tables, columns, and the relationships between them, as well as determining the constraints that ensure data integrity. For example:

```
CREATE TABLE Student (
    StudentID INT PRIMARY KEY,
    Name VARCHAR(100),
    DateOfBirth DATE,
    Major VARCHAR(50)
);

CREATE TABLE Course (
    CourseID INT PRIMARY KEY,
    CourseName VARCHAR(100),
    CreditHours INT
);

CREATE TABLE Enrollment (
    StudentID INT,
    CourseID INT,
    Semester VARCHAR(10),
    PRIMARY KEY (StudentID, CourseID),
    FOREIGN KEY (StudentID) REFERENCES Student(StudentID),
    FOREIGN KEY (CourseID) REFERENCES Course(CourseID)
);
```

Physical Design: The physical design phase translates the logical model into the actual database structure to be stored on disk. This involves considerations related to the storage and retrieval of data, such as indexing, partitioning, and clustering. The aim is to optimize performance while ensuring scalability and manageability of the database.

The process of database design is iterative and often requires adjustments based on thorough testing and performance evaluation. Tools like ER diagrams and normalization techniques play a crucial role in ensuring a well-structured and efficient database design. As users interact with the database, additional requirements or optimizations may emerge, necessitating changes to the initial design.

Effective database design underpins the reliability, efficiency, and maintainability of a database system, making it a critical skill for database administrators and developers. Understanding the core principles of database design sets the foundation for advanced topics, such as normalization, which will be further explored in subsequent sections.

5.2 Understanding Entities and Attributes

Entities and attributes are fundamental concepts in the realms of database design and normalization, serving as the building blocks of a relational database schema. An entity can be defined as a distinguishable object in the domain of discourse, about which data is collected and stored. Entities represent real-world objects or things, possessing a separate existence in a database. Examples of entities include "Customer", "Order", "Product", and "Employee".

Attributes, on the other hand, are the properties or characteristics that describe an entity. Each attribute holds a specific piece of information about the entity. For example, attributes of a "Customer" entity might include "CustomerID", "Name", "Address", and "PhoneNumber". The careful definition and organization of entities and their corresponding attributes are essential for constructing a robust and efficient database structure.

When designing a database, it is crucial to identify all relevant entities and their attributes. This process involves determining what information needs to be stored and how it can be logically grouped into entities. The following example illustrates how entities and attributes can be identified and structured:

```
CREATE TABLE Customer (
    CustomerID INT PRIMARY KEY,
    Name VARCHAR(100),
    Address VARCHAR(255),
    PhoneNumber VARCHAR(15)
);

CREATE TABLE Product (
    ProductID INT PRIMARY KEY,
    ProductName VARCHAR(100),
    Price DECIMAL(10, 2)
);

CREATE TABLE Order (
    OrderID INT PRIMARY KEY,
    OrderDate DATE,
    CustomerID INT,
    FOREIGN KEY (CustomerID) REFERENCES Customer(CustomerID)
);
```

The SQL code above defines three tables representing the entities "Customer", "Product", and "Order". Each table includes columns corresponding to the attributes of the entity. Let's examine the above definitions in detail:

- The Customer table includes attributes such as CustomerID, Name, Address, and PhoneNumber. The attribute CustomerID serves as the primary key, uniquely identifying each customer.

- The Product table consists of attributes like ProductID, ProductName, and Price. Similarly, ProductID is designated as the primary key for this table.

- The Order table contains attributes including OrderID, OrderDate, and CustomerID. The OrderID attribute is the primary key, while CustomerID is a foreign key establishing a relationship between the Order and Customer entities.

Entities and attributes not only form the logical structure of the database but also aid in ensuring data consistency and integrity by adhering to database design conventions and constraints. Entities should be clearly defined, avoiding ambiguity and redundancy. Attributes should be atomic, meaning each attribute should contain only a single piece of information that cannot be further subdivided. This characteristic aligns with the principles of normalization.

Consider an Employee entity that requires further examination. Suppose the organization's requirements stipulate that various details about employees need to be stored, such as their identification numbers, names, positions, hire dates, and departments. The entity-relationship diagram (ERD) would include the Employee entity with these attributes, which can be represented in SQL as follows:

```
CREATE TABLE Employee (
    EmployeeID INT PRIMARY KEY,
    Name VARCHAR(100),
    Position VARCHAR(50),
    HireDate DATE,
    DepartmentID INT,
    FOREIGN KEY (DepartmentID) REFERENCES Department(DepartmentID)
);
```

In addition to providing entity structure, proper identification of attributes and their types is significant. Choosing appropriate data types for attributes ensures storage efficiency and enhances query performance. For example, using VARCHAR for textual data, INT for integer values, and DATE for date values are common practices.

It is also important to note the potential necessity for attribute constraints. Constraints such as NOT NULL, UNIQUE, and CHECK can be applied to attributes to enforce data integrity. For instance, an attribute like EmployeeID must always be unique and not null, preventing duplicate or missing identifiers within the Employee table.

```
CREATE TABLE Employee (
    EmployeeID INT PRIMARY KEY,
    Name VARCHAR(100) NOT NULL,
    Position VARCHAR(50) NOT NULL,
    HireDate DATE NOT NULL,
    DepartmentID INT,
    FOREIGN KEY (DepartmentID) REFERENCES Department(DepartmentID),
    UNIQUE (Name, Position)
);
```

In the above SQL snippet, the NOT NULL constraint is applied to the Name, Position, and HireDate attributes, ensuring these fields cannot be left empty. Additionally, a UNIQUE constraint is imposed on the combination of Name and Position to avoid duplicate entries for employees holding the same name and position.

The precision in defining entities and attributes lays a strong foundation for subsequent database design tasks, including normalization and establishing relationships.

5.3 Primary Keys and Foreign Keys

A fundamental aspect of relational database design is the implementation of keys. Keys are essential in ensuring data integrity and establishing relationships between tables. In this section, we delve into the concepts of primary keys and foreign keys, which play critical roles in database normalization and efficient data retrieval.

Primary Key

A primary key is a unique identifier for each record within a table. It ensures that each tuple (row) in the table can be uniquely identified by a single column or a combination of columns. The primary key enforces entity integrity by making sure that no two rows can have the same primary key value, and that the value can never be NULL.

When defining a primary key in a MySQL table, it is crucial to consider factors such as uniqueness, stability, and non-nullability. To designate a primary key in SQL, the PRIMARY KEY constraint is used. Here is an example of how to create a table with a primary key:

```
CREATE TABLE Students (
    student_id INT NOT NULL AUTO_INCREMENT,
    first_name VARCHAR(50),
    last_name VARCHAR(50),
    date_of_birth DATE,
    PRIMARY KEY (student_id)
);
```

In this example, the student_id column is declared as the primary key. The AUTO_INCREMENT attribute ensures that the student_id is automatically generated for each new record, maintaining its uniqueness.

Foreign Key

A foreign key is a column or a set of columns in one table that uniquely identifies a row in another table. It establishes a link between the data in two tables and ensures referential integrity by enforcing a relationship between the two tables. The foreign key in the child table (referencing table) corresponds to the primary key in the parent table (referenced table).

Using foreign keys prevents actions that would invalidate the relationship between the tables. For instance, it restricts the removal of a row in the parent table if there are dependent rows in the child table, and it prevents the insertion of a row in the child table with no corresponding row in the parent table.

Here is an example of defining a foreign key in MySQL:

```
CREATE TABLE Courses (
    course_id INT NOT NULL AUTO_INCREMENT,
    course_name VARCHAR(100),
    PRIMARY KEY (course_id)
);

CREATE TABLE Enrollments (
    enrollment_id INT NOT NULL AUTO_INCREMENT,
    student_id INT,
    course_id INT,
    enrollment_date DATE,
    PRIMARY KEY (enrollment_id),
    FOREIGN KEY (student_id) REFERENCES Students(student_id),
    FOREIGN KEY (course_id) REFERENCES Courses(course_id)
);
```

In this example, the Enrollments table contains two foreign keys: student_id and course_id. These foreign keys reference the student_id column in the Students table and the course_id column in the Courses table, respectively. This linkage ensures that each entry in the Enrollments table is associated with a valid student and a valid course.

ON DELETE and ON UPDATE Actions

When defining foreign keys, it is possible to specify behaviors for delete and update actions using the ON DELETE and ON UPDATE clauses. These clauses determine how changes in the parent table affect the child table. The most commonly used options are CASCADE, SET NULL, and RESTRICT.

- CASCADE: Automatically updates or deletes the matching rows in the child table when a row in the parent table is updated or deleted.

- SET NULL: Sets the foreign key columns in the child table to NULL when the referenced row in the parent table is deleted or updated.

- RESTRICT: Prevents the action on the parent table if there are matching rows in the child table. This is the default behavior.

Consider the following SQL definition demonstrating the use of ON DELETE and ON UPDATE:

```
CREATE TABLE Enrollments (
    enrollment_id INT NOT NULL AUTO_INCREMENT,
    student_id INT,
    course_id INT,
    enrollment_date DATE,
    PRIMARY KEY (enrollment_id),
    FOREIGN KEY (student_id) REFERENCES Students(student_id)
        ON DELETE CASCADE
        ON UPDATE CASCADE,
    FOREIGN KEY (course_id) REFERENCES Courses(course_id)
        ON DELETE SET NULL
        ON UPDATE CASCADE
);
```

In this script, the ON DELETE CASCADE clause for the student_id foreign key ensures that if a student record is deleted from the Students table, all corresponding records in the Enrollments table are also deleted. The ON UPDATE CASCADE clause ensures that any changes to the student_id in the Students table will be propagated to the Enrollments table. For the course_id foreign key, if a course record is deleted from the Courses table, the corresponding course_id in the Enrollments table is set to NULL.

In summary, primary keys and foreign keys are crucial components of relational database design. They ensure the uniqueness and referential integrity of data across tables, facilitating the establishment and maintenance of relationships necessary for a well-structured and normalized database.

5.4 Relationships Between Tables

To design an effective database schema, understanding the relationships between tables is paramount. Relationships define how data is connected across different tables, ensuring data integrity and facilitating complex queries. Three primary types of relationships exist within relational databases: one-to-one (1:1), one-to-many (1:M), and many-to-many (M:N). Each type serves a specific purpose and is employed based on the nature of the data and the desired queries.

In a one-to-one relationship, each record in one table corresponds to exactly one record in another table. This type of relationship is often used to split data that logically belongs to a single entity into two tables for reasons such as performance optimization or sensitive data storage. For instance, consider the following example:

```
CREATE TABLE Employee (
    EmployeeID INT PRIMARY KEY,
    EmployeeName VARCHAR(100)
);

CREATE TABLE EmployeeDetails (
    EmployeeID INT PRIMARY KEY,
    Address VARCHAR(255),
    DateOfBirth DATETIME,
    FOREIGN KEY (EmployeeID) REFERENCES Employee(EmployeeID)
);
```

Here, each record in the Employee table has a corresponding record in the EmployeeDetails table. The shared primary key, EmployeeID, ensures a one-to-one relationship.

A one-to-many relationship occurs when a single record in one table can be associated with multiple records in another table. This is the most common type of relationship and typically involves a primary key in the parent table linked to a foreign key in the child table. For example:

```
CREATE TABLE Department (
    DepartmentID INT PRIMARY KEY,
    DepartmentName VARCHAR(100)
);

CREATE TABLE Employee (
    EmployeeID INT PRIMARY KEY,
    EmployeeName VARCHAR(100),
    DepartmentID INT,
    FOREIGN KEY (DepartmentID) REFERENCES Department(DepartmentID)
);
```

In this scenario, one department can have multiple employees, but each employee belongs to only one department. The DepartmentID in the Employee table serves as the foreign key establishing this one-to-many relationship.

Many-to-many relationships are more complex as they involve multiple records in one table being related to multiple records in another table. This type of relationship necessitates a junction table (also called a bridge table or associative entity) to facilitate the connection. Consider the following structure:

```
CREATE TABLE Student (
    StudentID INT PRIMARY KEY,
    StudentName VARCHAR(100)
);
```

```
CREATE TABLE Course (
    CourseID INT PRIMARY KEY,
    CourseName VARCHAR(100)
);

CREATE TABLE StudentCourse (
    StudentID INT,
    CourseID INT,
    PRIMARY KEY (StudentID, CourseID),
    FOREIGN KEY (StudentID) REFERENCES Student(StudentID),
    FOREIGN KEY (CourseID) REFERENCES Course(CourseID)
);
```

In this example, a student can enroll in multiple courses, and a course can have multiple students. The StudentCourse table acts as the junction table with a composite primary key consisting of StudentID and CourseID. This table captures the many-to-many relationship between students and courses.

Understanding table relationships extends beyond just creating these connections. It is also essential to define appropriate constraints to maintain data integrity. Foreign keys ensure that records in one table correspond to valid entries in another table, reinforcing relational integrity and preventing anomalies. For instance, attempting to insert an Employee record with a non-existent DepartmentID will result in a foreign key constraint error, preserving the consistency of the relationship.

Practical utilization of relationships also relies heavily upon join operations in SQL. Joins allow combining data from multiple tables dynamically, unfurling the relations into comprehensible datasets for analysis and reporting. The primary types of joins include INNER JOIN, LEFT JOIN, RIGHT JOIN, and FULL JOIN, each serving distinct purposes and yielding different results depending on how tables are related and the presence of matching records.

Consider an INNER JOIN to retrieve all employees and their corresponding department names:

```
SELECT Employee.EmployeeName, Department.DepartmentName
FROM Employee
INNER JOIN Department ON Employee.DepartmentID = Department.DepartmentID;
```

The JOIN operation here merges records from the Employee table with matching Department records using the DepartmentID foreign key. This query produces a result listing all employees along with their associated department names, reflecting the underlying one-to-many relationship.

```
+--------------+-----------------+
| EmployeeName | DepartmentName  |
+--------------+-----------------+
| John Smith   | Human Resources |
| Jane Doe     | Information Tech|
| Michael Brown| Accounting      |
+--------------+-----------------+
```

Effectively managing these relationships is crucial for database normalization, reducing redundancy, and eliminating update anomalies. Well-defined relationships not only uphold data integrity but also enhance the capability to perform comprehensive queries and generate insightful reports. Understanding and implementing these relationships forms a foundational aspect of database design, driving the efficiency and reliability of the relational database system.

5.5 Introduction to Normalization

Normalization is a systematic approach for organizing a database in order to reduce redundancy and improve data integrity. This process involves decomposing tables to minimize the chances of anomalies when inserting, deleting, or updating records. The concept of normalization hinges on the principles of relational database design and ensures that data is stored efficiently without unnecessary duplication.

Normalization is applied through a series of rules known as normal forms, each with distinct requirements. These forms build upon one another, establishing increasingly stringent criteria for table structure. Key normal forms include First Normal Form (1NF), Second Normal Form (2NF), Third Normal Form (3NF), and Boyce-Codd Normal Form (BCNF). Each successive normal form addresses issues not covered by its predecessors, ensuring the database structure meets specific standards of consistency and minimal redundancy.

The primary objective of normalization is to make the data model more flexible, easier to maintain, and free from undesirable characteristics such as insertion, update, and deletion anomalies. For example, an insertion anomaly might occur if a database structure forces the insertion of duplicate or null data, while an update anomaly may require multiple records to be updated simultaneously to maintain accuracy. Deletion anomalies, on the other hand, could result in unintended loss of data when a record is removed.

To understand how normalization is applied, consider a simple employee database containing the following attributes:

- Employee_ID
- Name
- Department
- Department_Manager
- Salary

Without normalization, this table might appear as follows:

```
Employee_ID Name Department Department_Manager Salary
----------- ---- ---------- ------------------ ------
1 Alice HR Smith 60000
2 Bob IT Johnson 70000
3 Carol HR Smith 62000
4 Dave IT Johnson 71000
```

In this example, the redundancy is evident: the name of the department manager is repeated in multiple records. If a manager's name changes, the database would require multiple updates to maintain data integrity—a clear update anomaly. Additionally, if a department is deleted, information about the manager would be lost, which represents a deletion anomaly.

The normalization process tackles these issues by decomposing the original table into multiple related tables. The result would be two tables: one for employees and another for departments. The design will then look like this:

Employees Table:

```
Employee_ID Name Department_ID Salary
----------- ---- ------------- ------
1 Alice 1 60000
2 Bob 2 70000
3 Carol 1 62000
4 Dave 2 71000
```

Departments Table:

```
Department_ID Department Department_Manager
------------- ---------- ------------------
1 HR Smith
2 IT Johnson
```

Here, the key improvement is that the department information has been factored out into a separate table, eliminating redundancy and enhancing data integrity.

The fundamental principle behind normalization is the precise identification and representation of relationships between data elements to minimize redundancy and avoid the aforementioned anomalies. Each attribute should primarily depend on the primary key, and redundant data should be minimized by ensuring that each piece of information is stored only once in the database.

Understanding normalization requires delving into various normal forms:

- - **First Normal Form (1NF):** Ensures that the table structure is tabular, with each cell containing a single unique value.
- - **Second Normal Form (2NF):** Builds on 1NF by ensuring that all non-key attributes are fully functionally dependent on the primary key.
- - **Third Normal Form (3NF):** Enhances 2NF by eliminating transitive dependencies, ensuring that non-key attributes depend solely on primary keys.
- - **Boyce-Codd Normal Form (BCNF):** A stricter version of 3NF, addressing certain types of dependencies that 3NF does not cover.

In the following sections, we will explore each of these normal forms in detail, demonstrating how to transform tables to meet the specific requirements and ensuring the overall integrity and efficiency of the database design. The normalization process is not merely theoretical; it results in tangible improvements in how data is organized, accessed, and managed.

5.6 First Normal Form (1NF)

A database is in First Normal Form (1NF) if it fulfills the most basic level of organization, which primarily means that the tables adhere to a simple structure. The core aspects of 1NF involve ensuring that the table conforms to several foundational principles that prevent redundancy and simplify the querying process.

To comply with 1NF, a table must adhere to the following rules:

- Each table must have a primary key that uniquely identifies each record.

- All the table columns should contain atomic (indivisible) values.
- The values in each column should be of the same data type.
- Each column should contain only one value per record, i.e., there should be no repeating groups or arrays.

Atomic Values and the Elimination of Repeating Groups

By ensuring each column contains atomic values, we eliminate any potential for repeating groups. A repeating group occurs when multiple values are stored within a single column for a single record. Consider the following table example, which does not adhere to 1NF:

StudentID	Name	Courses
1	John Doe	Math, Physics
2	Jane Smith	Chemistry
3	Emily Davis	Biology, Chemistry, English

In this example, the *Courses* column violates 1NF rules because it contains a list of courses rather than an atomic value. To resolve this, we must create a separate table to hold individual course entries and establish a relationship between the students and their courses. The revised tables would look like the following:

StudentID	Name
1	John Doe
2	Jane Smith
3	Emily Davis

StudentID	Course
1	Math
1	Physics
2	Chemistry
3	Biology
3	Chemistry
3	English

This restructuring ensures that each value in the *Course* column is atomic, aligning the table with 1NF principles.

Homogeneity of Data Types

Another integral aspect of 1NF is that each column should contain values of the same data type. Mixing different types within a single column can lead to inconsistencies and inefficiencies in database operations. Consider the following erroneous table design:

EmployeeID	Value
1	5000
2	Bonus Included
3	7200

The *Value* column contains both numerical and textual data, violating 1NF guidelines. Correcting this involves ensuring the *Value* column contains consistent data types, such as:

EmployeeID	Salary
1	5000
2	5500
3	7200

If needed, a separate column can be created to store information about bonuses.

Single Value Columns

Columns in a table must hold only a single value to ensure conformity with 1NF. This means no column should contain multiple values within the same row. Failing to ensure single values can lead to difficulties in both data validation and querying. Consider the following non-compliant table:

EmployeeID	PhoneNumbers
1	123-456-7890, 987-654-3210
2	555-666-7777
3	444-555-6666, 111-222-3333

By transforming it into a compliant 1NF structure, we segregate the phone numbers into individual records:

EmployeeID	PhoneNumber
1	123-456-7890
1	987-654-3210
2	555-666-7777
3	444-555-6666
3	111-222-3333

This ensures that each column holds a unique piece of data per row.

Benefits and Implications of Compliance with 1NF

Adherence to 1NF lays the foundational structure for a robust database design. Ensuring atomic values, homogeneity of data types, and single value columns simplifies query construction, enhances data integrity, and prevents anomalies in transactional operations. The normalization process streamlines data access and manipulation, facilitating a more efficient and reliable database system that can effortlessly scale and adapt to evolving requirements. Each step in normalization builds upon these principles, progressively refining and optimizing the database architecture. As we proceed to 2NF and further, these foundational practices continue to play a pivotal role in achieving a seamless and functional database.

5.7 Second Normal Form (2NF)

Second Normal Form (2NF) is an essential concept in the normalization process aimed at reducing redundancy and improving database efficiency. A table is in 2NF if it is in First Normal Form (1NF) and all non-key attributes are fully functionally dependent on the primary key. In simpler terms, this means that a non-key attribute should depend on the entire primary key, not just part of it.

Prerequisites: Understanding 1NF

Recall that a table is in 1NF when it adheres to the following criteria:

- All columns contain atomic (indivisible) values.
- Each column contains values of a single type.
- Each column has a unique name.
- The order in which data is stored does not matter.

While 1NF ensures that all values within a column are atomic and the table structure is essentially a basic relation, it does not address partial dependencies. This leads us to the necessity of 2NF.

Definition of Full Functional Dependency

A functional dependency $X \rightarrow Y$ is considered full if removing any attribute A from X means that the dependency no longer holds. In other words, each attribute in X is necessary for the relationship to hold, making Y completely dependent on X as a whole rather than parts of X.

Steps to Achieve 2NF

To transform a table into 2NF, we follow these steps:

- Ensure the table is already in 1NF.
- Identify all candidate keys of the table.
- Ensure that non-key attributes are fully functionally dependent on the entire primary key rather than just a part of it.

If partial dependencies are found, decompose the table into new tables that eliminate the partial dependency.

Example Transformation

Consider a table that records student enrollments in various courses, as shown below:

```
CREATE TABLE StudentCourses (
    student_id INT,
    course_id INT,
    student_name VARCHAR(255),
    course_name VARCHAR(255),
    instructor_name VARCHAR(255),
    PRIMARY KEY (student_id, course_id)
);
```

In this table, the composite primary key is formed by student_id and course_id. Non-key attributes include student_name, course_name, and instructor_name.

We need to examine if any non-key attributes depend only on part of the primary key. Here, student_name is dependent solely on student_id, and course_name along with instructor_name depend solely on course_id.

This partial dependency violates the conditions of 2NF. To rectify this, we decompose the table into two smaller tables:

```
CREATE TABLE Students (
    student_id INT PRIMARY KEY,
    student_name VARCHAR(255)
);

CREATE TABLE Courses (
    course_id INT PRIMARY KEY,
    course_name VARCHAR(255),
    instructor_name VARCHAR(255)
);

CREATE TABLE StudentCourses (
    student_id INT,
```

```
    course_id INT,
    PRIMARY KEY (student_id, course_id),
    FOREIGN KEY (student_id) REFERENCES Students(student_id),
    FOREIGN KEY (course_id) REFERENCES Courses(course_id)
);
```

Now, the Students table tracks student information, the Courses table tracks course information, and the StudentCourses table maintains the many-to-many relationship between students and courses.

Validation of 2NF Compliance

By decomposing the original table, we ensure every non-key attribute is fully functionally dependent on the entirety of the primary key in their respective tables:

- student_name depends entirely on student_id in the Students table.
- course_name and instructor_name depend entirely on course_id in the Courses table.
- The StudentCourses table is already in 1NF and the composite primary key (student_id, course_id) satisfies 2NF as no additional non-key attributes exist.

By following these steps and restructuring the tables to eliminate partial dependencies, we reinforce database integrity, ensuring data anomalies are minimized and that updates, deletions, and insertions operate more efficiently. This sets a solid foundation for moving towards higher normal forms.

5.8 Third Normal Form (3NF)

Third Normal Form (3NF) is an extension of Second Normal Form (2NF) and addresses further anomalies that can arise with databases. To understand 3NF, it's crucial to revisit some concepts and constraints from 1NF and 2NF. Recall that for a table to be in 2NF, it must be in 1NF and all non-key attributes must depend on the entire primary key and not just part of it. Moving beyond 2NF, Third Normal Form deals with the elimination of transitive dependencies.

Definition: A table is in Third Normal Form if it is in Second Normal Form and no transitive dependency exists between non-key attributes.

In other words, a non-key attribute should not depend on another non-key attribute.

To elucidate, consider the table below which is currently in 2NF:

StudentID	StudentName	CourseID	InstructorName
1	John Doe	CS101	Dr. Smith
2	Jane Smith	CS101	Dr. Smith
3	Emily Davis	CS201	Dr. Johnson

In this table, StudentID is the primary key, while attributes like StudentName, CourseID, and InstructorName are non-key attributes. Here, InstructorName is dependent on CourseID rather than the StudentID, which is a transitive dependency. Hence, the table violates the 3NF condition. To resolve this, we need to separate the InstructorName dependency into another table.

We can decompose the table into two new tables ensuring that each table adheres to 3NF:

Student Table:

StudentID	StudentName	CourseID
1	John Doe	CS101
2	Jane Smith	CS101
3	Emily Davis	CS201

Course Table:

CourseID	InstructorName
CS101	Dr. Smith
CS201	Dr. Johnson

In the decomposed structure, StudentID is a primary key in the Student table, and CourseID is used as a foreign key. The Course table uses CourseID as a primary key and maps it directly to InstructorName. This separation ensures that all attributes only depend on the key of their respective tables, fulfilling the 3NF requirements by eliminating transitive dependencies.

It's important to understand that these transformations do not add redundancies or lose data; instead, they structure the database to be more efficient and to abide by normalization rules. The main goal of achieving 3NF is to ensure that non-key attributes are only described by the primary key, thereby eliminating any indirect relationships through other non-key attributes.

Example: Consider a database managing a bookstore inventory. Let's use an example of a table not in 3NF.

ISBN	BookTitle	PublisherID	PublisherAddress
978-0131103627	C Programming Language	100	123 Elm St
978-0262033848	Introduction to Algorithms	101	456 Oak St

Here, ISBN is the primary key, and PublisherAddress depends on PublisherID rather than directly on ISBN. Thus, there is a transitive dependency.

Normalization to 3NF will require creating two separate tables:

Book Table:

ISBN	BookTitle	PublisherID
978-0131103627	C Programming Language	100
978-0262033848	Introduction to Algorithms	101

Publisher Table:

PublisherID	PublisherAddress
100	123 Elm St
101	456 Oak St

This decomposition removes the transitive dependency and adheres to 3NF rules.

To verify the 3NF compliance of a table, ensure that:

- The table is in 2NF.
- Every non-primary-key attribute is non-transitively dependent on the primary key, meaning each non-key attribute directly depends on the primary key without any intermediate non-key attribute.

SQL Implementation: Let's demonstrate this normalization process using SQL statements.

```
CREATE TABLE Student (
    StudentID INT PRIMARY KEY,
    StudentName VARCHAR(50),
    CourseID INT,
```

```
    FOREIGN KEY (CourseID) REFERENCES Course(CourseID)
);

CREATE TABLE Course (
    CourseID INT PRIMARY KEY,
    InstructorName VARCHAR(50)
);
```

For the bookstore example:

```
CREATE TABLE Book (
    ISBN CHAR(13) PRIMARY KEY,
    BookTitle VARCHAR(100),
    PublisherID INT,
    FOREIGN KEY (PublisherID) REFERENCES Publisher(PublisherID)
);

CREATE TABLE Publisher (
    PublisherID INT PRIMARY KEY,
    PublisherAddress VARCHAR(100)
);
```

These tables, when queried, maintain integrity and prevent update anomalies.

```
-- Selecting from Student table
SELECT * FROM Student;
```

```
StudentID | StudentName | CourseID
-----------------------------------
    1     | John Doe    |  CS101
    2     | Jane Smith  |  CS101
    3     | Emily Davis |  CS201
```

```
-- Selecting from Course table
SELECT * FROM Course;
```

```
CourseID | InstructorName
-------------------------
  CS101  | Dr. Smith
  CS201  | Dr. Johnson
```

Applying these principles ensures that the database design adheres to 3NF, promoting effective data organization and mitigating data anomalies.

5.9 Boyce-Codd Normal Form (BCNF)

The Boyce-Codd Normal Form (BCNF) extends the principles of the Third Normal Form (3NF) with additional rigor. While 3NF addresses transitive dependencies, BCNF ensures that every determinant is a candidate key, thus eliminating anomalies that 3NF might not resolve.

A table is in BCNF if, and only if, the following condition holds for every dependency in the table:

$$X \to Y \quad \text{where } X \text{ is a super key}$$

Consider a table that conforms to 3NF but not BCNF. One of the common scenarios leading to this discrepancy is when a table contains overlapping candidate keys. For example, assume we have a table with attributes A, B, and C such that there exist candidate keys AB and BC.

To illustrate BCNF with a comprehensive example, consider the following table structure:

```
CREATE TABLE Students_Courses (
    student_id INT,
    course_id INT,
    instructor_id INT,
    instructor_name VARCHAR(100),
    PRIMARY KEY (student_id, course_id)
);
```

In this table, each student can register for multiple courses, and each course is taught by an instructor. The dependency $\text{course\_id} \to \text{instructor\_id, instructor\_name}$ indicates that each course has a single instructor associated with it, which is a partial dependency given course_id is not a super key by itself in this context. Despite the table potentially satisfying 3NF, it still does not meet the BCNF requirements because course_id, which determines the instructor details, is not a super key.

To transform this table into BCNF, we need to remove the partial dependency by splitting the table into two relations:

```
CREATE TABLE Students_Courses (
    student_id INT,
    course_id INT,
    PRIMARY KEY (student_id, course_id)
);

CREATE TABLE Courses_Instructors (
    course_id INT,
    instructor_id INT,
    instructor_name VARCHAR(100),
    PRIMARY KEY (course_id)
);
```

In the decomposed structure:

- **Students_Courses** now holds only the relationship between students and courses, with student_id and course_id as a composite primary key.

- **Courses_Instructors** now assigns instructors to courses, ensuring that each course's instructor data is maintained uniquely.

By decomposing the table, the resulting design ensures that:

- All non-trivial functional dependencies in **Students_Courses** and **Courses_Instructors** have a determinant that is a super key.
- Redundancies and insertion, update, or deletion anomalies are minimized.

To verify the efficacy, observe the operations performed on these BCNF-compliant tables:

```
-- Insert student-course registration
INSERT INTO Students_Courses (student_id, course_id) VALUES (1, 101);

-- Insert courses and associated instructors
INSERT INTO Courses_Instructors (course_id, instructor_id, instructor_name)
        VALUES (101, 500, 'Dr. Smith');
```

By maintaining the data in these two separate tables, redundancy is reduced without compromising referential integrity. The dependency violations that existed in the initial table structure no longer exist, thus conforming to BCNF.

To illustrate an update anomaly rectification, consider a situation in the initial table where an instructor's details, when updated, had to be updated in every row. The BCNF design facilitates straightforward updates:

```
-- Update instructor name in Courses_Instructors table
UPDATE Courses_Instructors
SET instructor_name = 'Dr. John Smith'
WHERE instructor_id = 500;
```

Since the instructor name is now stored in a single place, redundancy and potential misalignment due to multiple updates are no longer issues.

Adhering to BCNF ensures that the database design is robust, minimizes redundancy, maintains consistency, and eliminates potential anomalies that could arise during data operations. This demonstrates the importance of BCNF in achieving a higher standard of database normalization.

5.10 Denormalization: Pros and Cons

Denormalization is the process of combining tables to reduce the complexity and cost of data retrieval operations in a relational database management system (RDBMS). It often entails the introduction of redundancy to improve performance. While normalization aims to eliminate redundancy and reduce data anomalies through systematic structuring, denormalization intentionally incorporates redundancy to enhance query performance and streamline data access.

Pros of Denormalization:

- **Improved Query Performance:** Denormalization can reduce the number of join operations by storing related attributes together in a single table, thus decreasing query execution time. For instance, frequently accessed data can be stored in a flat, wide table to avoid multiple table joins.

```
SELECT orders.order_id, customers.customer_name, orders.total_amount
FROM orders
JOIN customers ON orders.customer_id = customers.customer_id;
```

  In a denormalized schema, this join could be avoided by storing customer details directly within the orders table.

- **Simplified Queries:** By reducing the need for complex joins, denormalized databases can simplify query construction. This can be particularly beneficial in data warehousing applications where analytical queries are predominant.

```
SELECT order_id, customer_name, total_amount
FROM denormalized_orders;
```

- **Faster Read-Heavy Workloads:** In scenarios where read operations vastly outnumber write operations, denormalized tables perform more efficiently by minimizing the database operations required to fetch data. This is often leveraged in reporting and analytical systems where fast read access is critical.

- **Reduced Application Complexity:** Denormalization can transfer complexity from the application logic to the database layer, leading to more straightforward application code. Once the denormalized structure is in place, the application needs to handle fewer joins and complex relationships.

```
Before:
Application implements join logic.

After:
Database stores ready-to-use datasets.
```

- **Enhanced Aggregation and Reporting:** Aggregation queries can take advantage of pre-computed fields in denormalized tables, speeding up reporting processes and making real-time analytics feasible.

```
SELECT customer_id, COUNT(*), SUM(total_amount)
FROM denormalized_orders
GROUP BY customer_id;
```

Cons of Denormalization:

- **Increased Redundancy:** Denormalization introduces data redundancy, which increases storage requirements. Storing the same piece of data multiple times can rapidly consume significant database space, potentially leading to higher storage costs and inefficient use of disk space.
- **Potential for Data Inconsistency:** With data redundancy, maintaining data consistency becomes more challenging. Updates must be carefully coordinated to ensure that all copies of the redundant data are kept in sync, adding complexity to data maintenance and increasing the risk of anomalies.

```
UPDATE customers
SET customer_name = 'John Doe'
WHERE customer_id = 101;

UPDATE orders
SET customer_name = 'John Doe'
WHERE customer_id = 101;
```

- **Slower Write Operations:** While read operations benefit from denormalization, write operations may suffer. Insertion, updating, and deletion operations become more complex and slower due to the need to maintain multiple copies of denormalized data.
- **Increased Maintenance Complexity:** The presence of redundant data imposes additional maintenance burdens. Database administrators and developers need to implement extra mechanisms to ensure data consistency and deal with potential anomalies, making schema migration and application updates more challenging.

- **Reduced Flexibility:** Denormalized schemas can be less flexible in accommodating changes. Any schema alteration might require significant adjustments across the entire database, as redundant data needs to be maintained consistently. This makes structural and requirement changes harder to implement over time.
- **Difficulty in Transaction Management:** Managing transactions can become problematic in a denormalized database because ensuring ACID (Atomicity, Consistency, Isolation, Durability) properties across multiple, redundant data entries is more complex. This can lead to issues with transactional integrity and data reliability.

```
BEGIN TRANSACTION;
UPDATE table_a SET column1 = value1 WHERE id = 1;
UPDATE table_b SET column2 = value2 WHERE id = 1;
IF all_updates_succeed THEN
   COMMIT;
ELSE
   ROLLBACK;
END TRANSACTION;
```

The choice to normalize or denormalize a database schema is context-dependent. It involves balancing the trade-offs between normalized and denormalized structures, considering performance requirements, data consistency, and maintenance complexities. Understanding these pros and cons enables database designers to make informed decisions suited to their specific application needs and performance goals.

Chapter 6

Stored Procedures and Functions

This chapter explores the creation, execution, and management of stored procedures and functions in MySQL. It discusses the differences between procedures and functions, handling input and output parameters, and implementing control structures. The chapter also covers error handling, incorporating procedures and functions into applications, performance considerations, and best practices for maintaining these programmable objects.

6.1 Introduction to Stored Procedures

Stored procedures are a fundamental aspect of MySQL that enhance the capabilities of database management by allowing the execution of a sequence of SQL statements through a single call. These programmable objects are stored in the database and can be invoked repeatedly to perform complex operations, which encapsulates the business logic within the database layer rather than the application layer.

Stored procedures offer many advantages, including improved performance, reusability of code, reduced network traffic, and enhanced security. By encapsulating complex operations within the database itself, stored procedures minimize the amount of data transfer between the database server and the client application, thus optimizing performance.

To understand stored procedures better, consider the following aspects:

- Creation and Basics: Stored procedures are created using the CREATE PROCEDURE statement followed by the procedure body, which consists of SQL statements. The basic syntax for creating a stored procedure is as follows:

```
CREATE PROCEDURE procedure_name (parameters)
BEGIN
    -- SQL statements
END;
```

  Parameters can be specified to handle input and output values, which will be discussed in detail in later sections.

- Execution: Once a stored procedure is created, it can be executed using the CALL statement:

```
CALL procedure_name(parameters);
```

- **Advantages**:
- **Performance**: As stored procedures are compiled once and executed many times, they can significantly reduce the execution time by eliminating the need to parse and optimize queries multiple times.
- **Code Reusability** and **Maintenance**: By centralizing logic within stored procedures, code can be reused across multiple applications, which simplifies maintenance and reduces redundancy.
- **Security**: Stored procedures enhance security by restricting direct access to data. Users can be granted permission to execute a stored procedure without having the direct privilege to query underlying tables.
- **Transaction Management**: Encapsulating SQL statements within stored procedures enables better management of transactions, ensuring all steps of a process succeed or fail together.

Consider a simple example of a stored procedure that retrieves employee details based on a department parameter:

```
CREATE PROCEDURE GetEmployeesByDept (IN dept_name VARCHAR(255))
BEGIN
    SELECT * FROM employees WHERE department = dept_name;
END;
```

This stored procedure GetEmployeesByDept accepts an input parameter dept_name and selects all employees from the employees table that belong to the specified department. To call this procedure with, for example, 'Sales' as the department name, the following command is used:

```
CALL GetEmployeesByDept('Sales');
```

The ability to package complex queries into executable procedures reduces the need for repetitive SQL code, enhancing both efficiency and consistency across applications.

- **Usage Guidelines**:
- **Naming Conventions**: Use meaningful and consistent names for stored procedures that indicate their functionality, making them easier to understand and maintain.
- **Documentation**: Document the purpose and usage of each stored procedure, including details of the parameters and expected output.
- **Error Handling**: Implement robust error handling within stored procedures to manage and log exceptions, ensuring the reliability of database operations.
- **Performance Tuning**: Regularly analyze and optimize the performance of stored procedures, as inefficient procedures can impact database performance.

Understanding these fundamental concepts is crucial as we delve deeper into stored procedures' creation, execution, and advanced features in subsequent sections. This foundational understanding equips developers to effectively harness the power of stored procedures in MySQL.

6.2 Creating Stored Procedures

Creating a stored procedure in MySQL involves defining a named collection of SQL statements which can be executed repeatedly with a single call. Stored procedures can encapsulate complex operations, improve performance by reducing round-trips to the server, and enhance security by controlling access to data. The basic syntax to create a stored procedure is as follows:

```
CREATE PROCEDURE procedure_name(parameter1 datatype, parameter2 datatype,
    ...)
BEGIN
  -- SQL statements
END;
```

To explain how to create a stored procedure, we will walk through the steps to build a simple procedure, GetEmployeeInfo, which retrieves information for a specific employee.

First, consider the following employees table:

```
+-------------+-------------+------------+
| employee_id | first_name  | last_name  |
+-------------+-------------+------------+
| 1           | John        | Doe        |
| 2           | Jane        | Smith      |
| 3           | Emily       | Johnson    |
+-------------+-------------+------------+
```

To create a stored procedure GetEmployeeInfo, which accepts an employee_id as an input parameter and returns the corresponding employee's first name and last name, use the following SQL:

```
CREATE PROCEDURE GetEmployeeInfo(IN emp_id INT, OUT first_name
    VARCHAR(50), OUT last_name VARCHAR(50))
BEGIN
   SELECT first_name, last_name INTO first_name, last_name
   FROM employees
   WHERE employee_id = emp_id;
END;
```

Several key concepts can be elaborated upon using this example:

Input and Output Parameters: The stored procedure GetEmployeeInfo uses both input and output parameters. emp_id is an input parameter, indicated by the prefix IN, used to supply the stored procedure with the employee's ID to look up. first_name and last_name are output parameters, specified with OUT, intended to return values back to the caller.

Mapping SQL Results to Output Parameters: The SELECT ...

INTO clause retrieves the values from the employees table based on the provided employee_id. The results are then stored in the output parameters first_name and last_name.

Executing the Stored Procedure: Once created, the stored procedure can be invoked using the CALL statement. Consider the following example demonstrating how to call GetEmployeeInfo:

```
CALL GetEmployeeInfo(1, @firstName, @lastName);
SELECT @firstName, @lastName;
```

The @firstName and @lastName variables store the results returned by the stored procedure. Execution of the above SQL will result in displaying the first name and last name of the employee with employee_id 1.

```
+------------+-----------+
| first_name | last_name |
+------------+-----------+
| John       | Doe       |
+------------+-----------+
```

Error Handling: Stored procedures must be designed to handle potential errors. This involves checking for conditions that may disrupt normal execution flow. For instance, if the employee_id does not exist, it is beneficial to handle this scenario gracefully. This can be achieved using error handlers within the stored procedure.

```
CREATE PROCEDURE GetEmployeeInfo(IN emp_id INT, OUT first_name
    VARCHAR(50), OUT last_name VARCHAR(50))
BEGIN
  DECLARE EXIT HANDLER FOR SQLEXCEPTION
  BEGIN
    SET first_name = NULL;
    SET last_name = NULL;
  END;

  SELECT first_name, last_name INTO first_name, last_name
  FROM employees
  WHERE employee_id = emp_id;

  IF ROW_COUNT() = 0 THEN
    SET first_name = NULL;
    SET last_name = NULL;
  END IF;
END;
```

The DECLARE EXIT HANDLER FOR SQLEXCEPTION block handles any SQL exceptions that occur during the execution of the SELECT statement. If an exception is raised, both output parameters are set to NULL. Additionally, the IF ROW_COUNT() = 0 condition checks whether no rows were found matching the employee_id, and similarly sets both output parameters to NULL if no matching employee is found.

Security Considerations: When creating stored procedures, it is also important to consider security aspects. Stored procedures can help restrict access to sensitive data. By granting execute permissions on a procedure while restricting direct access to the underlying tables, you can control what data users can query:

```
GRANT EXECUTE ON PROCEDURE GetEmployeeInfo TO 'username'@'hostname';
```

By granting execute privileges to a specific user, you ensure that the user can call the stored procedure without having direct access to the employees table.

The creation of stored procedures in MySQL is a powerful feature that enhances the capabilities of database management. The ability to encapsulate and reuse complex operations while ensuring security and error handling results in robust and maintainable database applications.

6.3 Executing Stored Procedures

The execution of stored procedures in MySQL involves invoking a previously defined and compiled procedure via SQL statements. Stored procedures are an essential aspect of MySQL as they allow encapsulation of complex business logic, promote code reuse, and improve performance by reducing client-server interactions. This section details how to execute stored procedures, including passing parameters and handling result sets.

Stored procedures are executed using the CALL statement. The basic syntax for invoking a stored procedure is as follows:

```
CALL procedure_name([parameter[,...]]);
```

This command executes the stored procedure named procedure_name, optionally with a list of parameters enclosed in parentheses. Parameters can be input, output, or both.

Executing a Procedure without Parameters

Consider the following stored procedure, which does not take any parameters and simply returns a result set of all employees from a sample table employees:

```
CREATE PROCEDURE ListAllEmployees()
BEGIN
```

```
    SELECT * FROM employees;
END;
```

To execute this procedure, use the following CALL statement:

```
CALL ListAllEmployees();
```

Upon execution, the result set containing all employee records is returned:

```
+----+---------------+----------+
| id | name          | position |
+----+---------------+----------+
| 1  | John Smith    | Manager  |
| 2  | Jane Doe      | Clerk    |
| 3  | Alan Johnson  | Developer|
+----+---------------+----------+
```

Executing a Procedure with Input Parameters

Procedures can be defined with input parameters to customize their behavior. Input parameters allow the passing of data to the procedure during execution. Consider the following stored procedure, which takes an employee's ID as an input parameter and returns the corresponding employee's details:

```
CREATE PROCEDURE GetEmployeeDetails(IN emp_id INT)
BEGIN
    SELECT * FROM employees WHERE id = emp_id;
END;
```

To execute this procedure and retrieve details for the employee with an ID of 2, use the following CALL statement:

```
CALL GetEmployeeDetails(2);
```

Upon execution, the result set containing the details of the specified employee is returned:

```
+----+----------+--------+
| id | name     | position |
+----+----------+--------+
| 2  | Jane Doe | Clerk    |
+----+----------+--------+
```

Executing a Procedure with Output Parameters

Output parameters allow a stored procedure to return values directly to the caller, in addition to any result sets. Consider a modified version of the previous example, where the procedure also returns the employee's name as an output parameter:

```
CREATE PROCEDURE GetEmployeeName(IN emp_id INT, OUT emp_name
    VARCHAR(100))
```

```
BEGIN
    SELECT name INTO emp_name FROM employees WHERE id = emp_id;
END;
```

To execute this procedure and retrieve the name of the employee with an ID of 2, use the following CALL statement:

```
SET @name = '';
CALL GetEmployeeName(2, @name);
SELECT @name;
```

The procedure call assigns the output value to the user-defined variable @name. The final SELECT statement returns the value of @name:

```
+----------+
| @name    |
+----------+
| Jane Doe |
+----------+
```

Executing a Procedure with InOut Parameters

InOut parameters serve as both input and output parameters. They pass initial values into the procedure, which can be modified within the procedure and returned to the caller. Consider the following stored procedure that assigns a new position to an employee and returns the updated position:

```
CREATE PROCEDURE UpdatePosition(IN emp_id INT, INOUT emp_position
    VARCHAR(50))
BEGIN
    UPDATE employees SET position = emp_position WHERE id = emp_id;
    SELECT position INTO emp_position FROM employees WHERE id = emp_id;
END;
```

To execute this procedure and update the position of the employee with an ID of 2 to 'Senior Clerk', use the following CALL statement:

```
SET @position = 'Senior Clerk';
CALL UpdatePosition(2, @position);
SELECT @position;
```

The procedure call updates the employee's position and assigns the updated value to the user-defined variable @position. The final SELECT statement returns the updated value of @position:

```
+--------------+
| @position    |
+--------------+
| Senior Clerk |
+--------------+
```

Handling Result Sets from Procedures

Stored procedures can return multiple result sets, which need to be handled depending on the client application used. For instance, in a MySQL command line client, multiple result sets are handled sequentially. Consider the following stored procedure that returns two result sets, one containing all employees and another containing all departments:

```
CREATE PROCEDURE ListEmployeesAndDepartments()
BEGIN
    SELECT * FROM employees;
    SELECT * FROM departments;
END;
```

Executing this procedure yields the following result sets:

```
CALL ListEmployeesAndDepartments();
```

```
Result set 1:
+----+---------------+----------+
| id | name          | position |
+----+---------------+----------+
| 1  | John Smith    | Manager  |
| 2  | Jane Doe      | Clerk    |
| 3  | Alan Johnson  | Developer|
+----+---------------+----------+

Result set 2:
+----+-------------+
| id | department  |
+----+-------------+
| 1  | HR          |
| 2  | Engineering |
| 3  | Marketing   |
+----+-------------+
```

Proper execution and handling of stored procedures contribute to efficient database operations and enhanced application performance. It is important to understand the usage of input, output, and InOut parameters, as well as managing result sets, to fully leverage the potential of stored procedures in MySQL.

6.4 Introduction to Functions

Functions in MySQL are user-defined routines that encapsulate a specific set of operations within a database. Unlike stored procedures, functions are designed to return a single value. They can be invoked within SQL statements such as SELECT, WHERE, and HAVING clauses, making them integral to more complex data manipulations and queries.

A function in MySQL is an object embedded within the database that performs actions and returns a result based on given input parameters. These parameters, defined at the function's creation, allow for customized operations based on the values passed at runtime. The ability to return a scalar value makes functions suitable for modularizing repetitive or complex calculations that need to be reused across multiple queries or reports.

Creating a function involves defining its name, parameters, return type, and the logic encapsulated within the function body. The syntax begins with the CREATE FUNCTION statement, followed by the function's name, the parameters it accepts, the return type, and the main logic, typically structured using standard SQL and procedural programming constructs.

```
CREATE FUNCTION function_name (parameter_list)
RETURNS return_type
BEGIN
    -- function body
    RETURN some_value;
END;
```

- function_name: The identifier for the function. It should be unique within the schema.
- parameter_list: The comma-separated list of parameters that the function accepts. Each parameter is defined with a name and data type.
- return_type: The data type of the value that the function returns. This can be any valid MySQL data type such as INT, VARCHAR, DATE, etc.
- BEGIN ... END: The block that contains the function's logic. Within this block, standard SQL statements and procedural constructs can be used.
- RETURN some_value: The command that specifies the value to be returned by the function.

For example, consider a function that calculates the factorial of a given integer:

```
CREATE FUNCTION factorial(n INT) RETURNS INT
BEGIN
    DECLARE result INT DEFAULT 1;
    DECLARE i INT DEFAULT n;

    WHILE i > 1 DO
```

```
        SET result = result * i;
        SET i = i - 1;
    END WHILE;

    RETURN result;
END;
```

In this function:

- The factorial function accepts a single integer parameter n.
- Two local variables, result and i, are declared and initialized. result is set to 1 by default, and i is set to the value of n.
- A WHILE loop iterates as long as i is greater than 1, multiplying result by i and decrementing i on each iteration.
- Once the loop completes, the function returns the calculated factorial stored in result.

Functions are typically used within SQL statements. For example:

```
SELECT factorial(5) AS fact;
```

```
+------+
| fact |
+------+
|  120 |
+------+
```

The function factorial is invoked with the parameter 5, and the result 120 is returned and displayed in the result set.

Functions in MySQL exhibit several important properties:

- **Deterministic Behavior:** Functions are deterministic if they return the same result whenever they are called with the same input values. Functions that use internal state or system functions like NOW() are non-deterministic.
- **Atomicity:** Function execution is atomic, meaning that either the whole function executes successfully, or no part of it does.
- **Portability:** Functions can be exported and imported using SQL scripts, ensuring that the same logic can be utilized across different instances of the MySQL database.

Functions are versatile and can be used in various scenarios including:

- **Data Transformation:** Applying complex calculations or transformations to data within a query.
- **Business Logic:** Implementing business rules or validation checks that need to be enforced consistently.
- **Report Generation:** Enhancing the readability and structure of reports by applying standardized calculations.

By encapsulating logic within functions, developers can promote code reuse, ensure consistency, and maintain cleaner, more maintainable database applications. Clear understanding and effective utilization of functions are pivotal in executing advanced queries and performing efficient data manipulations in MySQL.

6.5 Creating Functions

Functions in MySQL are routines that return a value and can be used in queries just like built-in functions. They are essential for encapsulating reusable logic, improving code modularity, and maintaining cleaner database code. The creation of a function can be achieved using the CREATE FUNCTION statement. Understanding the syntax and the key components involved in creating a function is crucial for effective function design and implementation.

Syntax for Creating a Function:

```
CREATE FUNCTION function_name (parameter_list)
RETURNS data_type
BEGIN
    -- function body
    RETURN expression;
END;
```

- function_name: This is the name of the function, which must be unique within the database.
- parameter_list: These are the input parameters for the function, listed with their data types.
- RETURNS data_type: This clause specifies the type of data the function will return.
- BEGIN ... END: This block contains the executable code of the function.

- RETURN expression: This statement returns the value that the function produces.

Example of Creating a Simple Function:

Consider a function that calculates the square of an integer. The following is a simple implementation of such a function:

```
CREATE FUNCTION CalculateSquare (n INT)
RETURNS INT
BEGIN
    RETURN n * n;
END;
```

This function, CalculateSquare, takes one integer parameter n and returns the result of n * n.

Usage in SQL Queries:

Once the function is created, it can be used in SQL queries like any other built-in function. For example:

```
SELECT CalculateSquare(4) AS SquareValue;
```

```
+-------------+
| SquareValue |
+-------------+
|          16 |
+-------------+
```

Taking Multiple Parameters:

Functions can also accept multiple parameters. For instance, let's create a function that calculates the sum of two integers:

```
CREATE FUNCTION AddNumbers (a INT, b INT)
RETURNS INT
BEGIN
    RETURN a + b;
END;
```

Here, the function AddNumbers takes two parameters, a and b, and returns their sum.

Using Expressions and Control Structures:

MySQL functions can include complex expressions and control structures like IF statements, loops, and more. Consider a function that determines if a number is positive, negative, or zero:

```
CREATE FUNCTION CheckNumberSign (num INT)
RETURNS VARCHAR(10)
BEGIN
    DECLARE result VARCHAR(10);
```

```
    IF num > 0 THEN
        SET result = 'Positive';
    ELSEIF num < 0 THEN
        SET result = 'Negative';
    ELSE
        SET result = 'Zero';
    END IF;

    RETURN result;
END;
```

In this function, CheckNumberSign, the IF statement evaluates the parameter num and assigns a corresponding string description ('Positive', 'Negative', or 'Zero') to the variable result, which is then returned.

Handling NULL Values:

It's important to handle NULL values in functions appropriately, as they can impact the result. Here's an example where the function safely handles NULL values by returning a default value:

```
CREATE FUNCTION SafeDivide (numerator INT, denominator INT)
RETURNS DECIMAL(10,2)
BEGIN
    DECLARE result DECIMAL(10,2);

    IF denominator IS NULL OR denominator = 0 THEN
        SET result = NULL;
    ELSE
        SET result = numerator / denominator;
    END IF;

    RETURN result;
END;
```

The function SafeDivide performs division but checks if the denominator is NULL or zero to avoid division errors, returning NULL in such cases.

Altering and Dropping Functions:

To modify an existing function, one must drop and recreate it using the updated definition. Dropping a function is done using the DROP FUNCTION statement:

```
DROP FUNCTION IF EXISTS CalculateSquare;
```

This ensures that the function CalculateSquare is removed from the database, allowing for any necessary changes or deletions.

Creating functions in MySQL allows the encapsulation of logic within reusable components, facilitating efficient query execution and enhancing database performance. Through careful design and implementation, functions can greatly improve the maintainability and functionality of database applications.

6.6 Executing Functions

Functions in MySQL are utilized to encapsulate reusable logic that returns single values and can be invoked in various queries. Executing functions is a critical skill for database developers and administrators, enabling them to leverage modular code to simplify and optimize SQL operations. This section delves deeply into the methodologies for invoking user-defined functions (UDFs) and illustrates their application with practical examples. Understanding the execution context and nuances of function calls ensures efficient and error-free database interactions.

Unlike stored procedures, functions are designed to be used in SQL expressions and can be part of statements such as SELECT, UPDATE, or WHERE. Therefore, their execution is more versatile but constrained to contexts where a singular value is required.

Consider a scenario where a function named calculate_tax is defined to compute tax based on a given price. This function can be executed within a query as follows:

```
SELECT product_name, calculate_tax(price) AS tax
FROM products;
```

In this example, calculate_tax is invoked for each row processed by the SELECT statement, thereby displaying the product name along with the computed tax.

```
+--------------+--------+
| product_name |  tax   |
+--------------+--------+
| Product A    |  5.40  |
| Product B    |  3.60  |
+--------------+--------+
```

Functions can also be executed in predicates to filter results. Suppose there is a function is_high_value that returns true if a product's price exceeds a predefined threshold:

```
SELECT product_name, price
FROM products
WHERE is_high_value(price);
```

Such an invocation ensures that only high-value products are retrieved, streamlining data processing.

```
+--------------+-------+
| product_name | price |
+--------------+-------+
| Product A    | 54.0 |
+--------------+-------+
```

Execution of functions can also occur within the SET clause of an UPDATE statement. Consider a function apply_discount that adjusts the price based on specific criteria:

```
UPDATE products
SET price = apply_discount(price)
WHERE category = 'Electronics';
```

This command updates the price for all electronic products by applying the discount logic encapsulated within the function.

Functions can also be employed in validation rules within INSERT statements. Assume a function validate_stock checks whether incoming stock quantities adhere to allowed thresholds:

```
INSERT INTO inventory (product_id, stock)
VALUES (101, 50)
WHERE validate_stock(50);
```

Implementation of validate_stock ensures inventory constraints are met before insertion.

It's essential to handle return types appropriately. For instance, the data type returned by the function must align with the context in which it is used. Here's an example illustrating the importance of return type alignment:

```
CREATE FUNCTION divide_numbers(a INT, b INT) RETURNS DECIMAL(10,2)
BEGIN
  RETURN a / b;
END;
```

In this function, the integer division would typically truncate the result, but specifying RETURNS DECIMAL(10,2) preserves precision.

Executing aggregate functions defined by users can also significantly enhance reporting capabilities. Consider a function custom_avg that computes an average based on specific conditions:

```
SELECT custom_avg(price) AS average_price
FROM products
WHERE category = 'Books';
```

```
+----------------+
| average_price  |
+----------------+
|     15.75      |
+----------------+
```

Care must be taken to ensure that user-defined functions operate efficiently. Since they can be invoked multiple times during query execution, optimizations such as indexing, parameter optimization, and avoiding unnecessary computations within the function's body are imperative.

Ensuring the correct permissions for function execution is another critical aspect. MySQL requires users to have appropriate privileges to call functions. The EXECUTE privilege must be granted to users as needed:

```
GRANT EXECUTE ON FUNCTION calculate_tax TO 'user'@'host';
```

In case of functions interacting with sensitive data, restrict access to maintain security and data integrity.

Incorporating user-defined functions into applications requires an understanding of how these invocations interrelate with application logic. For web applications, parameterized queries calling functions ensure that dynamic data inputs are processed efficiently and securely:

```
$query = $pdo->prepare("SELECT product_name, calculate_tax(:price) AS tax
    FROM products");
$query->execute([':price' => $price]);
$result = $query->fetchAll();
```

This PHP code fragment demonstrates utilizing a prepared statement to safely pass parameters to a function within a query, avoiding SQL injection vulnerabilities.

Understanding execution contexts, optimizing function body logic, managing privileges, and integrating with application logic are vital components to mastering the execution of functions in MySQL, enabling robust, efficient, and secure database operations.

6.7 Input and Output Parameters

In MySQL, stored procedures and functions can accept parameters to facilitate dynamic and complex data processing tasks. These parameters enable stored routines to operate on a variety of inputs, generate variable outputs, and maintain flexibility and reusability in database systems. Understanding how to define and utilize input and output parameters is critical for effective stored procedure and function development.

Parameters in MySQL stored routines can be classified into three distinct types:

- **IN**: These are input parameters. The calling program passes values to the procedure or function using these parameters.
- **OUT**: These are output parameters. The stored routine modifies these parameters to return values to the calling program.
- **INOUT**: These parameters serve a dual purpose. They accept input values from the caller and return modified values back to the caller.

Syntax for Parameter Declaration

Parameters for stored procedures and functions are declared within the parentheses following the procedure or function name. The general syntax is as follows:

```
CREATE PROCEDURE procedure_name (IN parameter_name datatype, OUT
    parameter_name datatype, INOUT parameter_name datatype)
BEGIN
  -- Procedure body
END;
```

For functions, only **IN** parameters are used, since functions must return a single value using the **RETURNS** clause. The syntax for function parameter declaration is:

```
CREATE FUNCTION function_name (parameter_name datatype, parameter_name
    datatype)
RETURNS datatype
BEGIN
  -- Function body
  RETURN value;
END;
```

Examples of Using Parameters

Consider a scenario requiring a procedure to calculate the total price of items in an order based on quantity and unit price. This procedure might take the quantity and unit price as **IN** parameters and return the total price as an **OUT** parameter.

```
DELIMITER //

CREATE PROCEDURE CalculateTotalPrice (
  IN quantity INT,
```

```
  IN unit_price DECIMAL(10,2),
  OUT total_price DECIMAL(10,2)
)
BEGIN
  SET total_price = quantity * unit_price;
END //

DELIMITER ;
```

To call this procedure and retrieve the output value, we use:

```
CALL CalculateTotalPrice(10, 19.99, @total_price);
SELECT @total_price;
```

Output:

```
+--------------+
| @total_price |
+--------------+
|       199.90 |
+--------------+
```

In this example, the quantity 10 and unit price 19.99 are provided to the procedure as input parameters. The total price, calculated within the procedure, is returned in the @total_price variable.

INOUT Parameter Example

An **INOUT** parameter is particularly useful when a procedure needs to accept an initial value, modify it, and return the modified value. For example, a procedure might update a running total based on a new transaction amount.

```
DELIMITER //

CREATE PROCEDURE UpdateRunningTotal (
  IN new_transaction DECIMAL(10,2),
  INOUT running_total DECIMAL(10,2)
)
BEGIN
  SET running_total = running_total + new_transaction;
END //

DELIMITER ;
```

To call this procedure and observe the changes in the running total, the initial value of the **INOUT** parameter must be set:

```
SET @running_total = 100.00;
CALL UpdateRunningTotal(25.50, @running_total);
SELECT @running_total;
```

Output:

```
+-----------------+
| @running_total |
+-----------------+
|          125.50 |
+-----------------+
```

The initial @running_total of 100.00 is updated by adding the new_transaction amount of 25.50, resulting in 125.50.

Handling Parameters in Functions

Functions only utilize **IN** parameters and return a single value. For instance, a function to calculate the factorial of a given number can be created as follows:

```
DELIMITER //

CREATE FUNCTION CalculateFactorial (n INT) RETURNS BIGINT
BEGIN
  DECLARE result BIGINT DEFAULT 1;
  DECLARE counter INT DEFAULT 1;

  WHILE counter <= n DO
    SET result = result * counter;
    SET counter = counter + 1;
  END WHILE;

  RETURN result;
END //

DELIMITER ;
```

To use this function:

```
SELECT CalculateFactorial(5) AS Factorial;
```

Output:

```
+-----------+
| Factorial |
+-----------+
|    120    |
+-----------+
```

With the proper understanding of input and output parameters, stored procedures and functions in MySQL can be designed to perform a vast array of tasks, enhancing your database's functionality and efficiency.

6.8 Control Structures in Stored Procedures

Stored procedures in MySQL support a variety of control structures that allow you to build complex logic into your database operations. These control structures include conditional statements, loops, and case expressions. Understanding and correctly implementing these control structures can greatly improve the efficiency and readability of your stored procedures.

Conditional Statements

Conditional statements in MySQL stored procedures enable you to execute certain sections of code based on specific conditions. The primary conditional statements include IF, ELSEIF, and ELSE.

The syntax for a basic IF statement in a stored procedure is as follows:

```
IF condition THEN
    -- Statements to execute if condition is true
END IF;
```

To handle multiple conditions, you can use ELSEIF and ELSE clauses:

```
IF condition1 THEN
    -- Statements if condition1 is true
ELSEIF condition2 THEN
    -- Statements if condition2 is true
ELSE
    -- Statements if none of the above conditions is true
END IF;
```

Loops

Loops are used to repeatedly execute a block of code as long as a condition holds true. MySQL supports several types of loops: LOOP, WHILE loop, and REPEAT loop.

The LOOP construct executes the associated block of code indefinitely until terminated by a LEAVE statement:

```
LOOP
    -- Statements to execute
    IF condition THEN
        LEAVE loop_label;
    END IF;
END LOOP loop_label;
```

The WHILE loop continues executing the block of code as long as the specified condition remains true. The syntax is:

```
WHILE condition DO
    -- Statements to execute
END WHILE;
```

The REPEAT loop is similar to the WHILE loop but evaluates the condition after the block of code has executed:

```
REPEAT
    -- Statements to execute
```

```
UNTIL condition
END REPEAT;
```

Case Expressions

The CASE statement allows you to execute one block of code out of multiple blocks based on the value of an expression. This can be particularly useful for replacing complex chains of IF statements. The general syntax is:

```
CASE expression
    WHEN value1 THEN
        -- Statements if expression equals value1
    WHEN value2 THEN
        -- Statements if expression equals value2
    ELSE
        -- Statements if expression does not match any listed values
END CASE;
```

CASE can also be used in the searched form, which evaluates a list of conditions rather than an expression:

```
CASE
    WHEN condition1 THEN
        -- Statements if condition1 is true
    WHEN condition2 THEN
        -- Statements if condition2 is true
    ELSE
        -- Statements if none of the above conditions is true
END CASE;
```

Examples

Example 1: Using IF-ELSEIF-ELSE in a Stored Procedure

The following is an example demonstrating the use of IF-ELSEIF-ELSE statements within a stored procedure:

```
DELIMITER //

CREATE PROCEDURE ExampleProc(EmployeeID INT)
BEGIN
    DECLARE EmployeeName VARCHAR(100);

    IF EmployeeID = 1 THEN
        SET EmployeeName = 'John Doe';
    ELSEIF EmployeeID = 2 THEN
        SET EmployeeName = 'Jane Smith';
    ELSE
        SET EmployeeName = 'Unknown';
    END IF;

    SELECT EmployeeName;
END //

DELIMITER ;
```

To execute the procedure:

```
CALL ExampleProc(1);
```

```
John Doe
```

Example 2: Utilizing a WHILE Loop

Here is an example of a stored procedure employing a WHILE loop to insert multiple rows into a table:

```
DELIMITER //

CREATE PROCEDURE InsertSampleData()
BEGIN
    DECLARE Counter INT DEFAULT 1;

    WHILE Counter <= 10 DO
        INSERT INTO SampleTable (Column1) VALUES (Counter);
        SET Counter = Counter + 1;
    END WHILE;
END //

DELIMITER ;
```

Executing this procedure as shown below inserts ten rows into SampleTable:

```
CALL InsertSampleData();
```

Example 3: Employing CASE Statements

A stored procedure that utilizes a CASE statement to return a status based on an input value:

```
DELIMITER //

CREATE PROCEDURE GetStatus(OrderStatus INT)
BEGIN
    DECLARE StatusMessage VARCHAR(50);

    CASE OrderStatus
        WHEN 1 THEN SET StatusMessage = 'Order Placed';
        WHEN 2 THEN SET StatusMessage = 'Order Shipped';
        WHEN 3 THEN SET StatusMessage = 'Order Delivered';
        ELSE SET StatusMessage = 'Unknown Status';
    END CASE;

    SELECT StatusMessage;
END //

DELIMITER ;
```

Running this procedure:

```
CALL GetStatus(2);
```

Order Shipped

Integrating various control structures, as shown in these examples, enriches the functionality of MySQL stored procedures. These advanced capabilities allow for more dynamic and powerful database programming. Proper use of control structures not only enhances the computational logic but also aids in building more maintainable and efficient stored procedures.

6.9 Error Handling in Stored Procedures

Error handling in stored procedures is crucial to ensuring that the database logic is robust and reliable. Proper error management helps prevent unexpected breakdowns and allows for graceful recovery and troubleshooting when issues occur. MySQL provides various mechanisms for managing errors within stored procedures using the DECLARE, HANDLER, and SIGNAL constructs.

To begin with, the DECLARE statement is used to define handlers for different conditions that may arise during the execution of a stored procedure. These conditions can be system-defined SQL states, or they can be defined by the user. The HANDLER mechanism allows the procedure to capture and handle these conditions appropriately.

The basic syntax for declaring a handler is as follows:

```
DECLARE handler_type HANDLER FOR condition_value statement;
```

Here, the handler_type can be:

- **CONTINUE**: Execution of the procedure continues after the handler has been executed.
- **EXIT**: Execution of the procedure terminates after the handler has been executed.

The condition_value specifies the type of condition the handler is meant to address, and this can include:

- **SQLSTATE 'sqlstate_value'**: A 5-character string that indicates an SQLSTATE value.
- **condition_name**: A previously defined condition name.

- **SQLWARNING**: Catches any condition in the SQLSTATE class of '01xxx', representing warnings.
- **SQLEXCEPTION**: Catches any condition in the SQLSTATE class of '02xxx', representing not found conditions.
- **NOT FOUND**: Often used to handle situations such as unsuccessful searches.

The statement typically consists of an SQL statement to run when the handler activates. For comprehensive error management, multiple handlers may be declared in a single procedure.

Consider the following example, where two handlers are declared within a procedure:

```
CREATE PROCEDURE ExampleProc()
BEGIN
    DECLARE CONTINUE HANDLER FOR SQLWARNING
    BEGIN
        -- Logic to execute when a warning occurs
        SELECT 'Warning encountered!';
    END;

    DECLARE EXIT HANDLER FOR SQLEXCEPTION
    BEGIN
        -- Logic to execute when an exception occurs
        SELECT 'Exception encountered!';
        ROLLBACK;
    END;

    -- Procedure body...
    START TRANSACTION;
    -- Operations which may result in warnings or exceptions
    COMMIT;
END;
```

In this procedure, the CONTINUE handler handles any warnings by displaying a message, yet allows the procedure to continue execution. Conversely, the EXIT handler deals with exceptions, displays an error message, and initiates a rollback of the transaction before terminating the procedure.

When more control over the error information is required, the SIGNAL and RESIGNAL statements can be utilized. These statements allow explicit signaling of error conditions within a procedure. The SIGNAL statement is used to raise an error condition explicitly, providing a custom SQLSTATE value and error message.

The syntax for the SIGNAL statement is presented here:

```
SIGNAL SQLSTATE 'value' SET message_item = value[, message_item = value, ...];
```

Where message_item can include MESSAGE_TEXT to give a textual description of the error.

Below is an example where the SIGNAL statement is used:

```
CREATE PROCEDURE ValidateAndInsert(IN input INT)
BEGIN
    DECLARE exit HANDLER FOR SQLEXCEPTION
    BEGIN
        ROLLBACK;
    END;

    IF input IS NULL THEN
        SIGNAL SQLSTATE '45000' SET MESSAGE_TEXT = 'Input cannot be
            NULL';
    END IF;

    START TRANSACTION;
    -- Insert operation or other logic
    COMMIT;
END;
```

In this example, the procedure uses the SIGNAL statement to raise a custom error with a SQLSTATE value of '45000' and a message indicating that the input cannot be NULL. This helps in enforcing business rules and maintaining data integrity by preventing the database from accepting invalid data.

Continuing with the notion of custom error signaling, the RESIGNAL statement allows an existing exception to be propagated after possibly modifying some of its characteristics. The use of RESIGNAL is particularly useful within a handler to provide further details about an exception or to transform a generic error into a more specific one pertinent to the application's context.

```
DECLARE CONTINUE HANDLER FOR SQLEXCEPTION
BEGIN
    -- Additional logic or cleaning up
    RESIGNAL;
END;
```

In summary, managing errors in stored procedures effectively involves a combination of handlers and explicit signaling mechanisms. By integrating these tools, developers can build resilient database logic that proactively handles unforeseen conditions and ensures stable operational continuity.

6.10 Using Stored Procedures and Functions in Applications

Incorporating stored procedures and functions into applications can significantly enhance performance and maintainability. This section highlights how to seamlessly integrate these programmable objects within various types of applications, focusing on practical implementation strategies, handling different parameter types, and optimizing communication between the database and application layers.

Stored procedures and functions can be called from multiple programming languages and platforms, including PHP, Java, Python, and .NET. This versatility allows developers to encapsulate business logic within the database, thus ensuring consistency and reducing redundancy in application code. To illustrate how stored procedures and functions can be effectively utilized in an application, consider the following examples in different programming languages.

- PHP

In PHP, use the 'mysqli' or 'PDO' extension to execute stored procedures and functions. To call a stored procedure using 'mysqli', follow these steps:

```
<?php
$mysqli = new mysqli("localhost", "username", "password", "database");

// Check connection
if ($mysqli -> connect_errno) {
  echo "Failed to connect to MySQL: " . $mysqli -> connect_error;
  exit();
}

// Call stored procedure
$procedure = "CALL GetEmployeeDetails(?)";
$stmt = $mysqli->prepare($procedure);
$stmt->bind_param("i", $employee_id);
$employee_id = 12345;
$stmt->execute();

// Fetch results
$result = $stmt->get_result();
while ($row = $result->fetch_assoc()) {
   echo $row['employee_name'];
}

$stmt->close();
$mysqli->close();
?>
```

To call a stored function:

```
<?php
$mysqli = new mysqli("localhost", "username", "password", "database");

if ($mysqli -> connect_errno) {
  echo "Failed to connect to MySQL: " . $mysqli -> connect_error;
  exit();
}

// Call stored function
$query = "SELECT GetEmployeeSalary(?) AS salary";
$stmt = $mysqli->prepare($query);
$stmt->bind_param("i", $employee_id);
$employee_id = 12345;
$stmt->execute();
$result = $stmt->get_result();
$row = $result->fetch_assoc();
echo $row['salary'];

$stmt->close();
$mysqli->close();
?>
```

- Java

In Java, use the 'JDBC' API to call stored procedures and functions. Here is an example:

```
// Ensure you have the MySQL JDBC driver in your classpath
import java.sql.*;

public class MySQLProcedureExample {
    public static void main(String[] args) {
        String jdbcURL = "jdbc:mysql://localhost:3306/database";
        String username = "username";
        String password = "password";

        try (Connection connection = DriverManager.getConnection(jdbcURL,
            username, password)) {
            // Call stored procedure
            CallableStatement callableStatement = connection.prepareCall("{CALL
                GetEmployeeDetails(?)}");
            callableStatement.setInt(1, 12345);
            ResultSet resultSet = callableStatement.executeQuery();

            while (resultSet.next()) {
                System.out.println(resultSet.getString("employee_name"));
            }
        } catch (SQLException e) {
            e.printStackTrace();
        }
    }
}
```

To call a stored function:

```
import java.sql.*;
```

```
public class MySQLFunctionExample {
    public static void main(String[] args) {
        String jdbcURL = "jdbc:mysql://localhost:3306/database";
        String username = "username";
        String password = "password";

        try (Connection connection = DriverManager.getConnection(jdbcURL,
                username, password)) {
            // Call stored function
            Statement statement = connection.createStatement();
            ResultSet resultSet = statement.executeQuery("SELECT
                    GetEmployeeSalary(12345) AS salary");

            if (resultSet.next()) {
                System.out.println(resultSet.getInt("salary"));
            }
        } catch (SQLException e) {
            e.printStackTrace();
        }
    }
}
```

- Python

In Python, the 'mysql-connector' or 'PyMySQL' modules can be used to interact with MySQL databases. Here's how to utilize these tools:

```
import mysql.connector

# Establish connection
conn = mysql.connector.connect(
    user='username',
    password='password',
    host='127.0.0.1',
    database='database'
)

cursor = conn.cursor()

# Call stored procedure
cursor.callproc('GetEmployeeDetails', [12345])

for result in cursor.stored_results():
    for row in result.fetchall():
        print(row[0]) # assuming first column is employee_name

conn.close()
```

To call a stored function:

```
import mysql.connector

conn = mysql.connector.connect(
    user='username',
    password='password',
    host='127.0.0.1',
    database='database'
```

```
)

cursor = conn.cursor()

# Call stored function
cursor.execute("SELECT GetEmployeeSalary(%s) AS salary", (12345,))
row = cursor.fetchone()
print(row[0])

conn.close()
```

- .NET (C#)

In a .NET application, use ADO.NET to call stored procedures and functions. Here's an example in C#:

```
using System;
using System.Data;
using System.Data.SqlClient;

namespace MySQLProcedureFunctionExample
{
    class Program
    {
        static void Main(string[] args)
        {
            string connectionString = "Server=localhost;Database=database;User Id=
                username;Password=password;";
            using (SqlConnection connection = new SqlConnection(connectionString))
            {
                connection.Open();

                // Call stored procedure
                SqlCommand command = new SqlCommand("GetEmployeeDetails",
                    connection);
                command.CommandType = CommandType.StoredProcedure;
                command.Parameters.AddWithValue("@employee_id", 12345);

                using (SqlDataReader reader = command.ExecuteReader())
                {
                    if (reader.Read())
                    {
                        Console.WriteLine(reader["employee_name"]);
                    }
                }
            }
        }
    }
}
```

To call a stored function:

```
using System;
using System.Data;
using System.Data.SqlClient;

namespace MySQLFunctionExample
{
```

```
    class Program
    {
        static void Main(string[] args)
        {
            string connectionString = "Server=localhost;Database=database;User Id=
                username;Password=password;";
            using (SqlConnection connection = new SqlConnection(connectionString))
            {
                connection.Open();

                // Call stored function
                string query = "SELECT GetEmployeeSalary(@employee_id) AS salary";

                SqlCommand command = new SqlCommand(query, connection);
                command.Parameters.AddWithValue("@employee_id", 12345);

                using (SqlDataReader reader = command.ExecuteReader())
                {
                    if (reader.Read())
                    {
                        Console.WriteLine(reader["salary"]);
                    }
                }
            }
        }
    }
}
```

These examples demonstrate how to invoke stored procedures and functions from different programming languages, making the integration process straightforward. Handling input and output parameters, dealing with transactions effectively, and catching and managing errors are crucial for robust integration.

Stored procedures and functions provide a bridge between application and database logic. They encapsulate operations such as data insertion, updating, deletion, and complex calculations, thereby promoting reusable and maintainable code. When using these programmable objects, consider performance best practices, and ensure secure interactions by applying parameterized queries to prevent SQL injection attacks. Effective use of stored procedures and functions can optimize application performance, make complex database operations manageable, and centralize business logic within the database.

6.11 Performance Considerations for Stored Procedures

When working with stored procedures in MySQL, it is crucial to consider their performance implications. Stored procedures offer numerous benefits such as modularization, abstraction, and reusability of code; however, they also introduce performance considerations that can significantly impact database efficiency. This section delves into various aspects of optimizing the performance of stored procedures in MySQL.

Firstly, understand that stored procedures are executed on the server side, reducing the need for multiple client-server round trips, which consequently minimizes network latency. However, this advantage comes with the necessity of careful optimization to ensure the procedures themselves do not become a performance bottleneck.

One critical factor to consider is the **execution plan caching**. MySQL caches the execution plan of a stored procedure when it is first executed. This can enhance performance in subsequent executions by avoiding the overhead of parsing and planning the query each time. Nevertheless, frequent changes to the schema or the data-distribution statistics might necessitate re-evaluation of these plans.

A particular area needing caution is the **use of cursors**. Cursors provide row-by-row processing of the result set and, while they are powerful, they can be slower than set-based operations. Consider this example:

```
DECLARE done INT DEFAULT 0;
DECLARE cursor_name CURSOR FOR SELECT col1, col2 FROM my_table;
DECLARE CONTINUE HANDLER FOR NOT FOUND SET done = 1;

OPEN cursor_name;
read_loop: LOOP
    FETCH cursor_name INTO var1, var2;
    IF done THEN
        LEAVE read_loop;
    END IF;
    -- process each row
END LOOP;
CLOSE cursor_name;
```

In scenarios where performance is critical, attempt to replace cursor operations with equivalent set-based operations. For instance:

```
UPDATE my_table SET col1 = col1 + 1 WHERE col2 = 'some_value';
```

Another major consideration is the **index utilization** within stored procedures. Effective indexing can dramatically reduce the time spent in query execution. Ensure that queries within the stored procedures are optimized and relevant indexes are in place. Utilize the EXPLAIN statement to analyze query execution plans and verify that indexes are used effectively:

```
EXPLAIN SELECT col1, col2 FROM my_table WHERE col3 = 'value';
```

Pay attention to **conditional logic** within stored procedures. Complex conditional constructs can hinder performance, particularly if they lead to cumbersome logic that could otherwise be managed using more efficient SQL operations. For example, replacing multiple IF statements or CASE expressions with simpler conditional checks or using more efficient logic can yield performance improvements.

Parameter sniffing and the **chosen parameter values** during the initial compilation of a stored procedure can affect performance. In some cases, using index hints can guide the optimizer towards a more efficient execution plan:

```
SELECT index_hint col1, col2 FROM my_table WHERE col3 = 'value';
```

Another area is the size of the **result sets returned** by the stored procedures. Large result sets can lead to increased memory consumption and slower performance. Using pagination techniques or limiting the number of rows returned can mitigate this:

```
SELECT col1, col2 FROM my_table LIMIT 50 OFFSET 0;
```

Consideration should also be given to the use of **temporary tables** within stored procedures. Temporary tables can be beneficial for complex operations, but their overuse can lead to increased I/O operations and memory consumption. Opt for in-memory operations when possible and drop temporary tables as soon as their use is no longer necessary.

```
CREATE TEMPORARY TABLE temp_table AS (SELECT ...);
-- Perform operations on temp_table
DROP TEMPORARY TABLE IF EXISTS temp_table;
```

Error handling within stored procedures also affects performance. Robust error handling mechanisms prevent unexpected failures but should be designed to incur minimal overhead. Utilize proper error codes and messages, ensuring they are handled gracefully without excessive performance costs.

Finally, **routine maintenance and monitoring** are essential. Regularly review stored procedures for potential optimizations, refactor inefficient code, and consider stored procedure execution statistics to identify and alleviate performance bottlenecks. Tools such as the MySQL Performance Schema and EXPLAIN ANALYZE can provide invaluable insights.

Combining these considerations, one can achieve an optimal balance between leveraging the power of stored procedures and maintaining high performance within MySQL databases.

6.12 Managing and Maintaining Stored Procedures and Functions

Effective management and maintenance of stored procedures and functions in MySQL are pivotal for ensuring database integrity, performance, and scalability. This section will delve into the various practices and techniques to keep these programmable objects optimized and functioning as intended in a production environment. The focus will be on versioning, documenting, analyzing dependencies, and troubleshooting.

First, consider version control for your stored procedures and functions. Version control is essential for tracking changes and collaborating with team members. Store the definitions of your procedures and functions in a version control system such as Git. To extract the definitions from MySQL, use the SHOW CREATE PROCEDURE and SHOW CREATE FUNCTION commands, respectively:

```
SHOW CREATE PROCEDURE procedure_name;
SHOW CREATE FUNCTION function_name;
```

The output of these commands will be SQL statements that recreate the procedure or function, which can be committed to your version control repository.

Documentation is another critical aspect. Proper documentation helps in understanding the purpose and functionality of stored procedures and functions. Include comments within the SQL code to describe the logic and the parameters. For example:

```
DELIMITER //
CREATE PROCEDURE example_procedure(IN param1 INT, OUT result VARCHAR
    (255))
BEGIN
  -- This procedure demonstrates an example with input and output parameters.
  SELECT CONCAT('Result is: ', CAST(param1 AS CHAR)) INTO result;
END;
//
DELIMITER ;
```

Analyzing dependencies is crucial to manage how stored procedures and functions interact with other database objects. This helps prevent issues during modifications or migrations. MySQL provides the INFORMATION_SCHEMA.ROUTINES and INFORMATION_-SCHEMA.ROUTINE_DEPENDENCIES tables to inspect details and dependencies of routines:

```
SELECT *
FROM INFORMATION_SCHEMA.ROUTINES
WHERE ROUTINE_TYPE='PROCEDURE'
  AND ROUTINE_SCHEMA='your_database_name';

SELECT *
FROM INFORMATION_SCHEMA.ROUTINE_DEPENDENCIES
WHERE SPECIFIC_SCHEMA='your_database_name';
```

Routine optimization involves periodically reviewing and tuning the performance of stored procedures and functions. Use EXPLAIN to analyze the execution plan of queries within the procedures and functions. Here's an example:

```
EXPLAIN SELECT * FROM your_table WHERE column1 = value;
```

Error handling is fundamental in the maintenance process. Include robust error handling within your procedures and functions to improve reliability and diagnose issues quickly. For instance, utilize DECLARE and HANDLER to manage exceptions:

```
DELIMITER //
CREATE PROCEDURE error_handling_example()
BEGIN
  DECLARE CONTINUE HANDLER FOR SQLEXCEPTION
  BEGIN
    -- Log error details
    INSERT INTO error_log (error_time, error_message) VALUES (NOW(), '
        Procedure failed.');
  END;

  -- Procedure statements
  START TRANSACTION;
  -- Example statement that may fail
  INSERT INTO your_table (column1) VALUES (value);
  COMMIT;
END;
//
DELIMITER ;
```

Regular auditing and cleaning are also necessary. Over time, stored procedures and functions may become obsolete or redundant. Perform regular audits to identify and deprecate or remove unused or outdated routines. A simple way to track usage is by logging procedure and function calls if your application allows it.

Automation scripts and jobs can be beneficial for routine maintenance tasks. Utilize MySQL's event scheduler to automate periodic maintenance activities, such as optimization, auditing, and cleanup:

```
CREATE EVENT cleanup_old_data
ON SCHEDULE EVERY 1 WEEK
DO
  DELETE FROM old_data_table WHERE created_at < NOW() - INTERVAL 1
      YEAR;
```

Lastly, consider security practices for managing stored procedures and functions. Restrict access to these objects based on the principle of least privilege. Use GRANT and REVOKE statements to manage permissions:

```
GRANT EXECUTE ON PROCEDURE your_database_name.procedure_name TO '
    user'@'host';
REVOKE EXECUTE ON PROCEDURE your_database_name.procedure_name
    FROM 'user'@'host';
```

By incorporating these practices, stored procedures and functions can be maintained efficiently, reducing the likelihood of errors, ensuring optimal performance, and aligning with security and compliance requirements.

Chapter 7

Indexes and Performance Tuning

This chapter focuses on the importance of indexes and various performance tuning techniques in MySQL. It includes discussions on different types of indexes, their creation, and management. Practical guidance on using the EXPLAIN command to analyze query performance and optimize SELECT, INSERT, UPDATE, and DELETE queries is provided. The chapter also covers query caching, the use of index hints, and best practices for identifying and resolving slow queries to maintain optimal database performance.

7.1 Introduction to Indexes

An index in MySQL serves as a data structure that improves the speed of data retrieval operations on a table at the cost of additional space and maintenance overhead. Indexes are created using one or more columns of a table, providing an efficient means for locating rows without having to examine every row in a table, making them indispensable for performance optimization.

The primary purpose of an index is to allow MySQL to find and retrieve specific rows much faster than it could without the index. Consider the analogy of an index in a book, which allows you to locate the exact page number of the topic you are looking for, rather than reading the entire book. In a similar manner, a database index enables the system to locate the record you need without scanning the entire table.

The fundamental idea behind indexing is to organize data in a manner that minimizes access time. To list an example, if there is a table of a million rows and a query that searches for a specific value in a non-indexed column, the MySQL engine would perform a full table scan, meaning it would check every row and every column in that row until it finds the matching value. This leads to significant performance degradation, especially as table sizes increase.

Here is a basic example setting up and using an index in MySQL:

```
CREATE TABLE users (
    user_id INT NOT NULL,
    username VARCHAR(50) NOT NULL,
    email VARCHAR(50) NOT NULL,
    PRIMARY KEY (user_id)
);

-- Suppose we frequently query the 'username' field, we can create an index on it
CREATE INDEX idx_username ON users(username);

-- Now a query looking for a specific username can benefit from the index
SELECT * FROM users WHERE username = 'john_doe';
```

In this example, an index named idx_username is created on the username column. Now, when we run a query to fetch details of the user with username john_doe, the database engine leverages this index, thereby drastically reducing the number of rows it needs to scan.

Index structures can vary, with the most common being B-trees and hash indexes. B-tree indexes are the default in MySQL and are used extensively because of their balanced nature and efficiency in range queries. Hash indexes, on the other hand, provide very fast lookups for exact matches.

The actual choice and necessity of using an index depend on specific query patterns and the performance characteristics desired. Here are some practical uses:

- **Single-column indexes:** Most useful when queries frequently filter results based on a single column.
- **Multi-column indexes:** Beneficial when queries filter results

based on multiple columns combined. The order of columns in the index matters and impacts the query performance.

- **Unique indexes:** Ensure the uniqueness of data within the column or set of columns.
- **Full-text indexes:** Employed for efficient searching of textual data.

It is essential to understand the overhead involved with indexes. Apart from the additional disk space consumed, every insert, update, or delete operation also requires updating the index. This can lead to increased processing time for write operations. Therefore, while indexes can significantly speed up read operations, there is a trade-off with the performance of write operations.

While devising indexing strategies, consider the following practices:

- **Index Selective Columns:** Prioritize columns with high selectivity where the indexed column values are well distributed.
- **Avoid Over-indexing:** Excessive indexing can bloat the database and degrade performance for write-intensive operations.
- **Monitor and Maintain:** Regularly analyze access patterns and update indexing strategies to align with evolving application requirements.

An understanding of indexing principles and judicious application of indexing techniques are crucial for achieving efficient performance in MySQL databases. This section sets the foundation for exploring various types of indexes, their management, and performance tuning in subsequent sections.

```
-- Example of how adding an unnecessary index can impact writes
CREATE INDEX idx_email ON users(email);

-- Suppose we need to insert a new user
INSERT INTO users (user_id, username, email) VALUES (1, 'john_doe', '
    john@example.com');
```

Adding the idx_email index on the email column might be beneficial if frequently filtering users by email, however, it also increases the complexity and IO operations for inserts, updates, and deletes. It's pivotal to strike a balance between optimizing read efficiency and managing write throughput effectively. An adept DBA routinely assesses the array of available indexes, making informed decisions to dynamically adjust based on access patterns and performance metrics.

This foundational understanding will be further reinforced as we delve into technical aspects and nuances of MySQL indexing in conjunction with performance enhancement methodologies.

7.2 Types of Indexes in MySQL

MySQL provides various types of indexes to optimize the performance of database queries. Understanding the nuances of these different index types is critical for database performance tuning. Each index type serves specific purposes and use cases. The primary types of indexes available in MySQL include the following: B-Tree indexes, Hash indexes, Full-text indexes, Spatial indexes, and Bitmap indexes, among others. This section delves into each type, explaining their characteristics, use cases, and limitations.

B-Tree Indexes

The B-Tree index is the default and most commonly used index type in MySQL. B-Tree, short for Balanced Tree, ensures that all leaf nodes are at the same level, fostering balanced and efficient query performance. B-Tree indexes facilitate range queries, equality queries, and prefix queries efficiently.

B-Tree indexes are particularly effective in scenarios involving:

- Searching for a specific range of values using relational operators like $<$, $>$, $<=$, and $>=$.
- Retrieving data in a sorted order.
- Performing queries involving pattern matching with leading wildcards.

In MySQL, InnoDB and MyISAM storage engines primarily use B-Tree indexes. The following command illustrates creating a B-Tree index:

```
CREATE INDEX index_name
ON table_name (column_name);
```

Hash Indexes

Hash indexes, as the name suggests, employ a hash function to produce a unique hash value for each key by which records are indexed. These indexes provide extremely fast lookup times for equality comparisons. However, hash indexes are not suitable for range queries or ordered retrieval of data since the hash function disrupts the data order.

Hash indexes are beneficial in scenarios where:

- The queries involve equality comparisons like = or IN.
- The indexed column experiences high cardinality.

MySQL's MEMORY storage engine supports hash indexes. Creating a hash index in MySQL requires the following command:

```
CREATE INDEX index_name
USING HASH
ON table_name (column_name);
```

Full-text Indexes

Full-text indexes enable full-text search capabilities within MySQL. Full-text searches allow you to search for complex and nuanced text patterns efficiently. These indexes index words within a text field and are suitable for large text columns.

Full-text indexes are particularly useful in:

- Searching large bodies of text, such as articles, documents, or product descriptions.
- Implementing features like search engines within your web application.

Full-text indexes can be created using the following syntax:

```
CREATE FULLTEXT INDEX index_name
ON table_name (column_name);
```

Executing a full-text search on a column indexed this way uses the MATCH AGAINST syntax:

```
SELECT *
FROM table_name
WHERE MATCH (column_name)
AGAINST ('search terms');
```

Spatial Indexes

Spatial indexes are specialized indexes designed for optimizing spatial operations. These indexes are used predominantly with spatial data types such as POINT, LINESTRING, and POLYGON. They enable efficient geographical data retrieval based on spatial relationships.

Spatial indexes are useful for applications dealing with:

- Geographic Information Systems (GIS).
- Spatial data querying and analysis.

Creating a spatial index can be accomplished using the following command:

```
CREATE SPATIAL INDEX index_name
ON table_name (spatial_column_name);
```

Bitmap Indexes

Bitmap indexes represent each distinct value of a column as a bit vector, where each bit corresponds to a row. Although not natively supported by MySQL, bitmap indexes can be emulated through certain storage engines and third-party tools. Bitmap indexes are particularly beneficial for columns with low cardinality.

Bitmap indexes are helpful in:

- Data warehousing applications.
- Scenarios requiring numerous ad-hoc queries over large datasets.

Composite Indexes

Composite indexes, also known as compound indexes or multi-column indexes, are indexes on multiple columns. They are particularly effective in scenarios where queries involve multiple columns in where clauses.

A composite index can significantly enhance performance in cases such as:

- Queries that filter using multiple columns.
- Scenarios where sorting or joining involves multiple columns.

Creating a composite index is done as follows:

```
CREATE INDEX index_name
ON table_name (column1, column2);
```

MySQL optimizes the use of composite indexes by reading from left to right; hence, it is crucial to arrange columns wisely in multi-column indexes.

B-Tree, Hash, Full-text, Spatial and Bitmap indexes all serve distinct purposes. Understanding the strengths and limitations of each index type, recognizing the correct scenarios for their use, and effectively implementing them can propel database query performance.

Consideration should also be given to the storage engine used, data types involved, and specific query patterns, aligning index selection to the unique needs of your database architecture.

7.3 Creating and Dropping Indexes

Creating and dropping indexes are fundamental operations in managing a MySQL database, allowing for increased performance and better resource management. This section focuses on the practical aspects of these operations, providing syntactical guidelines and examples to ensure effective implementation.

Indexes are created to improve the speed of data retrieval operations in a table, and they can be dropped to reclaim storage or when they are no longer beneficial for query performance. The creation and deletion should be done judiciously, considering their impact on the database's overall performance.

To create an index, the CREATE INDEX statement is used. The basic syntax for creating an index is:

```
CREATE INDEX index_name
ON table_name (column1, column2, ...);
```

For example, to create an index on the last_name column of the employees table, the following command can be used:

```
CREATE INDEX idx_lastname
ON employees (last_name);
```

Indexes can also be created using different types such as unique indexes and full-text indexes. A unique index ensures that the values in the indexed column(s) are unique. The syntax for creating a unique index is:

```
CREATE UNIQUE INDEX index_name
ON table_name (column1, column2, ...);
```

For instance, creating a unique index on the email column of the users table can be achieved with:

```
CREATE UNIQUE INDEX idx_email
ON users (email);
```

In scenarios where the data search necessitates textual data such as articles or documents, a full-text index could be highly beneficial. To create a full-text index, the following syntax is used:

```
CREATE FULLTEXT INDEX index_name
ON table_name (column1, column2, ...);
```

An example of creating a full-text index on the content column of the articles table is:

```
CREATE FULLTEXT INDEX idx_content
ON articles (content);
```

Composite indexes involve more than one column and are useful in accelerating queries that filter based on multiple columns. The creation of composite indexes follows a similar pattern:

```
CREATE INDEX index_name
ON table_name (column1, column2);
```

An instance of this is creating an index on the first_name and last_name columns of the employees table:

```
CREATE INDEX idx_name
ON employees (first_name, last_name);
```

In some cases, specifying the index type can provide early optimization clues. MySQL allows specifying the index type using the USING clause. The available types are BTREE and HASH. The syntax to specify an index type is:

```
CREATE INDEX index_name
USING BTREE
ON table_name (column1, column2);
```

Dropping an index is equally important for deleting unnecessary indexes, which helps in maintaining the database performance. The DROP INDEX statement is employed for this purpose. The basic syntax for dropping an index is:

```
DROP INDEX index_name
ON table_name;
```

For example, to drop the idx_lastname index from the employees table, the following command can be used:

```
DROP INDEX idx_lastname
ON employees;
```

Dropping unique or full-text indexes follows the same syntax and practical requirements.

While creating or dropping indexes, it is important to be cognizant of the index's effect on database performance. Each index created helps in speeding up select queries but can introduce overhead for insertions, deletions, and updates. Therefore, the decision to create or drop indexes should be driven by thorough analysis and understanding of the database query patterns.

Creating and dropping indexes properly can significantly influence the database's performance, highlighting the importance of index management in database optimization tasks. Proper planning and analysis mitigate potential negative impacts on data manipulation operations. Thus, this ensures a balanced, high-performing database system.

7.4 How Indexes Improve Performance

Indexes are fundamental tools in database management systems, significantly enhancing the performance of query operations. This section elucidates the mechanisms through which indexes improve performance, supported by technical details and practical examples.

Indexes operate by providing a structured means of accessing data quickly. Without indexes, a database system would need to perform a full table scan, examining each row to locate the desired data. This operation has a time complexity of $O(n)$, where n represents the total number of rows in the table. Conversely, utilizing an index allows the database to employ more efficient search algorithms, often reducing the time complexity to $O(\log n)$.

```
CREATE INDEX idx_customer_lastname ON customers(last_name);
```

The above command creates an index named idx_customer_lastname on the column last_name in the customers table. This index enables MySQL to quickly locate rows where the last_name matches a specified value.

```
SELECT * FROM customers WHERE last_name = 'Smith';
```

For this query, MySQL utilizes the idx_customer_lastname index to rapidly pinpoint rows where last_name is 'Smith', bypassing the need for a full table scan.

B-Tree Indexes

One commonly used index structure is the B-tree. B-trees maintain sorted data and allow searches, sequential access, insertions, and deletions in logarithmic time. A B-tree index is optimal for range queries and exact matches. Most MySQL indexes use a B-tree structure by default.

When a query involves a range condition, such as:

```
SELECT * FROM orders WHERE order_date BETWEEN '2023-01-01' AND '
    2023-03-31';
```

The B-tree index on order_date enables MySQL to efficiently retrieve all rows within the specified date range, significantly reducing the I/O operations compared to a table scan.

Full-Text Indexes

Full-text indexes are specialized structures designed to facilitate text searching capabilities. They improve the performance of search operations over large text fields. A full-text index in MySQL can be created on columns to support complex text queries.

```
CREATE FULLTEXT INDEX idx_article_content ON articles(content);
```

This index accelerates text search queries:

```
SELECT * FROM articles WHERE MATCH(content) AGAINST('database
    performance tuning');
```

The MATCH() function leverages the full-text index to perform a fast and efficient search, returning relevant rows that contain the search terms.

Spatial Indexes

Spatial indexes are used for geospatial data types, enabling efficient processing of spatial operations. These indexes are crucial for queries involving geographical data.

```
CREATE SPATIAL INDEX idx_location ON spatial_data(location);
```

A spatial query example:

```
SELECT * FROM spatial_data WHERE ST_Contains(location, ST_GeomFromText('
    POINT(1 1)'));
```

The spatial index allows this query to efficiently determine whether a given point lies within the defined spatial data.

Composite Indexes

Composite indexes are indexes on multiple columns. They enhance performance for queries that filter on multiple columns by using the combined index more effectively.

```
CREATE INDEX idx_user_activity ON user_activities(user_id, activity_date);
```

A query benefiting from the composite index:

```
SELECT * FROM user_activities WHERE user_id = 5 AND activity_date = '
    2023-10-01';
```

In this query, MySQL employs the composite index to quickly locate rows matching both user_id and activity_date criteria.

Index Selectivity

Index selectivity is a measure of the uniqueness of data in a column. High selectivity indicates that the indexed column contains many unique values, which results in more efficient indexing. For instance, an index on a column with high cardinality, like a primary key, provides greater performance benefits compared to an index on a column with low cardinality.

Query Execution Plan

To illustrate the impact of indexes on query performance, consider using the EXPLAIN command to view the execution plan of a query.

```
EXPLAIN SELECT * FROM customers WHERE last_name = 'Smith';
```

The EXPLAIN output might look like this:

```
+----+-------------+----------+------------+------+----------------------+----------------------+---------+-------+------+----------+-------+
| id | select_type | table    | partitions | type | possible_keys        | key                  | key_len | ref   | rows | filtered | Extra |
+----+-------------+----------+------------+------+----------------------+----------------------+---------+-------+------+----------+-------+
|  1 | SIMPLE      | customers| NULL       | ref  | idx_customer_lastname | idx_customer_lastname | 102     | const |    1 |   100.00 | NULL  |
+----+-------------+----------+------------+------+----------------------+----------------------+---------+-------+------+----------+-------+
```

The EXPLAIN output indicates that the query uses the idx_customer_lastname index, resulting in a filtered row set of 1, confirming the efficiency of the index in this context.

Indexes are indispensable assets in enhancing database query performance. Efficient indexing can markedly reduce query response times, optimize resource usage, and ensure scalability for large datasets. Understanding and adeptly applying different types of indexes in MySQL arms database administrators and developers with the essential tools to maintain robust and high-performance database systems.

7.5 Analyzing Query Performance with EXPLAIN

The EXPLAIN command is an indispensable tool for database administrators and developers to analyze and optimize the performance of MySQL queries. By providing insights into how MySQL executes a query, EXPLAIN helps identify potential bottlenecks and areas for improvement. This section delves into the syntax and output of the EXPLAIN command, while also exploring techniques to interpret the results for effective query optimization.

To utilize the EXPLAIN command, prefix your query with the keyword EXPLAIN. Consider the following example query:

```
EXPLAIN SELECT * FROM employees WHERE department_id = 5;
```

When executed, MySQL returns a detailed description of the query execution plan. The output consists of several key columns, each providing specific information about the query components:

```
+----+-------------+-----------+------------+------+---------------+------+---------+------+---------+----------+-------------+
| id | select_type | table     | partitions | type | possible_keys | key  | key_len | ref  | rows    | filtered | Extra       |
+----+-------------+-----------+------------+------+---------------+------+---------+------+---------+----------+-------------+
|  1 | SIMPLE      | employees | NULL       | ref  | dept_index    | dept_index | 5 | const| 3       | 100.00   | Using index |
+----+-------------+-----------+------------+------+---------------+------+---------+------+---------+----------+-------------+
```

Column Descriptions:

- **id**: This column indicates the unique identifier for each select in the query. It helps in understanding the execution sequence among multiple queries.
- **select_type**: Represents the type of SELECT query. Common types include SIMPLE, PRIMARY, UNION, DEPENDENT UNION, SUBQUERY, etc.
- **table**: Specifies the name of the table to which the row of the output refers.

- **partitions**: Displays the matching partitions if the table is partitioned.
- **type**: Indicates the join type. It is a crucial column for understanding query performance. Types range from system, const, eq_ref, ref, range, index, to ALL. The ALL type signifies a full table scan, which is the least efficient and should be avoided.
- **possible_keys**: Lists the potential indexes MySQL can use to find the rows in the table.
- **key**: Displays the actual index selected by the query optimizer.
- **key_len**: Shows the length of the key used. This value aids in diagnosing which part of the index MySQL uses.
- **ref**: Indicates the columns or constants used with the key to select rows from the table.
- **rows**: Provides an estimate of the number of rows examined by MySQL to produce the output. Although it is an approximation, it helps gauge the query's efficiency.
- **filtered**: Represents the percentage of rows filtered by the conditions upon table access.
- **Extra**: Contains additional information about the query execution plan. Common values include Using index, Using where, Using temporary, and Using filesort, each with distinct implications for performance.

Interpreting EXPLAIN **Output**:
An essential component of query optimization involves interpreting the EXPLAIN output to identify inefficiencies. Consider the following principles:

1. **Join Type**: - The ideal join types are system and const. - Types such as eq_ref, ref, and range indicate reasonable performance. - index and ALL suggest potential performance issues, with ALL being the most severe as it indicates a full table scan.

2. **Key Length**: - Ensure that the key_len value is optimal because longer keys could signal inefficient index usage.

3. **Rows**: - The rows value should be as low as possible, as a higher value implies more rows are scanned, leading to reduced query performance.

4. **Extra**: - The Using index value implies a coverage index, which generally boosts performance. - The presence of Using temporary or Using filesort suggests the use of temporary tables or file sorts, respectively, which can degrade performance and should be minimized.

Optimizing Based on EXPLAIN:

By leveraging the insights gained from EXPLAIN, several optimization strategies can be implemented:

- **Indexing**: - Create appropriate indexes on columns frequently used in WHERE clauses, JOIN conditions, and ORDER BY statements.

```
ALTER TABLE employees ADD INDEX idx_department_id (department_id);
```

- **Query Rewrite**: - Rewrite queries to improve efficiency. For example, breaking complex queries into simpler fragments where feasible.
- **Index Hints**: - Utilize index hints to guide the query optimizer in selecting the optimal index.

```
SELECT /*+ INDEX(employees idx_department_id) */ * FROM employees
    WHERE department_id = 5;
```

- **Analyze and Optimize Joins**: - Ensure join operations are performed using the most efficient paths and reduce unnecessary full table scans.

The ability to effectively analyze and interpret EXPLAIN output is fundamental for database performance tuning. Through systematic examination and strategic optimizations, significant enhancements in query performance can be achieved.

7.6 Using the Query Cache

The query cache is a mechanism in MySQL designed to improve query performance by storing the results of SELECT statements and reusing those results when the same query is executed multiple times. This can significantly reduce the workload on the server and speed up response times for repeated queries.

Enabling the Query Cache

To use the query cache, it must first be enabled. This can be done by adjusting the MySQL server configuration. The following parameters in the MySQL configuration file (my.cnf or my.ini) control the behavior of the query cache:

```
query_cache_type = 1
query_cache_size = 128M
```

query_cache_type can be set to one of the following values:

- **0**: Disable the query cache.
- **1**: Enable the query cache.
- **2**: Enable the query cache, but only cache queries marked explicitly.

query_cache_size determines the memory allocated for the cache. A value of 128M allocates 128 megabytes of memory to the query cache. The size can be adjusted according to the system memory and workload requirements.

Query Cache Usage

Once the query cache is enabled, MySQL will automatically cache the results of SELECT queries if all of the following conditions are met:

- The query is a SELECT statement.
- The query does not use functions that produce non-deterministic results (e.g., NOW(), RAND()).
- Tables used in the query have not been modified since the query was cached.
- The query does not reference user-defined variables.

To check if a query result was fetched from the cache, the following command can be used:

```
SHOW STATUS LIKE 'Qcache_hits';
```

If the number increases after executing a query, it indicates a cache hit.

Explicit Query Caching

When query_cache_type is set to 2, only queries explicitly marked for caching will utilize the query cache. This is useful for controlling the caching behavior in a fine-grained manner.

To explicitly cache a query, the SQL_CACHE keyword can be used:

```
SELECT SQL_CACHE field1, field2 FROM table WHERE condition;
```

To explicitly bypass the query cache, the SQL_NO_CACHE keyword can be used:

```
SELECT SQL_NO_CACHE field1, field2 FROM table WHERE condition;
```

Monitoring and Maintenance

Monitoring the query cache involves checking various status variables. The following table summarizes important status variables related to the query cache:

Status Variable	Description
Qcache_queries_in_cache	Number of queries currently in the query cache.
Qcache_hits	Number of query cache hits.
Qcache_inserts	Number of queries added to the query cache.
Qcache_lowmem_prunes	Number of queries pruned from the cache due to low memory.
Qcache_not_cached	Number of non-cached queries (e.g., due to non-deterministic functions).

Queries are removed from the cache when tables involved in the query are altered. This can result in the cache being invalidated frequently if the underlying data changes often.

Best Practices

While the query cache can significantly boost performance for read-heavy applications, there are caveats to its use:

- The query cache is beneficial for applications with frequent identical queries.
- For write-heavy workloads, frequent cache invalidation can reduce the effectiveness of the query cache.
- Cache size should be monitored and adjusted based on application needs. Over-allocating memory to the query cache can reduce the memory available for other database operations.
- Periodic monitoring of query cache status variables helps in understanding cache performance and tuning parameters accordingly.

Proper configuration and use of the query cache can lead to noticeable performance improvements by reducing query execution times and offloading pressure from the server's query processing engine.

7.7 Optimizing SELECT Queries

Optimizing SELECT queries is crucial for maintaining high performance in MySQL databases. A well-optimized SELECT query can significantly reduce the load on database servers and improve the response time of applications. This section delves into various strategies for optimizing SELECT queries, focusing on indexing, query execution analysis, and query design patterns.

The efficiency of a SELECT query heavily depends on its access to the necessary data and the minimization of redundant data scans. One of the primary tools at your disposal is the index. Proper indexing enables quick lookups and efficient retrieval of rows. However, indexing is only one part of the optimization process. You must also consider the structure and execution plan of your queries, as well as how they interact with your database schema.

To begin, the proper use of indexes can dramatically improve query performance. Consider the following query on a table named employees:

```
SELECT first_name, last_name, email FROM employees WHERE department_id = 3;
```

If there is an index on the department_id column, MySQL can quickly locate the rows that match the WHERE clause condition, avoiding a full table scan. You can create an index for the department_id column as follows:

```
CREATE INDEX idx_department_id ON employees(department_id);
```

MySQL uses indexes to create a balanced tree structure, allowing rapid access to records. However, over-indexing can lead to performance degradation during data modification operations like INSERT, UPDATE, and DELETE. Therefore, it's essential to find a balance and only create indexes that are necessary for query optimization.

The next tool for query optimization is the EXPLAIN command. EXPLAIN provides insights into how MySQL executes a query, displaying information about the tables involved, join types, possible keys, key usage, and the number of rows MySQL needs to examine. Using EXPLAIN for the previous query:

```
EXPLAIN SELECT first_name, last_name, email FROM employees WHERE
    department_id = 3;
```

The output will be displayed in a tabular format:

```
+----+-------------+-----------+-------+---------------+--------------------+---------+-------+--------+-------------+
| id | select_type | table     | type  | possible_keys | key                | key_len | ref   | rows   | Extra       |
+----+-------------+-----------+-------+---------------+--------------------+---------+-------+--------+-------------+
|  1 | SIMPLE      | employees| ref   | idx_department| idx_department (ref) | 4       | const|      30| Using where |
+----+-------------+-----------+-------+---------------+--------------------+---------+-------+--------+-------------+
```

The type column indicates the join type MySQL is using. In this case, ref indicates that MySQL is using an index to find rows quickly based on the department_id. The key column confirms that the idx_department_id index is used.

Another critical aspect of query optimization is ensuring efficient join operations. When joining tables, using indexed columns in the ON or USING clause can significantly reduce execution time. For instance:

```
SELECT e.first_name, e.last_name, d.department_name
FROM employees e
JOIN departments d ON e.department_id = d.department_id
WHERE d.location_id = 100;
```

Both employees.department_id and departments.department_id should be indexed to facilitate this join. Here's how you might create these indexes:

```
CREATE INDEX idx_emp_dept_id ON employees(department_id);
CREATE INDEX idx_dept_id ON departments(department_id);
```

Efficient query design also includes selecting only the necessary columns. Avoid using SELECT * since it retrieves all columns, which may be unnecessary and increase resource usage. For example, instead of:

```
SELECT * FROM employees WHERE department_id = 3;
```

Specify only the needed columns:

```
SELECT first_name, last_name, email FROM employees WHERE department_id = 3;
```

Filtering data early in your queries is another effective optimization strategy. Using indexed columns in the WHERE clause helps reduce the dataset size before performing any further operations. Consider indexes in the following composite query:

```
SELECT e.first_name, e.last_name, d.department_name
FROM employees e
JOIN departments d ON e.department_id = d.department_id
WHERE e.join_date > '2020-01-01' AND d.location_id = 100;
```

Here, indexing employees.join_date and departments.location_id will optimize the retrieval process.

Lastly, consider using temporary tables or derived tables for complex queries involving multiple joins and aggregations. Temporary tables can store intermediary results, which can then be indexed for faster access in subsequent operations.

Throughout all optimization efforts, consistent testing and analysis are crucial. Use sample datasets and the EXPLAIN command to evaluate the impact of indexes and query structures, making adjustments as needed for optimal performance.

7.8 Optimizing INSERT, UPDATE, and DELETE Queries

Ensuring the optimal performance of INSERT, UPDATE, and DELETE operations in MySQL is crucial for maintaining the efficiency and responsiveness of your database. This section addresses key strategies and techniques to optimize these Data Manipulation Language (DML) operations, enhancing their throughput and reducing potential bottlenecks.

Optimizing INSERT Queries

INSERT queries add new rows to tables and can be resource-intensive. The following strategies help optimize INSERT operations:

- **Batch Inserts**: Instead of inserting rows one at a time, use bulk insert operations to reduce the overhead associated with multiple single-row insert operations.

```
INSERT INTO table_name (column1, column2) VALUES
(value1_1, value1_2),
(value2_1, value2_2),
(value3_1, value3_2);
```

- **Disable Indexes and Foreign Key Checks**: Temporarily disabling indexes and foreign key checks during bulk insert operations can significantly improve performance. After the operation, re-enable them.

```
SET FOREIGN_KEY_CHECKS = 0;
ALTER TABLE table_name DISABLE KEYS;
```

```
INSERT INTO table_name (column1, column2) VALUES
(value1_1, value1_2),
(value2_1, value2_2),
(value3_1, value3_2);

ALTER TABLE table_name ENABLE KEYS;
SET FOREIGN_KEY_CHECKS = 1;
```

- **Use Appropriate Storage Engines**: Different storage engines offer different performance characteristics. For instance, the InnoDB engine provides transactional support and performance improvements for INSERT operations through its use of clustered indexes and row-level locking.
- **Optimize Table Design**: Ensure that the table is properly indexed and normalized to reduce the overhead during INSERT operations.
- **Utilize Load Data Infile**: For extremely large datasets, the LOAD DATA INFILE statement can be much faster than multiple INSERT statements.

```
LOAD DATA INFILE 'file_path'
INTO TABLE table_name
FIELDS TERMINATED BY ','
LINES TERMINATED BY '\n'
(column1, column2, column3);
```

Optimizing UPDATE Queries

UPDATE queries modify existing rows in a table and can lock resources, affecting performance. Consider the following approaches to optimize UPDATE operations:

- **Index Relevant Columns**: Ensure columns used in the WHERE clause are indexed to expedite search and reduce the number of rows that need to be updated.

```
CREATE INDEX idx_column1 ON table_name (column1);

UPDATE table_name
SET column2 = new_value
WHERE column1 = specific_value;
```

- **Update in Batches**: For large datasets, updating rows in smaller batches can reduce lock contention and improve performance.

```
UPDATE table_name
SET column2 = new_value
```

```
WHERE column1 = specific_value
LIMIT 1000;
```

- **Avoid Unnecessary Updates**: Ensure that updates only occur if necessary, especially when new values are calculated or derived from existing ones.

```
UPDATE table_name
SET column2 = new_value
WHERE column1 = specific_value AND column2 != new_value;
```

- **Reduce Index Overhead**: If many rows are updated, consider temporarily disabling non-essential indexes to minimize write amplification.

Optimizing DELETE Queries

DELETE queries remove rows from a table and can be particularly taxing in terms of performance. Utilize these optimization techniques:

- **Index WHERE Clause Columns**: Similar to UPDATE operations, ensure that the columns used in the WHERE clause are indexed to narrow down the scope quickly.

```
CREATE INDEX idx_column1 ON table_name (column1);

DELETE FROM table_name
WHERE column1 = specific_value;
```

- **Delete in Batches**: For deleting large numbers of rows, executing the DELETE in smaller batches can help in reducing lock contention and improving throughput.

```
DELETE FROM table_name
WHERE column1 = specific_value
LIMIT 1000;
```

- **Use Secondary Tables**: When deleting a significant portion of a table, it might be more efficient to create a new table with the required rows and then replace the original table.

```
CREATE TABLE new_table AS
SELECT * FROM table_name WHERE condition;

DROP TABLE table_name;

RENAME TABLE new_table TO table_name;
```

- **Consider** TRUNCATE **for Full Table Deletes**: The TRUNCATE command is faster than DELETE when you need to remove all rows from a table because it deallocates the data pages rather than logging individual row deletions.

```
TRUNCATE TABLE table_name;
```

Understanding Impact with Example

To illustrate the practical impact of these optimization techniques, consider the following example database operations on a table named users:

```
CREATE TABLE users (
    id INT PRIMARY KEY AUTO_INCREMENT,
    username VARCHAR(50) NOT NULL,
    email VARCHAR(100) NOT NULL,
    signup_date DATETIME
);
```

```
Insert 10,000 rows individually took 5 minutes.
Batch inserting 10,000 rows took 1 minute.
```

```
-- Disable foreign key checks and bulk insert users
SET FOREIGN_KEY_CHECKS = 0;

INSERT INTO 'users' ('username', 'email', 'signup_date') VALUES
('user1', 'user1@example.com', '2022-01-01 10:00:00'),
('user2', 'user2@example.com', '2022-01-01 10:01:00'),
...
('user10000', 'user10000@example.com', '2022-01-02 10:00:00');

SET FOREIGN_KEY_CHECKS = 1;
```

Updating 10,000 users individually versus updating in batches:

```
Update 10,000 rows individually took 4 minutes.
Batch updating 10,000 rows took 1.5 minutes.
```

```
-- Adding an index on signup_date for efficient updates
CREATE INDEX idx_signup_date ON users (signup_date);

-- Update users in smaller batches
UPDATE users SET email = 'updated@example.com'
WHERE signup_date < '2022-01-02 00:00:00'
LIMIT 1000;
```

Deleting 10,000 rows individually versus using batches or truncating:

```
Delete 10,000 rows individually took 3 minutes.
Batch deleting 10,000 rows took 1 minute.
```

```
-- Deleting rows in smaller batches
DELETE FROM users
WHERE signup_date < '2022-01-02 00:00:00'
LIMIT 1000;
```

```
-- Truncating the table
TRUNCATE TABLE users;
```

By carefully implementing these strategies, the performance of INSERT, UPDATE, and DELETE operations can be significantly improved, ensuring efficient and responsive database interactions.

7.9 Understanding and Using Index Hints

In MySQL, index hints are directives that instruct the query optimizer to use or ignore specific indexes when executing a query. This can be particularly useful when the optimizer's default index selection is suboptimal for certain queries. By understanding and utilizing index hints effectively, one can exert greater control over query execution plans and potentially enhance performance.

To use index hints in a SQL query, the USE INDEX, IGNORE INDEX, and FORCE INDEX clauses are employed. These clauses can be included in the SELECT, UPDATE, and DELETE statements.

```
SELECT column_list
FROM table_name
USE INDEX (index_name)
WHERE conditions;
```

The USE INDEX hint suggests to the optimizer to consider using the specified index or indexes for the query. Below is an example of a query that instructs the optimizer to use a specific index:

```
SELECT name, age
FROM employees
USE INDEX (idx_name_age)
WHERE age > 30;
```

In this example, the optimizer is directed to use the idx_name_age index while executing the query on the employees table.

The IGNORE INDEX hint advises the optimizer to ignore the specified index or indexes. This is useful if the optimizer chooses an index that is known to result in suboptimal performance.

```
SELECT name, age
FROM employees
IGNORE INDEX (idx_age)
WHERE age > 30;
```

Here, the optimizer is discouraged from using the idx_age index, even if it ordinarily might select it.

The FORCE INDEX hint mandates that the optimizer use the specified index. This hint should be used cautiously, as forcibly directing the optimizer may lead to inefficient query plans if the chosen index is not the optimal one.

```
SELECT name, age
FROM employees
FORCE INDEX (idx_name_age)
WHERE age > 30;
```

In this query, the idx_name_age index is forced upon the optimizer, ensuring its usage.

It is possible to combine multiple index hints within a single query. For example, specifying that the optimizer should use one index while ignoring another:

```
SELECT name, department
FROM employees
USE INDEX (idx_department)
IGNORE INDEX (idx_age)
WHERE department = 'HR' AND age > 30;
```

This query hints to the optimizer to consider the idx_department index and disregard the idx_age index.

Understanding the context in which to use these hints requires familiarity with the query patterns and underlying data distribution. Index hints can be particularly advantageous in these situations:

- The query optimizer consistently selects a non-optimal index.
- Certain queries have specific performance requirements that are not met by the default index selection.
- Index usage needs to be enforced or restricted for analysis or experimental purposes.

While index hints provide a means to influence the query optimizer directly, they should not be the primary approach to query optimization. Properly designed indexes and comprehensive query analysis should precede the usage of hints. Overusing index hints can lead to maintenance challenges and may result in unforeseen performance issues.

Practical usage of index hints can be evaluated using the EXPLAIN statement. By running EXPLAIN on a hinted query, one can scrutinize the query execution plan and verify that the desired index is being applied:

```
EXPLAIN SELECT name, age
FROM employees
USE INDEX (idx_name_age)
WHERE age > 30;
```

The output from the EXPLAIN command will reveal if the index hint was respected and which index was ultimately utilized by the optimizer.

Below is an example output from the EXPLAIN command:

```
+----+-------------+-----------+------------+------+---------------+--------------+---------+-------+------+----------+-------------+
| id | select_type | table     | partitions | type | possible_keys | key          | key_len | ref   | rows | filtered | Extra       |
+----+-------------+-----------+------------+------+---------------+--------------+---------+-------+------+----------+-------------+
|  1 | SIMPLE      | employees | NULL       | ref  | idx_name_age  | idx_name_age| 4       | const |  100 |   100.00 | Using where |
+----+-------------+-----------+------------+------+---------------+--------------+---------+-------+------+----------+-------------+
```

This output indicates that the idx_name_age index was used in executing the query, as specified by the hint.

By mastering the application of index hints, database administrators and developers can fine-tune query performance, ensuring efficient and expedient access to data stored within MySQL databases.

7.10 Maintaining and Rebuilding Indexes

To maintain optimal performance in a MySQL database, it is essential to periodically maintain and rebuild indexes. Indexes, while crucial for improving read operations, can become fragmented or obsolete over time due to updates, inserts, and deletes. This can severely impact query performance. Proper maintenance of indexes involves several tasks such as analyzing, optimizing, and occasionally rebuilding them.

Index fragmentation occurs when the physical order of index keys becomes out of sync with their logical order, leading to inefficient disk I/O operations. To mitigate this, the ANALYZE TABLE, OPTIMIZE TABLE, and ALTER TABLE statements are employed.

To analyze an index, the ANALYZE TABLE command gathers statistics about the distribution of table key values, which the query optimizer uses to make informed decisions. The syntax is as follows:

```
ANALYZE TABLE table_name;
```

After executing this command, the optimizer has updated statistics, enhancing its ability to formulate efficient query execution plans.

Optimizing a table, which also defragments the associated indexes, can be accomplished with the OPTIMIZE TABLE statement. This operation reclaims unused space and defragments the data and index files, effectively rebuilding the indexes associated with the table:

```
OPTIMIZE TABLE table_name;
```

Running this command is particularly effective when a table undergoes numerous updates and deletions, leading to considerable fragmentation and unused space.

In cases where indexes are heavily fragmented, or when significant structural changes occur, manually rebuilding the indexes may be necessary. This can be achieved using the ALTER TABLE command. To force an index rebuild, the table structure is altered, typically by performing a null operation:

```
ALTER TABLE table_name ENGINE=InnoDB;
```

While the command appears to change the storage engine, it effectively rebuilds all indexes without altering the current storage engine.

Another scenario requiring attention is the impact of index maintenance on system performance. These operations can be resource-intensive, potentially causing downtime or degraded performance. Scheduling maintenance during off-peak hours is advisable. For large datasets, consider using the pt-online-schema-change tool from the Percona Toolkit, which allows index rebuilding with minimal downtime by performing schema changes online.

Indexes may also need to be changed, for instance, when the data distribution changes significantly or when query patterns evolve. This involves dropping and recreating indexes:

```
ALTER TABLE table_name DROP INDEX index_name;
ALTER TABLE table_name ADD INDEX index_name (column_name);
```

Regularly reviewing the efficiency of existing indexes against current query workloads ensures that the most effective indexes are in place.

It is also important to monitor the size and growth of indexes. Large indexes can consume significant storage and impact the performance of maintenance operations. Using the SHOW INDEX statement provides valuable insights into index usage and storage:

```
SHOW INDEX FROM table_name;
```

Periodically evaluating the output of this command can highlight indexes that are candidates for optimization or removal. Furthermore, implementing proper index naming conventions and documentation facilitates easier index management.

Careful planning, execution of maintenance routines, and keeping abreast of changes in the dataset and query patterns are critical for sustaining the performance benefits provided by indexes.

7.11 Identifying and Resolving Slow Queries

Effective database performance management necessitates the identification and resolution of slow queries. Slow queries can significantly impact the responsiveness and efficiency of a database system. Addressing these queries involves a systematic approach to identifying performance bottlenecks, analyzing query execution plans, optimizing queries, and ensuring proper indexing strategies.

The most fundamental tool for identifying slow queries in MySQL is the slow query log. This feature provides detailed information about queries that exceed a specified duration threshold.

```
SET GLOBAL slow_query_log = 'ON';
SET GLOBAL long_query_time = 1; -- log queries longer than 1 second
```

Once the slow query log is enabled, it begins logging all queries that take longer than the specified duration to execute. The file path for the slow query log can be specified in the MySQL configuration file (my.cnf or my.ini):

```
[mysqld]
slow_query_log = 1
slow_query_log_file = /var/log/mysql/slow-query.log
long_query_time = 1
```

To parse and analyze the slow query log, the pt-query-digest tool from Percona Toolkit is highly effective. It provides a comprehensive analysis of slow queries, grouping similar queries, and highlighting the most impactful ones.

```
pt-query-digest /var/log/mysql/slow-query.log
```

Typical output from pt-query-digest includes the count of query occurrences, execution time statistics, and a sample of the most time-consuming queries. With this data, database administrators can prioritize which queries to optimize first.

To further analyze the execution plan of a specific slow query, the EXPLAIN command is indispensable. The EXPLAIN command provides insights into how MySQL executes a particular query, detailing aspects such as the order of table processing, the join types used, and the indexes being utilized.

```
EXPLAIN SELECT column1, column2 FROM table WHERE condition1 AND
    condition2;
```

The EXPLAIN command output includes several columns, each providing critical information about the query execution process:

- **id** - The identifier for the SELECT query, useful for distinguishing subqueries and compound queries.
- **select_type** - The type of SELECT operation, indicating if it's a simple SELECT, a UNION, or a subquery.
- **table** - The table from which rows are retrieved.
- **type** - The join type, ranging from "system" (best) to "ALL" (worst).
- **possible_keys** - The indexes that MySQL could potentially use to find rows.
- **key** - The actual index used by MySQL for the query.
- **key_len** - The length of the used key.
- **ref** - The columns or constants compared to the indexed columns.
- **rows** - The estimated number of rows to be examined.
- **extra** - Additional information about the query execution.

Consider the following EXPLAIN output for a sample query:

```
+----+-------------+-------+-------+---------------+---------+---------+------+------+-------------+
| id | select_type | table | type  | possible_keys | key     | key_len | ref  | rows | Extra       |
+----+-------------+-------+-------+---------------+---------+---------+------+------+-------------+
|  1 | SIMPLE      | table | range | idx_col1      | idx_col1| 4       | NULL | 1000 | Using where |
+----+-------------+-------+-------+---------------+---------+---------+------+------+-------------+
```

This output reveals that the query uses an index (idx_col1), processes rows in a range scan, and applies a WHERE clause filter.

Optimizing slow queries often involves ensuring proper indexing. Missing indexes can lead to full table scans, which are expensive in terms of performance. To add an appropriate index:

```
CREATE INDEX idx_column1 ON table(column1);
```

For complex queries involving multiple tables, examining join operations is crucial. Inefficient joins, due to lack of indexing on join columns, can also cause slow performance. Adding composite indexes on join columns can significantly improve query performance.

Another technique in query optimization is rewriting inefficient queries. Consider the following query, which uses a correlated subquery that might be slow:

```
SELECT a.column1,
       (SELECT b.column2
        FROM table2 b
        WHERE b.foreign_key = a.primary_key)
FROM table1 a;
```

Rewriting it using a join can enhance performance:

```
SELECT a.column1, b.column2
FROM table1 a
JOIN table2 b ON a.primary_key = b.foreign_key;
```

Query caching, if enabled, can also improve performance by storing the results of frequently executed queries. This reduces the need for repeated execution of the same query:

```
SET GLOBAL query_cache_type = 1;
SET GLOBAL query_cache_size = 1048576; -- 1MB
```

However, modern MySQL versions have deprecated the query cache due to its inefficiency in multi-core environments. Hence, application-level caching or utilizing an in-memory database like Redis may be preferable for performance gains.

Upon identifying and resolving slow queries, ongoing monitoring is essential to ensure sustained database performance. This includes regularly reviewing the slow query log, keeping EXPLAIN analyses up-to-date, and adjusting indexes as the schema or query patterns evolve. By meticulously applying these techniques, the performance of MySQL databases can be significantly optimized, ensuring robust and efficient data operations.

7.12 Performance Tuning Best Practices

Effective performance tuning requires a systematic and strategic approach to ensure databases operate optimally. Adhering to best practices is essential for maintaining performance as data volume and system complexity increase. This section elaborates on key practices that should be routinely followed:

Regularly Monitor Performance: Continuous monitoring of database performance is critical. Tools like MySQL's Performance Schema and third-party monitoring solutions can provide insights into various performance metrics. Monitoring allows for the timely detection of performance degradations and facilitates proactive tuning.

Proper Indexing: Indexes should be judiciously used to speed up query execution. However, over-indexing can lead to excessive overhead, particularly for write operations. Use the EXPLAIN command frequently to understand how queries interact with indexes and refine indexes as needed.

Query Optimization: Avoid writing suboptimal queries. Utilize indexing, joins, and proper filtering to make queries efficient. Simplifying complex queries can reduce the load on the database. For example, instead of using subqueries, consider rewriting them as joins when possible.

```
SELECT orders.order_id, customers.customer_name
FROM orders
JOIN customers ON orders.customer_id = customers.customer_id
WHERE customers.region = 'North America';
```

Use Prepared Statements: Prepared statements are beneficial as they allow MySQL to parse and compile queries only once, even if they are executed multiple times with different parameters. This can significantly reduce the overhead of query parsing.

```
PREPARE stmt FROM 'SELECT * FROM users WHERE user_id = ?';
SET @user_id = 1;
EXECUTE stmt USING @user_id;
```

Efficient Schema Design: A well-designed schema can drastically improve performance. Normalize databases to eliminate redundancy but denormalize selective areas for read-intensive operations. Understand the trade-offs between normalization and denormalization in the context of performance.

Leverage Query Caching: Utilize MySQL's query cache for applications that perform frequent, repetitive queries. Caching can reduce the time taken to serve queries by storing results of previously executed queries. However, consider the cache's invalidation costs and the nature of your workload.

Partition Large Tables: Table partitioning can improve performance for large datasets by dividing a table into smaller, more manageable pieces. It can enhance query performance and simplify maintenance tasks. MySQL supports several partitioning types, such as range, list, and hash partitioning.

```
CREATE TABLE sales (
  sale_id INT,
  sale_date DATE,
  amount DECIMAL(10,2)
) PARTITION BY RANGE (YEAR(sale_date)) (
  PARTITION p0 VALUES LESS THAN (2000),
  PARTITION p1 VALUES LESS THAN (2010),
  PARTITION p2 VALUES LESS THAN (2020)
);
```

Optimize Hardware Utilization: Ensure the database server has adequate resources (CPU, memory, and storage). Proper hardware provisioning and configuration can prevent bottlenecks. Analyze and upgrade hardware periodically to keep pace with growing data and usage.

Routine Maintenance Tasks: Regularly perform maintenance tasks such as analyzing and optimizing tables, updating statistics, and cleaning up unused indexes. MySQL provides commands like ANALYZE TABLE and OPTIMIZE TABLE which help maintain database health.

```
ANALYZE TABLE my_table;
OPTIMIZE TABLE my_table;
```

Backup and Recovery Planning: Regular backups are essential. Ensure that backups are taken without disrupting performance. Develop a recovery plan to minimize downtime and data loss in the case of system failure.

Minimize Lock Contention: Database locks are necessary to ensure data consistency but can also hinder performance. To reduce lock contention, aim for shorter transactions, use locking hints wisely, and consider using MySQL's isolation levels that align with application requirements.

Audit and Debug: Periodic audits and debugging can identify hidden issues. Use the MySQL slow query log to find and optimize long-running queries. Profiling tools can also help diagnose and pinpoint performance bottlenecks.

```
# Enable slow query logging
SET GLOBAL slow_query_log = 'ON';
SET GLOBAL long_query_time = 2; # Queries longer than 2 seconds
```

Leverage Replication and Sharding: Distribute the load by using replication, which involves creating copies of the database that can be hosted on separate servers. Sharding, or partitioning data across multiple databases, can further improve performance for extremely large datasets.

Documentation and Version Control: Maintain detailed documentation of all database configurations, schemas, and significant queries. Implement version control to manage and track changes. This practice enhances traceability and collaboration among team members.

Adopting these best practices helps ensure the database performs optimally under varying loads and conditions. Regular review and adaptation based on performance metrics and system requirements will contribute significantly to achieving and maintaining efficient database operations.

Chapter 8

Transactions and Concurrency

This chapter covers the principles of transactions and concurrency control in MySQL. It explains the ACID properties, how to start and end transactions, and the use of savepoints and rollbacks. Topics also include isolation levels, deadlock avoidance, and MySQL's locking mechanisms. The chapter discusses transaction management within stored procedures, employing concurrency control methods, and the differences between optimistic and pessimistic concurrency. Additionally, it addresses transaction monitoring best practices.

8.1 Introduction to Transactions

A transaction is a sequence of one or more SQL operations treated as a single unit of work. A transaction ensures that the operations either all succeed or all fail, maintaining database integrity. At its core, a transaction is designed to ensure data consistency, durability, and reliability across various manipulations. This section delves into the fundamental aspects of transactions in MySQL, elucidating their significance and implementation.

To delineate the concept with practical clarity, consider the following procedural steps in a typical transaction scenario. Begin a transaction, perform various operations, and either commit or roll back the transaction. Here is how these actions are carried out in MySQL:

```
START TRANSACTION;

-- Series of SQL operations
INSERT INTO accounts (account_id, amount) VALUES (1, 1000);
UPDATE accounts SET amount = amount - 100 WHERE account_id = 1;
UPDATE accounts SET amount = amount + 100 WHERE account_id = 2;

-- Decide to commit or rollback based on the operations' success
COMMIT;
-- or
-- ROLLBACK;
```

In the above code snippet, the transaction initiates with START TRANSACTION. It includes an INSERT and two UPDATE statements. If all these operations complete successfully, the changes are made permanent with COMMIT. If any step fails, a ROLLBACK reverts all operations, ensuring no partial updates are saved.

Transactions are pivotal in multi-step processes where atomicity, consistency, isolation, and durability (ACID) are necessary. For instance, in banking systems, transferring money involves debiting one account and crediting another. Using transactions guarantees that both operations either complete successfully or are both undone.

Understanding the concept of transactions involves recognizing specific properties:

- * Atomicity ensures that all components of the transaction are completed; if not, the system reverts to its original state.
- * Consistency maintains the integrity of the database before and after the transaction.
- * Isolation guarantees that transactions do not affect each other, ensuring concurrent transactions proceed as if they were executed sequentially.
- * Durability ensures that once a transaction is committed, its effects persist even in the event of a system failure.

These properties collectively define the robustness of transaction handling in MySQL and other relational database systems.

Consider the following SQL example, showcasing a scenario where transactions prevent data corruption:

```
START TRANSACTION;

-- Deduct amount from sender's account
UPDATE accounts SET balance = balance - 100 WHERE account_id = 1;

-- Simulate a failure scenario
-- Incorrect column name causes a failure
UPDATE accounts SET balancee = balance + 100 WHERE account_id = 2;

-- Incorrect column name causes error; this line won't be reached
COMMIT;
```

In this example, the second UPDATE statement contains a typographical error (balancee instead of balance). Due to the error, the transaction aborts, and the ROLLBACK operation (implicitly invoked) ensures that the first UPDATE, which debits the sender's account, is undone, preserving data integrity.

Here is an illustration of its execution:

```
START TRANSACTION;
Query OK, 0 rows affected (0.00 sec)

UPDATE accounts SET balance = balance - 100 WHERE account_id = 1;
Query OK, 1 row affected (0.01 sec)

UPDATE accounts SET balancee = balance + 100 WHERE account_id = 2;
ERROR 1054 (42S22): Unknown column 'balancee' in 'field list'

ROLLBACK;
Query OK, 0 rows affected (0.01 sec)
```

Due to the transactional approach, although the first update operation succeeds, the second operation's failure causes the rollback, undoing the first update. This behavior underscores the transaction's role in preventing partial updates and preserving the database's consistency state.

By using transactions, consistency and integrity are maintained even in the presence of unforeseen errors or interruptions, which are inherent to real-world systems. As such, mastering their application is crucial for developers aiming to build reliable, robust databases and applications.

Understanding how and when to use transactions effectively is fundamental to proficient database management and operation. Mastery of these principles lays a strong foundation for advanced topics such as isolation levels, concurrency control, and transaction management in stored procedures, which are discussed in subsequent sections.

8.2 ACID Properties

The acronym ACID stands for Atomicity, Consistency, Isolation, and Durability. These properties are fundamental for ensuring reliable transaction processing in relational databases. By adhering to the ACID properties, MySQL guarantees that transactions are processed in a secure, predictable, and reliable manner. Each property plays a critical role in maintaining the integrity and coherence of database operations.

Atomicity

Atomicity is the property that ensures a transaction is treated as a single, indivisible unit. This means that all operations within a transaction must be completed successfully for the transaction to be committed. If any operation within the transaction fails, the entire transaction is rolled back, leaving the database in its previous state before the transaction began. This all-or-nothing approach is crucial for maintaining data integrity and preventing partial updates.

In MySQL, atomicity can be demonstrated through the following example:

```
START TRANSACTION;
INSERT INTO accounts (user_id, balance) VALUES (1, 100);
UPDATE accounts SET balance = balance - 50 WHERE user_id = 1;
INSERT INTO accounts (user_id, balance) VALUES (2, 50);
COMMIT;
```

If all the statements execute without error, the transaction is committed, and the changes are permanently applied. Should an error occur in any of the statements, a ROLLBACK command is issued, aborting the transaction and undoing all changes:

```
START TRANSACTION;
INSERT INTO accounts (user_id, balance) VALUES (1, 100);
UPDATE accounts SET balance = balance - 50 WHERE user_id = 1;
INSERT INTO accounts (user_id, balance) VALUES (2, 50);
-- Suppose this last statement fails
ROLLBACK;
```

After the rollback, the database reflects its state prior to the initiation of the START TRANSACTION command.

Consistency

Consistency ensures that a transaction brings the database from one valid state to another, maintaining database invariants. In other words, any data written to the database must be valid according to all defined rules, including constraints, cascades, and triggers. Consistency checks ensure data integrity by enforcing these rules both before and after the transaction.

To illustrate consistency, consider a scenario where a financial application must ensure that the sum of deposits in two accounts remains constant. Suppose a transaction involves transferring money between these two accounts. The database schema enforces a check constraint on the total balance:

```
CREATE TABLE accounts (
    user_id INT PRIMARY KEY,
    balance DECIMAL(10,2) CHECK (balance >= 0)
);
```

A consistency violation occurs if a transaction attempts to withdraw more money than the available balance, leading to a negative balance. MySQL's constraint enforcement will abort the transaction and thus ensure consistency.

Isolation

Isolation ensures that concurrently executing transactions do not interfere with each other. A transaction should be unaware of other concurrently running transactions. Through isolation, MySQL avoids potential conflicts and anomalies such as dirty reads, non-repeatable reads, or phantom reads. MySQL uses several isolation levels to balance performance and consistency. These are:

- READ UNCOMMITTED
- READ COMMITTED
- REPEATABLE READ
- SERIALIZABLE

Each isolation level provides a different degree of concurrency control. For instance, SERIALIZABLE isolation level avoids all concurrency issues by ensuring complete isolation but at the expense of performance. In contrast, READ UNCOMMITTED offers the highest performance but allows for dirty reads.

Durability

Durability guarantees that once a transaction is committed, its changes are permanent, even in the event of a system failure. MySQL ensures durability by writing transaction logs and periodically flushing these logs to persistent storage. Commit operations are only acknowledged when all transaction data is reliably stored.

InnoDB, the default storage engine in MySQL, employs a mechanism known as the double-write buffer to ensure durability. When changes are made, they are first written to a transactional log file. Only after the data is safely flushed to disk are these changes committed and reflected in the database.

To demonstrate, consider the following MySQL configuration parameter adjustments that influence durability:

```
[mysqld]
innodb_flush_log_at_trx_commit=1
sync_binlog=1
```

Setting innodb_flush_log_at_trx_commit to 1 ensures that InnoDB flushes the log buffer to the transaction log after each transaction commit, ensuring durability. Similarly, setting sync_binlog to 1 forces MySQL to synchronize the binary log to disk after each transaction commit, further enhancing durability.

By implementing these parameters, MySQL ensures the successful execution and persistence of committed transactions, maintaining database reliability and stability.

These four ACID properties are fundamental to transactional systems, providing a robust framework for reliable and consistent database operations.

8.3 Starting and Ending Transactions

In MySQL, transactions are units of work that are treated as a single, indivisible operation. Each transaction ensures that all operations within it are completed successfully before being permanently applied to the database. If any operation within the transaction fails, the entire transaction can be rolled back, ensuring that no partial or inconsistent data is committed.

To manage transactions effectively, understanding how to properly start and end them is crucial. This section delves into the syntax and mechanisms provided by MySQL to initiate and conclude transactions, thereby maintaining data integrity and consistency.

Beginning a Transaction

A transaction begins with the START TRANSACTION or BEGIN statement. The selection between these two is a matter of preference, as they function equivalently. By issuing either of these commands, the database context shifts to transactional mode, meaning that subsequent SQL statements are executed within the confines of the current transaction.

```
START TRANSACTION;
-- or
BEGIN;
```

Once a transaction has started, all subsequent operations are part of that transaction until it is explicitly concluded.

Ending a Transaction

A transaction can conclude in one of two ways: by committing the changes or by rolling them back.

- **Commit:** The COMMIT statement finalizes the transaction, making all modifications permanent. Once committed, the changes are visible to all other transactions and users.

```
COMMIT;
```

- **Rollback:** The ROLLBACK statement aborts the transaction, undoing all changes made during the transaction. This capability is essential for maintaining data consistency when an operation fails or an error is encountered.

```
ROLLBACK;
```

Consider the following sequence of SQL commands as an example:

```
START TRANSACTION;

INSERT INTO accounts (user_id, balance) VALUES (1, 1000);
UPDATE accounts SET balance = balance - 100 WHERE user_id = 1;
UPDATE accounts SET balance = balance + 100 WHERE user_id = 2;

COMMIT;
```

In this example, the transaction begins with START TRANSACTION. It performs multiple operations on the accounts table, ensuring that either all operations are applied successfully or none at all. The COMMIT statement finalizes the transaction, making the changes permanent.

In case an error occurs during the transaction, the transaction can be rolled back to revert all changes:

```
START TRANSACTION;

INSERT INTO accounts (user_id, balance) VALUES (1, 1000);
UPDATE accounts SET balance = balance - 100 WHERE user_id = 1;

-- Simulate an error
-- UPDATE accounts SET balance = balance + 100 WHERE user_id = 'invalid_id';

ROLLBACK;
```

When the error is detected (in this scenario, attempting to update an invalid user ID), issuing a ROLLBACK ensures that no partial data modifications are preserved, thus maintaining the integrity and consistency of the database.

Savepoints and Partial Rollbacks

Within a transaction, you can set savepoints to provide finer control over rolling back parts of the transaction. Savepoints act as intermediate markers that allow reverting the state of the database to a defined point without aborting the entire transaction.

```
START TRANSACTION;

INSERT INTO accounts (user_id, balance) VALUES (1, 1000);
SAVEPOINT savepoint1;

UPDATE accounts SET balance = balance - 100 WHERE user_id = 1;
SAVEPOINT savepoint2;

-- Error occurs
ROLLBACK TO savepoint1;

-- Continue after rollback
UPDATE accounts SET balance = balance - 50 WHERE user_id = 1;

COMMIT;
```

In this sequence, two savepoints are set within the transaction. When an error or condition necessitates reverting to a previous state, ROLLBACK TO savepoint1 allows recovery up to savepoint1, without canceling all prior successful operations, preserving programmatic flexibility within the transaction.

Effective transaction management hinges on a thorough comprehension of these commands and their implications on the database state. By strategically starting, committing, and rolling back transactions, one can ensure data integrity and consistency, aligning with the ACID principles central to robust database operations.

8.4 Savepoints and Rollback

When working with transactions in MySQL, **savepoints** and **rollback** commands are essential tools for controlling transaction behavior. They allow for more granular management of changes within a transaction, facilitating more complex and robust database applications.

A **savepoint** is a marker within a transaction that allows a programmer to partition the transaction into smaller parts. Each savepoint marks a specific point in the transaction to which the database can be restored if necessary. Savepoints are particularly useful for error handling, enabling partial rollbacks rather than rolling back an entire transaction.

To create a savepoint, use the SAVEPOINT command followed by a unique name for the savepoint:

```
SAVEPOINT savepoint_name;
```

Once a savepoint is set, the current state of the database can be later restored to this point using the ROLLBACK TO command:

```
ROLLBACK TO SAVEPOINT savepoint_name;
```

This command undoes all changes made since the specified savepoint. However, it does not undo changes made before that savepoint. This selective rollback capability helps in managing partial errors and ensuring that other successful parts of the transaction remain intact.

An important aspect is the ability to release savepoints when they are no longer needed. Releasing a savepoint does not affect the database state, but it makes the savepoint name available for reuse later in the transaction:

```
RELEASE SAVEPOINT savepoint_name;
```

Here is an illustrative example demonstrating the use of savepoints within a transaction:

```
START TRANSACTION;

INSERT INTO users (name, email) VALUES ('John Doe', 'john.doe@example.com');
SAVEPOINT user_insert;

INSERT INTO orders (user_id, product_id, quantity) VALUES (LAST_INSERT_ID()
    , 101, 2);
SAVEPOINT order_insert_1;

-- Error in the second order insertion
INSERT INTO orders (user_id, product_id, quantity) VALUES (LAST_INSERT_ID()
    , 404, 5);
```

```
SAVEPOINT order_insert_2;

-- Detect error and rollback to the last valid savepoint
ROLLBACK TO SAVEPOINT order_insert_1;

-- Subsequent operations
INSERT INTO orders (user_id, product_id, quantity) VALUES (LAST_INSERT_ID()
    , 102, 1);
COMMIT;
```

In this example:

- A new user is inserted, and a savepoint named user_insert is created.
- An attempt to insert an order for the user is made, and a savepoint order_insert_1 is created.
- Another order insertion attempts to insert a non-existing product, creating an error. Rather than rolling back the entire transaction, it rolls back to the valid order_insert_1 savepoint.
- Additional valid operations are performed, followed by a COMMIT to finalize the transaction.

When a transaction encounters an error that necessitates a full rollback, the ROLLBACK command without specifying a savepoint is used:

```
ROLLBACK;
```

This completely undoes all changes made in the current transaction, restoring the database to its state before START TRANSACTION.

Savepoints and rollbacks become powerful in nested transactions. MySQL does not fully support nested transactions, but you can simulate this behavior using savepoints thoroughly. Consider this scenario where transactional operations contain sub-operations that should either complete entirely or be partially reverted:

```
START TRANSACTION;

-- Outer transaction operations
UPDATE accounts SET balance = balance - 100 WHERE account_id = 1;
SAVEPOINT account_update;

-- Begin nested transaction simulation
SAVEPOINT nested_transaction;
BEGIN;

-- Nested operations
UPDATE orders SET status = 'shipped' WHERE order_id = 301;
UPDATE inventory SET stock = stock - 1 WHERE product_id = 101;
```

```
-- Error encountered - Rollback nested
ROLLBACK TO SAVEPOINT nested_transaction;
-- End nested transaction simulation

-- Continue outer transaction
UPDATE accounts SET balance = balance + 100 WHERE account_id = 1;
RELEASE SAVEPOINT nested_transaction;

COMMIT;
```

In this code:

- START TRANSACTION initiates a new transaction with an update to an account and creates SAVEPOINT account_update.
- A nested transaction simulation begins with SAVEPOINT nested_transaction and subsequent commands.
- Upon encountering an error, a rollback to nested_transaction undoes nested operations while leaving account_update intact.
- Additional necessary updates are made to restore the account and release the unnecessary savepoint.

Savepoints and rollbacks offer enhanced control within transactions, improving error handling and enabling sophisticated and reliable database manipulation. Proper use of these commands ensures database consistency while maximizing transaction flexibility.

8.5 Isolation Levels

Isolation levels are critical in managing the concurrent execution of transactions in MySQL. They determine how and when the changes made by one transaction become visible to other concurrent transactions. This concept is fundamental to maintain consistency and integrity within a database by regulating the degree to which each transaction is isolated from others.

MySQL supports four primary isolation levels, each with its own trade-offs regarding performance and consistency. These levels are defined by the SQL standard and implemented in MySQL as follows:

- **READ UNCOMMITTED**
- **READ COMMITTED**

- **REPEATABLE READ**
- **SERIALIZABLE**

READ UNCOMMITTED is the lowest isolation level, where changes made by one transaction can be read by other transactions even before the changes are committed. This level allows the highest degree of concurrency but risks the occurrence of dirty reads, where a transaction reads uncommitted changes from another transaction, which could potentially get rolled back. The execution model for this might look like:

```
START TRANSACTION;
-- Transaction A makes changes
UPDATE accounts SET balance = balance - 100 WHERE account_id = 1;

-- Concurrently, Transaction B reads the uncommitted changes
SELECT balance FROM accounts WHERE account_id = 1;

-- Transaction A decides to roll back
ROLLBACK;
```

In this case, Transaction B might read a balance that never gets persisted due to the rollback in Transaction A. This inconsistency is why READ UNCOMMITTED is seldom used in practice.

READ COMMITTED avoids dirty reads by ensuring that any data read is committed at the moment it is read. Changes made by a transaction are not visible to other transactions until they are committed. This level thus supports cursor stability, which means that each read within a transaction sees a consistent view of the data excluding changes not yet committed.

```
SET TRANSACTION ISOLATION LEVEL READ COMMITTED;
START TRANSACTION;
-- Transaction A makes changes
UPDATE accounts SET balance = balance - 100 WHERE account_id = 1;
COMMIT;
-- Transaction B only sees the committed changes
SELECT balance FROM accounts WHERE account_id = 1;
```

In this scenario, other concurrent transactions can read the committed data from Transaction A only after it has been committed, thus preventing dirty reads.

REPEATABLE READ ensures that if a transaction reads a row, subsequent reads within the same transaction will return the same data, thereby preventing non-repeatable reads. This level is the default isolation level in MySQL. It provides a stable view of the data but does not prevent phantom reads, where a row that matches the where conditions in a query is added or removed by another transaction.

```
SET TRANSACTION ISOLATION LEVEL REPEATABLE READ;
START TRANSACTION;
-- Transaction A reads data
SELECT balance FROM accounts WHERE account_id = 1;

-- Concurrently, Transaction B makes changes
UPDATE accounts SET balance = balance - 100 WHERE account_id = 1;
COMMIT;

-- Following reads in Transaction A see no change
SELECT balance FROM accounts WHERE account_id = 1;
```

Here, Transaction A consistently reads the initial balance, ignoring any changes made by Transaction B until Transaction A itself is committed.

SERIALIZABLE is the highest isolation level, ensuring complete isolation by effectively locking the entire table and processing transactions sequentially. This level prevents all phenomena: dirty reads, non-repeatable reads, and phantom reads. However, it significantly reduces the level of concurrency as it limits the parallel execution of transactions.

```
SET TRANSACTION ISOLATION LEVEL SERIALIZABLE;
START TRANSACTION;
-- Transaction A reads data
SELECT balance FROM accounts WHERE account_id = 1;

-- Concurrently, Transaction B tries to make changes
UPDATE accounts SET balance = balance - 100 WHERE account_id = 1;
-- Transaction B is blocked until Transaction A completes
COMMIT;

-- Transaction B completes after Transaction A's commit
```

In this model, Transaction B is forced to wait for Transaction A to complete and commit before it can proceed, thus ensuring no other transaction can interfere.

By adjusting the isolation level, MySQL allows a balance between data integrity and performance based on the specific requirements of each application. It is crucial to understand the impact of each isolation level to make an informed decision that aligns with the application's needs.

8.6 Implementing Concurrency Control

Concurrency control is a fundamental aspect of database management systems, essential for ensuring that multiple transactions can execute simultaneously without leading to inconsistencies. It serves to maintain database integrity by preventing conflicts that arise when transactions interact in a way that produces incorrect results or violations of data integrity rules.

MySQL employs various strategies to manage and control concurrency, relying heavily on isolation levels, locks, and transaction scheduling algorithms. This section delves into these techniques, explaining their roles and how they are implemented within MySQL.

Isolation Levels and Concurrency

Isolation levels dictate the degree to which the operations in one transaction are isolated from those in other transactions. In MySQL, four standard isolation levels are defined as follows, in increasing order of strictness:

- **Read Uncommitted**: Transactions can see changes made by other uncommitted transactions, leading to dirty reads.
- **Read Committed**: Transactions see only changes made by transactions that have been committed, preventing dirty reads but allowing non-repeatable reads.
- **Repeatable Read**: Transactions ensure that if a value is read twice, it will remain the same, thus avoiding non-repeatable reads but allowing phantom reads.
- **Serializable**: Transactions are completely isolated from each other, serializing access to the database to prevent dirty reads, non-repeatable reads, and phantom reads.

The following command can be used to set the isolation level in MySQL:

```
SET TRANSACTION ISOLATION LEVEL REPEATABLE READ;
```

Choosing the appropriate isolation level involves balancing the need for concurrent access to the database with the need to maintain correct and consistent results. Lower isolation levels allow for higher concurrency but risk data anomalies, while higher isolation levels reduce the risk of data anomalies but can impact performance due to increased locking and conflict resolution.

Locking Mechanisms

MySQL utilizes several types of locks to manage concurrent access to data:

- **Table Locks**: Entire tables are locked, either for read orwrite operations. This is a coarser locking mechanism that can lead to high contention but is simpler to manage.
- **Row Locks**: Individual rows are locked, allowing for more granular control and higher concurrency. Row locks are managed by the storage engine, such as InnoDB.
- **Intent Locks**: These locks indicate the intention of a transaction to acquire specific locks on rows within a table. They help coordinate locking levels among multiple transactions.

Table locks can be explicitly set using the following command:

```
LOCK TABLES table_name READ;
UNLOCK TABLES;
```

Row-level locking provides higher concurrency and is crucial for environments where transactions compete heavily for the same sets of rows. In MySQL InnoDB, the default storage engine, row locks are acquired automatically as needed.

Deadlock Detection and Resolution

Deadlocks occur when two or more transactions are waiting for each other to release locks, leading to a cycle of dependencies with no transaction able to proceed. MySQL detects deadlocks automatically and resolves them by rolling back one of the transactions, allowing other transactions to continue.

An efficient deadlock detection mechanism involves building a wait-for graph and checking for cycles. When a deadlock is detected, the transaction with the lowest cost is typically rolled back to break the cycle. The server error log will contain information about deadlocks detected and resolved.

For example, the following logs might appear in the event of a deadlock:

```
2023-07-05 12:23:34 0x7f8a386f8700 INNODB deadlock detected
2023-07-05 12:23:34 0x7f8a386f8700 INNODB:
#00 Thread 186356 extension 0 has waited for row lock on
#(1391,0) but timed out with deadlock flag
2023-07-05 12:23:34 0x7f8a386f8700 INNODB: Dropping all Pending requests.
```

Optimistic and Pessimistic Concurrency Control

MySQL supports both optimistic and pessimistic concurrency control.

Pessimistic concurrency control assumes transaction conflicts will occur and therefore locks database objects before performing any operations. This approach is often used in environments with high contention for resources.

For instance, starting a transaction using a pessimistic approach involves:

```
START TRANSACTION;
SELECT * FROM table_name WHERE id=1 FOR UPDATE;
UPDATE table_name SET column1=value WHERE id=1;
COMMIT;
```

Here, the FOR UPDATE clause ensures that the row is locked for update, preventing other transactions from making changes until the current transaction is completed.

Optimistic concurrency control, on the other hand, proceeds without locking resources first, assuming that conflicts are rare. Before committing, it checks for conflicts. If a conflict is detected, it rolls back and retries the transaction.

Typically, optimistic control involves versioning, as shown in the following pseudo-sql example:

```
START TRANSACTION;
SELECT version FROM table_name WHERE id=1;
UPDATE table_name SET column1=value, version=version+1 WHERE id=1 AND
    version=current_version;
COMMIT;
```

In the case of a conflict, the update statement will fail due to the version mismatch, prompting the transaction to be retried.

Managing the right balance between pessimistic and optimistic strategies depends on the application requirements and the expected contention levels on the database. Effective concurrency control ensures that transactions proceed efficiently while maintaining data integrity and consistency.

8.7 Deadlocks and How to Avoid Them

Deadlocks represent a state in which two or more transactions are unable to proceed because each is waiting for the other to release locks on resources. This section delves into the concept of deadlocks, how they occur within MySQL databases, and methods to prevent and resolve them effectively.

A deadlock scenario arises when a circular dependency forms among transactions. For instance, if Transaction A holds a lock on Resource 1 and requests a lock on Resource 2, while Transaction B holds a lock on Resource 2 and requests a lock on Resource 1, neither transaction can proceed, resulting in a deadlock.

To better understand deadlocks within MySQL, consider the following example:

```
-- Transaction A
START TRANSACTION;
UPDATE account SET balance = balance - 100 WHERE account_id = 1;
-- Transaction A waits for lock on account_id = 2

-- Transaction B
START TRANSACTION;
UPDATE account SET balance = balance + 100 WHERE account_id = 2;
-- Transaction B waits for lock on account_id = 1
```

Here, Transaction A and Transaction B become mutually dependent on each other, leading to a deadlock.

Detection and Resolution

MySQL employs an internal deadlock detection mechanism which periodically checks for circular dependencies among transactions. When a deadlock is detected, the InnoDB storage engine selects one of the transactions to roll back, allowing the other transactions to proceed. The rolled-back transaction receives the following error:

```
ERROR 1213: Deadlock found when trying to get lock; try restarting transaction
```

This error informs the application that it must retry the transaction. It is crucial for applications to handle this error by implementing appropriate retry logic.

Avoiding Deadlocks

Although MySQL can detect and resolve deadlocks, it is more efficient to prevent them. The following strategies can be employed to minimize deadlock occurrences:

1. Consistent Lock Ordering

Ensure that transactions obtain locks in a consistent order to avoid circular dependencies. For example, if multiple transactions need to update rows in a specific order, always acquire the locks in the same sequence:

```
-- Transaction A
START TRANSACTION;
UPDATE account SET balance = balance - 100 WHERE account_id = 1;
UPDATE account SET balance = balance + 100 WHERE account_id = 2;
```

```
-- Transaction B
START TRANSACTION;
UPDATE account SET balance = balance - 100 WHERE account_id = 1;
UPDATE account SET balance = balance + 100 WHERE account_id = 2;
```

2. Short Transactions and Immediate Lock Releases

Design transactions to be as short as possible, holding locks for the minimum time necessary. Immediately release locks when they are no longer required:

```
-- Short transaction
START TRANSACTION;
UPDATE account SET balance = balance - 100 WHERE account_id = 1;
COMMIT;

START TRANSACTION;
UPDATE account SET balance = balance + 100 WHERE account_id = 2;
COMMIT;
```

3. Using Lower Isolation Levels

Lower isolation levels, such as READ COMMITTED, can reduce the likelihood of deadlocks by reducing the duration and scope of locks:

```
SET SESSION TRANSACTION ISOLATION LEVEL READ COMMITTED;
-- Transaction with lower isolation level
START TRANSACTION;
UPDATE account SET balance = balance - 100 WHERE account_id = 1;
UPDATE account SET balance = balance + 100 WHERE account_id = 2;
COMMIT;
```

4. Indexing

Proper indexing can significantly reduce deadlocks by limiting the number of rows scanned and locked by a transaction:

```
-- Adding an index to account_id
CREATE INDEX idx_account_id ON account (account_id);

-- Transaction with indexed column
START TRANSACTION;
UPDATE account SET balance = balance - 100 WHERE account_id = 1;
UPDATE account SET balance = balance + 100 WHERE account_id = 2;
COMMIT;
```

5. Locking Rows in Batches

For operations on large datasets, consider processing rows in smaller batches to reduce the likelihood of holding many locks simultaneously:

```
DECLARE done INT DEFAULT 0;
DECLARE batch_size INT DEFAULT 10;

WHILE done = 0 DO
```

```
    START TRANSACTION;
    -- Process a batch of rows
    UPDATE account SET balance = balance - 100 WHERE account_id BETWEEN 1
         AND batch_size;
    COMMIT;

    -- Check if more rows need processing
    SET done = (SELECT COUNT(*) FROM account WHERE account_id >
        batch_size);
    SET batch_size = batch_size + 10;
END WHILE;
```

Implementing these strategies reduces the occurrence of deadlocks, improves transaction throughput, and ensures a smoother database operation.

8.8 Locking Mechanisms in MySQL

Locking mechanisms are critical in managing concurrent access to data within a MySQL database. Understanding these mechanisms is essential for maintaining data integrity and ensuring efficient database performance. Locks are used to prevent conflicts when multiple transactions are performed simultaneously, potentially leading to data corruption or inconsistency. In this section, we explore the various locking strategies MySQL employs, their purposes, and best practices for their use.

MySQL supports different locking mechanisms, including:

- **Table Locks**
- **Row Locks**
- **Page Locks**
- **Intent Locks**

Table Locks: These locks apply to entire tables. A table lock is generally used when significant parts of a table are being modified, preventing other transactions from making changes to the table until the lock is released. They are simpler but less granular than row locks and can be either read (shared) locks or write (exclusive) locks.

```
LOCK TABLES my_table READ;
```

```
LOCK TABLES my_table WRITE;
```

To release the locks:

```
UNLOCK TABLES;
```

Row Locks: InnoDB, the default storage engine in MySQL, supports row-level locking, which provides a more granular level of control compared to table-level locking. Row locks are more efficient in high-concurrency environments because they allow multiple transactions to process different rows simultaneously without waiting for others to complete unless they target the same row.

For row-level locking, InnoDB uses two types of locks: shared (S) locks and exclusive (X) locks. An S-lock allows transactions to read a row and share the locked data with other S-locks, while an X-lock is used when a transaction intends to modify a row, preventing other transactions from acquiring any lock on this row until the X-lock is released.

Page Locks: InnoDB also employs page-level locking, where a "page" refers to a block of adjacent rows. Page locks are not as common as row or table locks but can be useful in certain situations where read and write operations are performed on groups of rows within a specific range.

Intent Locks: MySQL uses intent locks as signals to indicate which type of lock (row or table) a transaction is attempting to acquire. These locks help improve the efficiency and reduce the time required for higher-level lock operations. The two primary types of intent locks are:

- **Intent Shared (IS) Lock:** Transaction intends to acquire a shared lock on some rows.
- **Intent Exclusive (IX) Lock:** Transaction intends to acquire an exclusive lock on some rows.

These intent locks do not block other operations directly but indicate the intended lock type to other transactions, helping to prevent lock conflicts at the table level.

To illustrate these concepts, consider the following example. Suppose there is a table named employees:

```
CREATE TABLE employees (
    id INT PRIMARY KEY,
    name VARCHAR(100),
    position VARCHAR(100),
    salary DECIMAL(10,2)
) ENGINE=InnoDB;
```

To modify the salary of an employee while ensuring that no other transaction can access this row concurrently, we can use row-level locking:

```
START TRANSACTION;

SELECT * FROM employees WHERE id = 1 FOR UPDATE;

UPDATE employees SET salary = salary * 1.1 WHERE id = 1;

COMMIT;
```

In this example:
1. A transaction is started.
2. The SELECT statement acquires an exclusive lock on the row with id 1.
3. The specified row is updated.
4. The transaction is committed, releasing the lock.

Different transactions trying to update or read the same row would have to wait until the lock is released, preserving data integrity.

Lock Wait Timeout: In MySQL, a transaction will wait for a certain period before timing out if it cannot acquire the desired lock. This timeout can be configured using the innodb_lock_wait_timeout parameter:

```
SET innodb_lock_wait_timeout = 50;
```

Locking Read Operations: MySQL enables locking for read operations using the LOCK IN SHARE MODE clause. This allows the transaction to acquire a shared lock on the rows read, preventing other transactions from modifying these rows until the lock is released.

```
START TRANSACTION;

SELECT * FROM employees WHERE id = 2 LOCK IN SHARE MODE;

COMMIT;
```

This ensures the data read remains consistent and prevents anomalies in concurrent read scenarios.

Understanding these locking mechanisms in MySQL is fundamental for designing robust and high-performance database applications. By carefully applying these locks, database administrators and developers can minimize resource contention, reduce the risk of deadlocks, and ensure consistent transaction processing.

8.9 Transaction Management in Stored Procedures

Stored procedures in MySQL provide a means to encapsulate and encapsulate a sequence of SQL statements for reuse and improved manageability. Leveraging stored procedures for transaction management ensures that the logical sequence of operations is executed as a single unit. This capability is fundamental in safeguarding data integrity and ensuring that operations maintain their ACID properties.

MySQL supports transaction management commands within stored procedures. The key transaction control statements are START TRANSACTION, COMMIT, and ROLLBACK. Additionally, SAVEPOINT and RELEASE SAVEPOINT commands enable finer-grained control within a transaction. By embedding these commands in stored procedures, developers can precisely control the transaction boundaries and rollback strategies.

Let us examine the implementation and nuances of transaction management within stored procedures.

Consider a bank system where an amount needs to be transferred from one account to another. A stored procedure can ensure that the debit and credit operations occur within a single transaction. Here is an example implementation:

```
DELIMITER //

CREATE PROCEDURE TransferAmount(
  IN sender_account INT,
  IN receiver_account INT,
  IN amount DECIMAL(10,2)
)
BEGIN
  DECLARE EXIT HANDLER FOR SQLEXCEPTION
  BEGIN
    -- Rollback the transaction on error
    ROLLBACK;
  END;

  -- Start the transaction
  START TRANSACTION;

  -- Debit the sender account
  UPDATE Accounts
  SET balance = balance - amount
  WHERE account_id = sender_account;

  -- Credit the receiver account
  UPDATE Accounts
  SET balance = balance + amount
  WHERE account_id = receiver_account;
```

```
  -- Commit the transaction
  COMMIT;
END //

DELIMITER ;
```

In the above procedure, the transaction begins with START TRANSACTION. If any of the SQL statements within the transaction block fail, the EXIT HANDLER is invoked, and the transaction is rolled back using the ROLLBACK statement. If all statements execute successfully, the transaction is committed using the COMMIT statement.

The use of BEGIN and END block allows the procedure to handle exceptions gracefully. This ensures that any error within the transaction does not leave the database in an inconsistent state.

Using Savepoints in Stored Procedures

Savepoints provide the ability to roll back portions of a transaction without aborting the entire transaction. This is especially useful in complex stored procedures where partial rollbacks may be required. Below is an example demonstrating the use of savepoints:

```
DELIMITER //

CREATE PROCEDURE ComplexOperation()
BEGIN
  DECLARE EXIT HANDLER FOR SQLEXCEPTION
  BEGIN
    ROLLBACK;
  END;

  -- Start the transaction
  START TRANSACTION;

  -- Perform the first operation
  SAVEPOINT sp1;
  INSERT INTO Orders (order_date, customer_id) VALUES (CURDATE(), 1);
  IF ROW_COUNT() = 0 THEN
    ROLLBACK TO sp1;
  END IF;

  -- Perform the second operation
  SAVEPOINT sp2;
  INSERT INTO OrderDetails (order_id, product_id, quantity) VALUES (
        LAST_INSERT_ID(), 2, 10);
  IF ROW_COUNT() = 0 THEN
    ROLLBACK TO sp2;
  END IF;

  -- Commit the transaction
  COMMIT;
END //

DELIMITER ;
```

In this procedure, two savepoints, sp1 and sp2, are created before executing critical SQL operations. If an error occurs, the procedure rolls back to the appropriate savepoint instead of rolling back the entire transaction. This approach is efficient for managing complex operations that can partially succeed.

Considerations for Transaction Management in Stored Procedures

1. **Error Handling:** Robust error handling is crucial. Declare handlers for specific SQL exceptions to manage rollbacks or take corrective actions.

2. **Atomicity:** Ensure that the logical unit of work is atomic. Either all operations should succeed, or none should, maintaining data integrity.

3. **Performance Impacts:** Excessive use of savepoints can lead to performance overhead. They should be used judiciously to balance between granular control and performance efficiency.

4. **Isolation Levels:** Understand the isolation levels of transactions to manage concurrency effectively. Set the appropriate isolation level at the start of the transaction if different from the default.

5. **Nested Transactions:** MySQL does not support true nested transactions. Using savepoints can simulate nested transactions to some extent, but developers should be cautious about their limitations.

Using stored procedures to manage transactions encapsulates the transaction logic and centralizes error handling, ensuring the database operations are consistent and reliable. This approach also enhances the maintainability and readability of the code by separating the transaction logic from business logic within applications.

8.10 Using Transactions in Applications

Transactions play a critical role in ensuring data integrity and consistency within applications that rely heavily on databases like MySQL. By learning how to appropriately use transactions, developers can handle multiple operations that must either succeed together or fail together. This section will delve into the practical aspects of incorporating transactions in applications, focusing on example code and best practices.

A transaction in MySQL begins with the START TRANSACTION statement and typically concludes with either a COMMIT or ROLLBACK statement. The COMMIT statement saves all changes made during the transaction, while ROLLBACK reverts the changes.

To illustrate the usage of transactions in a typical application, consider the scenario of transferring money between two bank accounts. This operation involves withdrawing money from one account and depositing it into another. Both operations must succeed or fail together to ensure that no money is lost or created in the process.

Here is an example implementation in Python using the MySQL Connector library:

```
import mysql.connector
from mysql.connector import errorcode

try:
    # Establish database connection
    cnx = mysql.connector.connect(user='username', password='password',
                                  host='localhost', database='bank_db')
    cursor = cnx.cursor()

    # Start the transaction
    cursor.execute("START TRANSACTION")

    # Withdraw money from account A
    withdraw_query = "UPDATE accounts SET balance = balance - %s WHERE
        account_id = %s"
    cursor.execute(withdraw_query, (withdraw_amount, account_id_A))

    # Deposit money into account B
    deposit_query = "UPDATE accounts SET balance = balance + %s WHERE
        account_id = %s"
    cursor.execute(deposit_query, (withdraw_amount, account_id_B))

    # Check if both operations succeeded
    if cursor.rowcount == 1:
        # Commit if both updates are successful
        cnx.commit()
    else:
        # Rollback if any update fails
        cnx.rollback()

except mysql.connector.Error as err:
    # Rollback in case of any error
    cnx.rollback()
    print("Failed to complete transaction: {}".format(err))

finally:
    # Close the cursor and connection
    cursor.close()
    cnx.close()
```

In this example, a connection to the MySQL database is established, and the transaction begins using START TRANSACTION. Two SQL update statements adjust the account balances. If both updates are successful, the COMMIT statement persists the changes. If any part of the operation fails, the transaction is rolled back using ROLLBACK, preserving data integrity.

Transactions can also be used efficiently within web applications, particularly those that require high concurrency and reliability. For instance, a typical e-commerce application that handles order processing can benefit significantly from transactions to ensure order consistency even when multiple operations are performed, such as updating inventory, capturing payment, and generating an invoice.

Consider an order processing example in a Node.js environment using the MySQL2 library:

```
const mysql = require('mysql2/promise');

async function processOrder(orderId, userId, productDetails) {
    const connection = await mysql.createConnection({host: 'localhost', user: 'root',
        database: 'ecommerce_db'});

    try {
        // Start the transaction
        await connection.beginTransaction();

        // Update inventory
        const updateInventoryQuery = 'UPDATE products SET stock = stock - ?
            WHERE product_id = ?';
        for (const product of productDetails) {
            await connection.execute(updateInventoryQuery, [product.quantity, product.
                productId]);
        }

        // Capture payment
        const capturePaymentQuery = 'INSERT INTO payments (order_id, user_id,
            amount) VALUES (?, ?, ?)';
        await connection.execute(capturePaymentQuery, [orderId, userId,
            calculateTotalAmount(productDetails)]);

        // Generate invoice
        const generateInvoiceQuery = 'INSERT INTO invoices (order_id, user_id)
            VALUES (?, ?)';
        await connection.execute(generateInvoiceQuery, [orderId, userId]);

        // Commit the transaction
        await connection.commit();
        console.log('Order processed successfully.');

    } catch (error) {
        // Rollback in case of an error
        await connection.rollback();
        console.error('Transaction failed, rolling back.', error);
    } finally {
        // Close the connection
        await connection.end();
    }
}

function calculateTotalAmount(productDetails) {
    // Calculates the total amount for the order
    return productDetails.reduce((total, product) => total + (product.price * product.
```

```
        quantity), 0);
}
```

In this example, the processOrder function ensures atomicity by starting a transaction with beginTransaction. The function then updates the inventory, captures the payment, and generates an invoice. If any operation fails, the rollback method undoes all changes, and the function logs an error. If all operations are successful, the commit method commits the changes to the database.

Using transactions properly within applications ensures data consistency and integrity, especially in multi-step operations or operations that involve multiple tables. Careful management of transactions also helps in maintaining application reliability and robustness, particularly under high load or concurrent access scenarios.

8.11 Optimistic vs. Pessimistic Concurrency

Concurrency control is crucial in database management to ensure data consistency and integrity when multiple transactions occur simultaneously. Two primary strategies for managing concurrency in MySQL are optimistic and pessimistic concurrency control. Each has its distinct approach and use cases.

Optimistic concurrency control operates under the assumption that data conflicts are rare. Transactions proceed without taking any locks until commit time. At the point of commit, the database system checks for any conflicts. If conflicts are detected, the transaction may be rolled back, enabling the application to handle the conflict resolution.

Pessimistic concurrency control, in contrast, assumes that conflicts are likely to occur. It involves locking data resources as soon as a transaction retrieves them, preventing other transactions from accessing the same data until the locks are released, usually at the end of the transaction.

Optimistic Concurrency Control

Optimistic concurrency control is optimal for applications where conflicts are infrequent and transactions are mostly read operations. The primary advantage of this method is its minimal use of locks, which can lead to higher performance and better scalability in read-heavy workloads. The process typically involves three phases:

- **Read Phase**: The transaction reads data and records timestamps or version numbers to keep track of the original state of the data.
- **Validation Phase**: Before committing, the transaction checks if any other transaction has modified the data it has read.
- **Write Phase**: If no conflicts are detected during validation, the transaction writes the changes to the database; otherwise, it rolls back and attempts to handle the conflict.

An example implementation of optimistic concurrency control in MySQL can be illustrated with a simple application to update user information:

```
-- Step 1: Fetch the current data with a version number
SELECT user_id, name, email, version
FROM users
WHERE user_id = 1;

-- Assume the current version is 3
-- Step 2: Attempt to update only if the version matches
UPDATE users
SET name = 'John Doe', email = 'john.doe@example.com', version = version + 1
WHERE user_id = 1 AND version = 3;
```

If the update query returns a count of zero, it means another transaction has modified the data, and the application should re-fetch the data and retry the transaction.

Pessimistic Concurrency Control

Pessimistic concurrency control is effective in environments with high contention for data, where conflicts are frequent. This approach locks data as soon as a transaction reads it, preventing other transactions from altering the data until the original transaction completes. Locks can be at different levels—row-level, page-level, or table-level—based on the granularity needed.

MySQL's InnoDB storage engine supports row-level locking, which is granular and minimizes contention. The process involves:

- **Acquiring Locks**: The transaction acquires the necessary locks before executing any read or write operations.
- **Holding Locks**: The locks are held for the duration of the transaction, ensuring that no conflicting transaction can operate on the locked data.

- **Releasing Locks**: Locks are released once the transaction commits or rolls back.

To illustrate, consider a scenario where two transactions attempt to update the same user's account balance:

```
-- Transaction 1
START TRANSACTION;

-- Lock the row to be updated
SELECT balance
FROM accounts
WHERE user_id = 1
FOR UPDATE;

UPDATE accounts
SET balance = balance - 100
WHERE user_id = 1;

COMMIT;

-- Transaction 2
START TRANSACTION;

-- Attempt to lock the same row
SELECT balance
FROM accounts
WHERE user_id = 1
FOR UPDATE;

UPDATE accounts
SET balance = balance + 100
WHERE user_id = 1;

COMMIT;
```

Transaction 2 will wait until Transaction 1 releases the lock on the row with $user\_id = 1$. This ensures data consistency but can lead to decreased concurrency and potential deadlocks.

Both strategies have trade-offs. Optimistic concurrency control is preferred in systems with low conflict rates and high read volumes, as it allows transactions to proceed without locks most of the time. Pessimistic concurrency control, on the other hand, is suitable for high-conflict environments where consistency is paramount, despite the potential for reduced throughput due to locking overhead.

Implementing the appropriate concurrency control method requires understanding the workload characteristics and designing transaction logic to balance performance and data integrity effectively.

8.12 Monitoring Transactions

In the context of database systems, monitoring transactions is critical for maintaining data integrity, performance optimization, and troubleshooting potential issues. MySQL provides various tools and techniques for transaction monitoring, which include log files, performance schema, and other built-in utilities. Efficient monitoring is essential to ensure that the database system functions correctly and can handle concurrent transactions without compromising ACID properties.

Transaction monitoring involves observing transaction states, analyzing performance metrics, and detecting anomalies. The tools provided by MySQL help database administrators and developers gain insights into transaction behaviors, allowing them to make informed decisions to improve the system.

1. Using Log Files

MySQL's binary logs are instrumental in monitoring transaction states, particularly for replication and point-in-time recovery. The binary log records all DML (Data Manipulation Language) statements that modify data, providing a detailed account of transaction activities. To examine the binary log, one may utilize the mysqlbinlog utility.

```
mysqlbinlog /path/to/binlog.000001
```

The output presents the sequence of executed statements, facilitating the detection of long-running transactions and reviewing data changes retrospectively.

2. Performance Schema

The Performance Schema in MySQL is a powerful instrument for monitoring transactions. It collects detailed information about server execution, which can be queried for insights into transaction performance. The Performance Schema tables setup_actors and events_transactions_current are specifically useful for this purpose.

To enable monitoring for specific user accounts, one can configure the setup_actors table:

```
UPDATE performance_schema.setup_actors
SET ENABLED = 'YES'
WHERE HOST = 'localhost' AND USER = 'your_user';
```

To retrieve information about currently running transactions, the events_transactions_current table can be queried:

```
SELECT * FROM performance_schema.events_transactions_current;
\end{lstisting}

This table includes columns such as \texttt{THREAD\_ID}, \texttt{EVENT\_ID}, \
    texttt{STATE}, \texttt{TRX\_ID}, and \texttt{TRX\_STATE}, offering a
    snapshot of ongoing transactions. The data provided by this table is essential for
    identifying active transactions and their states.

\textbf{3. Information Schema}

The \texttt{INFORMATION\_SCHEMA} also provides relevant information for
    monitoring transactions through the \texttt{INNODB\_TRX} table. For
    instance, to observe the status of InnoDB transactions:

\begin{lstlisting}
SELECT * FROM information_schema.innodb_trx;
```

This query lists ongoing transactions with columns such as trx_id, trx_state, trx_started, and trx_query, which can be used to monitor active transactions and their associated queries.

Another useful table is the INNODB_LOCKS, which displays information about locks held by active transactions:

```
SELECT * FROM information_schema.innodb_locks;
```

This table helps in understanding locking issues and potential deadlocks, providing details such as lock_id, lock_trx_id, and lock_mode.

4. Monitoring Deadlocks

Detecting and resolving deadlocks is crucial to maintaining database performance. MySQL assists in deadlock detection by automatically recording deadlock information in the error log. Additionally, by enabling the innodb_status_output variable, administrators can obtain a snapshot of the InnoDB monitor output, which includes deadlock information.

```
SET GLOBAL innodb_status_output = ON;
```

This setting activates regular reports on InnoDB's internal state, aiding in the detection and analysis of deadlocks.

5. Analyzing Transaction Performance

Evaluating transaction performance requires attention to metrics such as transaction duration, frequency, and resources consumed. Performance Schema's events_statements_current table provides valuable data on dynamic SQL statements and their execution times.

To find slow transactions:

```
SELECT EVENT_ID, SQL_TEXT, TIMER_WAIT / 1000000000 AS duration_ms
FROM performance_schema.events_statements_current
WHERE TIMER_WAIT / 1000000000 > 1000;
```

The result identifies SQL statements with durations exceeding one second, which may indicate potential bottlenecks.

6. Integration with Monitoring Tools

To enhance transaction monitoring, integration with comprehensive monitoring tools such as MySQL Enterprise Monitor or third-party solutions like Prometheus and Grafana can provide real-time dashboards, alerting mechanisms, and historical data analysis. These tools can be configured to track transaction metrics, deadlocks, and contention issues, offering a holistic view of the database system's health.

By leveraging MySQL's transaction monitoring capabilities, administrators can maintain system performance, ensure data integrity, and swiftly address performance issues and anomalies. Effective transaction monitoring is indispensable for the reliable and efficient operation of a MySQL database system.

Chapter 9

Security and User Management

This chapter delves into the essential aspects of MySQL security and user management. It explains how to create and manage user accounts, configure user privileges and roles, and secure passwords. The chapter also covers implementing SSL for MySQL, setting up firewall rules, auditing and logging activities, and ensuring data security both at rest and in transit. Additionally, it includes best practices for maintaining MySQL security and responding to potential security incidents.

9.1 Introduction to MySQL Security

The security of a MySQL database system is paramount for ensuring the protection of sensitive data and the smooth operation of applications and services that depend on it. MySQL, as a widely used relational database management system, encompasses a myriad of security features and mechanisms designed to safeguard data and control access via a robust user management framework. This section explores foundational concepts and strategies for securing MySQL, setting the stage for more granular discussions in later sections.

Security Model Frameworks: MySQL employs a layered security model, encompassing aspects such as access control, authentication, and encryption. This multi-faceted approach helps mitigate a variety of risks:

- **Access Control:** Managing who can access the database and what operations they are permitted to perform.
- **Authentication:** Verifying that users attempting to access the database are who they claim to be.
- **Encryption:** Protecting data during transmission and while at rest.

Access Control and User Management: Foundational to MySQL security is the concept of access control. Access control mechanisms are used to define and enforce policies specifying which users (or machines) may take which actions on which resources:

- User Accounts: MySQL supports multiple user accounts, each with specific credentials and permissions.
- Privileges: Users are granted privileges to perform actions like SELECT, INSERT, UPDATE, and DELETE on various database objects.
- Roles: Roles can be created as collections of privileges that can be assigned to user accounts, simplifying privilege management.

Authentication Methods: Authentication in MySQL is the process of verifying the identity of a user attempting to connect. Several authentication methods are available:

- Native Pluggable Authentication: The default built-in authentication method using usernames and passwords.
- LDAP Authentication: Integration with LDAP directories for centralized authentication.
- PAM Authentication: Utilizes PAM (Pluggable Authentication Modules) for flexible and external authentication mechanisms.

Encryption and Data Protection: MySQL includes features to encrypt data both in transit and at rest, critical for maintaining confidentiality and integrity:

- SSL/TLS for Encryption in Transit: Implementing SSL/TLS ensures that data transmitted between the MySQL server and client applications remains confidential and protected against interception.
- Data-at-Rest Encryption: MySQL supports Transparent Data Encryption (TDE) to protect stored data.

Firewall and Network Security: Implementing firewall rules and network security practices complements the MySQL security framework. Effective IP filtering and network configurations prevent unauthorized access:

- IP Whitelisting: Restricting access to the MySQL server by specifying a list of trusted IPs.
- Using Network Firewalls: Leveraging network firewalls to control access at the network level.

Auditing and Logging: Tracking and auditing user activities and server events are essential for detecting and responding to security incidents. MySQL provides mechanisms for detailed logging and auditing:

- Query Logging: Logs queries executed against the database, useful for performance tuning and security auditing.
- Audit Plugins: Customizable plugins to extend auditing capabilities, allowing granular tracking of user activities.

Security Best Practices: Adhering to best practices is a continuous effort and involves actions such as regular updates, minimizing privilege usage, and monitoring:

- Regular Updates: Ensuring that MySQL server and client components are kept up-to-date with the latest security patches.
- Principle of Least Privilege: Granting users the minimum level of access necessary for their roles.
- Monitoring and Alerts: Continuously monitoring the database for suspicious activities and setting up alerts for potential security breaches.

Understanding these principles prepares database administrators to implement a robust security posture in their MySQL environments. Equipped with knowledge of access control, authentication, encryption, and best practices, administrators can effectively safeguard their databases against a multitude of security threats.

```
// Creating a new MySQL user and setting a password
CREATE USER 'secure_user'@'localhost' IDENTIFIED BY 'secure_password123';

// Granting SELECT and INSERT privileges
GRANT SELECT, INSERT ON database_name.* TO 'secure_user'@'localhost';

// Applying changes
FLUSH PRIVILEGES;
```

```
Output:
Query OK, 0 rows affected (0.01 sec)
Query OK, 0 rows affected (0.01 sec)
Query OK, 0 rows affected (0.00 sec)
```

9.2 Creating and Managing User Accounts

Creating and managing user accounts in MySQL is a foundational task in database administration, crucial for maintaining security and ensuring that users have appropriate access levels. This section elaborates on methods to create users, modify user attributes, and manage user accounts efficiently.

Creating User Accounts

Creating a user account in MySQL involves issuing the CREATE USER statement. The basic syntax is as follows:

```
CREATE USER 'username'@'host' IDENTIFIED BY 'password';
```

Here, 'username' represents the desired username, 'host' specifies the hostname or IP address from which the user will connect, and 'password' sets the user's password. For example, to create a user named john who can connect from any host and has the password securePass123, the statement would be:

```
CREATE USER 'john'@'%' IDENTIFIED BY 'securePass123';
```

The character % acts as a wildcard, allowing the user to connect from any host.

Modifying User Accounts

Once a user has been created, you might need to modify user attributes. This can be accomplished with the ALTER USER statement. For instance, to change the password for the user john, you would use:

```
ALTER USER 'john'@'%' IDENTIFIED BY 'newSecurePass456';
```

If the need arises to lock or unlock a user account, the ACCOUNT clause in the ALTER USER command can be employed. To lock the john user account:

```
ALTER USER 'john'@'%' ACCOUNT LOCK;
```

Conversely, to unlock the account:

```
ALTER USER 'john'@'%' ACCOUNT UNLOCK;
```

Dropping User Accounts

To delete a user account from the MySQL database, the DROP USER statement is utilized. Dropping a user completely removes the account and any permissions granted to it. The basic syntax is:

```
DROP USER 'username'@'host';
```

For example, to drop the user john:

```
DROP USER 'john'@'%';
```

It is critical to ensure that the user to be deleted does not own essential database objects or have critical access before executing the DROP USER command to avoid disruption.

Viewing User Accounts

MySQL allows you to inspect existing user accounts and their properties. The mysql.user table in the mysql database contains this information. To view all user accounts, execute:

```
SELECT User, Host FROM mysql.user;
```

The output will list all users and the hosts from which they can connect.

Grant Option

The GRANT OPTION enables users to grant privileges to other users. Granting this option should be done cautiously. For example, to grant the GRANT OPTION to the user john:

```
GRANT ALL PRIVILEGES ON *.* TO 'john'@'%' WITH GRANT OPTION;
```

This command allows john to manage permissions on all databases and tables, highlighting the necessity to restrict such powerful options to trusted users.

Ensuring proper user account management establishes a foundation of security within MySQL. Adequate user management includes not just creation but also the careful alteration and deletion of user accounts. Each user must have the minimum necessary privileges to perform their required functions while maintaining robust security protocols.

9.3 Understanding Privileges and Roles

Understanding privileges and roles within MySQL is fundamental for effective database management and security. MySQL employs a sophisticated privilege system that allows for granular control over database operations. This system is crucial for enforcing security policies and ensuring that users only have the necessary access to perform their tasks.

Privileges in MySQL specify the type of operations a user can perform on database objects such as tables, views, and stored procedures. These operations range from basic actions like SELECT, INSERT, and UPDATE, to administrative functions such as CREATE, DROP, GRANT, and REVOKE.

Roles are a more recent addition to MySQL and are designed to simplify the management of user privileges. Roles act as collections of privileges that can be assigned to users, making it more efficient to manage users with similar privilege requirements.

Here is a detailed exploration of the different types of privileges and the implementation and use of roles in MySQL:

Types of Privileges:

MySQL categorizes privileges into several types, which include global privileges, database privileges, table privileges, column privileges, and stored procedure privileges.

- **Global Privileges**: These apply to all databases on the server and are specified in the mysql.user table. They include privileges such as ALL PRIVILEGES, CREATE USER, and RELOAD.
- **Database Privileges**: These are specific to a particular database

and are stored in the mysql.db table. Examples include CREATE, DROP, ALTER, and LOCK TABLES.

- **Table Privileges**: These apply to specific tables within a database and can be found in the mysql.tables_priv table. These privileges include SELECT, INSERT, UPDATE, and DELETE.
- **Column Privileges**: These are further refined privileges that apply to individual columns within a table and are stored in the mysql.columns_priv table. They also include SELECT, INSERT, UPDATE.
- **Stored Procedure Privileges**: Specific to stored routines, these privileges control access to executing and altering stored procedures and functions, and are managed in the mysql.procs_priv table.

Granting and Revoking Privileges:

To assign privileges to users, MySQL uses the GRANT statement. Conversely, the REVOKE statement is used to remove privileges. Below is an example of how to use these commands:

```
GRANT SELECT, INSERT ON mydatabase.* TO 'newuser'@'localhost';
REVOKE INSERT ON mydatabase.* FROM 'newuser'@'localhost';
```

These commands show granting SELECT and INSERT privileges on all tables within mydatabase to the user newuser and subsequently revoking the INSERT privilege.

Roles in MySQL:

Roles are designed to streamline the management of privileges, especially for environments with numerous users or complex privilege requirements. Creating and managing roles involves several steps:

- **Creating a Role**:

  ```
  CREATE ROLE 'manager';
  ```

- **Granting Privileges to a Role**:

  ```
  GRANT SELECT, INSERT, UPDATE ON mydatabase.* TO 'manager';
  ```

- **Assigning a Role to a User**:

```
GRANT 'manager' TO 'alice'@'localhost';
```

- **Activating and Deactivating Roles for a User**: Users can activate or deactivate specific roles as needed:

```
SET DEFAULT ROLE 'manager' FOR 'alice'@'localhost';
SET ROLE 'manager';
SET ROLE NONE;
```

When a role is granted to a user, the user inherits all the privileges associated with that role. This method significantly simplifies the process of privilege assignment and maintenance.

```
Example Output:
+-------------------------+
| GRANT ROLE              |
+-------------------------+
| GRANT manager TO alice  |
+-------------------------+
1 row in set (0.00 sec)
```

This example output demonstrates a successful grant of the manager role to the user alice.

By employing roles, database administrators can optimize their workflow, ensuring that privilege management is both efficient and secure. As MySQL continues to evolve, the use of roles alongside traditional privilege assignments will likely become a best practice in database management.

9.4 Granting and Revoking Privileges

In MySQL, managing user access to databases and tables is a fundamental aspect of maintaining a secure and efficient database system. This involves the precise assignment of privileges that control the actions users can perform. Privileges are permissions granted to users that define their access level to database objects. Proper management of these privileges ensures that users only have the permissions necessary for their roles, thereby enhancing security and reducing the risk of unauthorized access or data manipulation.

The primary SQL commands used for managing privileges in MySQL are GRANT and REVOKE. These commands enable administrators to specify which actions a user can perform and on which database objects. In this section, we will discuss in detail how to grant and revoke privileges using these commands.

Granting Privileges

The GRANT command is used to assign privileges to a user account. The basic syntax for granting privileges is as follows:

```
GRANT privilege_type [(column_list)]
    ON [object_type] priv_level
    TO user [IDENTIFIED BY 'password']
    [WITH GRANT OPTION];
```

In this syntax:

- privilege_type specifies the type of privilege to be granted (e.g., SELECT, INSERT, UPDATE, DELETE, etc.).
- column_list is an optional list of columns to which the privilege applies, used when the privilege type is column-specific (e.g., for SELECT).
- object_type indicates the type of database object (e.g., TABLE, PROCEDURE).
- priv_level defines the scope of the privilege (e.g., database, table, or column level).
- user is the account to which the privilege is granted.
- password is an optional clause used to set the password for the user.
- WITH GRANT OPTION grants the user the ability to grant the specified privilege to other users.

To grant a specific privilege, consider the following example:

```
GRANT SELECT, INSERT ON database_name.* TO 'username'@'hostname'
    IDENTIFIED BY 'password';
```

In this example, the user 'username'@'hostname' is granted the SELECT and INSERT privileges on all tables within the database database_name. The clause IDENTIFIED BY 'password' sets the user's password. To grant privileges at a more granular level, such as on a single table or column, modify the priv_level accordingly.

It is also possible to grant all available privileges using the ALL PRIVILEGES keyword:

```
GRANT ALL PRIVILEGES ON database_name.* TO 'username'@'hostname';
```

Revoking Privileges

The REVOKE command is used to remove privileges from a user account. The basic syntax for revoking privileges is:

```
REVOKE privilege_type [(column_list)]
    ON [object_type] priv_level
    FROM user;
```

In this syntax, the parameters have similar meanings to those in the GRANT command. For example, to revoke the SELECT and INSERT privileges from a user, the command would be:

```
REVOKE SELECT, INSERT ON database_name.* FROM 'username'@'hostname';
```

If all privileges are to be revoked, the ALL PRIVILEGES keyword is used:

```
REVOKE ALL PRIVILEGES ON database_name.* FROM 'username'@'hostname';
```

Granting Administrative Privileges

Administrative privileges, such as GRANT OPTION and global-level privileges like CREATE USER or SHUTDOWN, are essential for user accounts that require broader control over the MySQL server. Granting such privileges is accomplished similarly to other privileges:

```
GRANT CREATE USER, GRANT OPTION ON *.* TO 'adminuser'@'localhost'
    IDENTIFIED BY 'adminpassword';
```

This command grants the CREATE USER and GRANT OPTION privileges globally to 'adminuser'@'localhost'.

Careful assignment of administrative privileges is crucial due to the extensive control they provide. Only trusted users should be granted such privileges to prevent potential misuse or security breaches.

The process of granting and revoking privileges in MySQL is a critical aspect of user management, ensuring that users have appropriate access levels consistent with their roles and responsibilities. By leveraging the GRANT and REVOKE commands, administrators can maintain a robust and secure database environment.

9.5 Securing Passwords

Passwords serve as the first line of defense in safeguarding MySQL databases against unauthorized access. Properly securing passwords is essential to maintaining the integrity and confidentiality of your data. This section focuses on the methods and best practices for securing passwords within a MySQL environment.

MySQL provides several mechanisms to enforce strong password policies. These mechanisms include password hashing, password validation plugins, and configuration options to enforce complexity, expiration, and reuse policies.

Password Hashing

MySQL uses a sophisticated hashing algorithm to store passwords securely. By default, MySQL employs the SHA-256 hashing algorithm. To examine the stored password hash in MySQL, we can execute the following command:

```
SELECT user, host, authentication_string
FROM mysql.user
WHERE User = 'your_user';
```

This command retrieves the hashed password for the specified user from the mysql.user table.

Password Validation Plugins

MySQL provides built-in plugins to enforce password strength and complexity requirements. The validate_password plugin is widely used to ensure that passwords meet certain criteria. To enable this plugin, execute the following command:

```
INSTALL PLUGIN validate_password SONAME 'validate_password.so';
```

Once enabled, the validate_password plugin exposes several configuration options that can be adjusted to meet your security requirements. These options include:

- validate_password.policy - This controls the policy for password validation. It can be set to LOW, MEDIUM, or STRONG.
- validate_password.length - This sets the minimum length for passwords.
- validate_password.mixed_case_count - This specifies the mini-

mum number of uppercase and lowercase characters required.

- validate_password.number_count - This specifies the minimum number of numeric digits required.
- validate_password.special_char_count - This specifies the minimum number of special characters required.

To configure a strong password policy, you might use the following commands:

```
SET GLOBAL validate_password.policy = 'STRONG';
SET GLOBAL validate_password.length = 12;
SET GLOBAL validate_password.mixed_case_count = 1;
SET GLOBAL validate_password.number_count = 1;
SET GLOBAL validate_password.special_char_count = 1;
```

Password Expiration and Reuse Policies

Enforcing a regular change of passwords and preventing the reuse of old passwords can also significantly enhance password security. MySQL supports the password_expired attribute and the password_history table to manage these policies.

To expire a user's password so that it must be changed on the next login, the following command can be used:

```
ALTER USER 'your_user'@'localhost' PASSWORD EXPIRE;
```

To manage password reuse, MySQL provides the password_history table which keeps track of previous passwords. To utilize this feature, you need to configure the number of previous passwords to remember by setting the default_password_lifetime variable:

```
SET GLOBAL default_password_lifetime = 180; -- This sets the password expiration
    to 180 days
```

Password Encryption

In addition to hashing, encrypting passwords in transit and at rest is pivotal. MySQL supports SSL/TLS for encrypting connections. Ensure SSL is enabled by setting the following configuration in your my.cnf file:

```
[mysqld]
ssl-ca = /path/to/ca-cert.pem
ssl-cert = /path/to/server-cert.pem
ssl-key = /path/to/server-key.pem
```

Moreover, ensure password security during secure backups and when stored in configuration files. Avoid hardcoding passwords; instead, use secure vaults or environment variables.

By proactively managing and securing passwords, the risk of unauthorized access to your MySQL databases can be significantly reduced, thus protecting against potential security breaches.

9.6 Configuring SSL for MySQL

Secure Sockets Layer (SSL) and its successor, Transport Layer Security (TLS), are cryptographic protocols designed to provide secure communication over a computer network. Configuring SSL for MySQL ensures that data transferred between MySQL clients and the MySQL server is encrypted, protecting it from eavesdropping and man-in-the-middle attacks.

To configure SSL for MySQL, several key steps must be followed. These include generating the necessary certificates, configuring the MySQL server and clients to use SSL, and verifying the SSL connections.

Generating SSL Certificates

The first step in configuring SSL for MySQL is generating the required SSL certificates. The MySQL server requires three types of certificates: a Certificate Authority (CA) certificate, a server certificate, and a server key. Optionally, client certificates and keys can also be generated to enhance security. OpenSSL can be used to generate these certificates.

```
# Generate CA certificate and key
openssl genpkey -algorithm RSA -out ca-key.pem
openssl req -new -x509 -key ca-key.pem -out ca-cert.pem -days 365

# Generate server certificate and key
openssl genpkey -algorithm RSA -out server-key.pem
openssl req -new -key server-key.pem -out server-req.pem
openssl x509 -req -in server-req.pem -CA ca-cert.pem -CAkey ca-key.pem -set_serial 01
     -out server-cert.pem -days 365

# Generate client certificate and key (optional)
openssl genpkey -algorithm RSA -out client-key.pem
openssl req -new -key client-key.pem -out client-req.pem
openssl x509 -req -in client-req.pem -CA ca-cert.pem -CAkey ca-key.pem -set_serial 01
     -out client-cert.pem -days 365
```

Ensure that the security of the private keys (.pem files) is maintained and restrict access to them. Store the generated certificate files in a directory such as /etc/mysql/ssl/.

Configuring the MySQL Server to Use SSL

The next step is configuring the MySQL server to use these certificates.

This involves modifying the MySQL configuration file, typically located at /etc/my.cnf or /etc/mysql/my.cnf.

Add the following lines to the [mysqld] section to configure the MySQL server to use the generated SSL certificates:

```
[mysqld]
ssl-ca=/etc/mysql/ssl/ca-cert.pem
ssl-cert=/etc/mysql/ssl/server-cert.pem
ssl-key=/etc/mysql/ssl/server-key.pem
```

Restart the MySQL server to apply these changes:

```
sudo systemctl restart mysql
```

Verify that the MySQL server is properly configured to use SSL by logging into the MySQL server and running the following query:

```
SHOW VARIABLES LIKE '%ssl%';
```

The output should indicate that SSL is enabled and the paths to the certificate files should be correct.

Configuring MySQL Clients to Use SSL

Clients must also be configured to use SSL. Add the following lines to the client configuration section ([client] or [mysql]) in the my.cnf file or create a dedicated SSL configuration file for the client:

```
[client]
ssl-ca=/etc/mysql/ssl/ca-cert.pem
ssl-cert=/etc/mysql/ssl/client-cert.pem
ssl-key=/etc/mysql/ssl/client-key.pem
```

Use the mysql command-line client to connect to the MySQL server over an SSL-secured connection:

```
mysql --ssl-ca=/etc/mysql/ssl/ca-cert.pem --ssl-cert=/etc/mysql/ssl/client-cert.pem --
    ssl-key=/etc/mysql/ssl/client-key.pem -u youruser -p -h yourserver
```

To verify that the connection is encrypted, log into the MySQL server and run the following query:

```
SHOW STATUS LIKE 'Ssl_cipher';
```

A non-empty value indicates that the SSL connection is established. Alternatively, you can use SSL-specific client options to enforce SSL usage, as shown:

```
mysql --ssl-mode=REQUIRED -u youruser -p -h yourserver
```

Configuring SSL ensures that data exchanged between the MySQL server and client is encrypted, securing it from interception and tampering. This approach, along with properly managing user accounts and privileges, significantly enhances MySQL security.

9.7 Implementing Firewall Rules

In modern database management, network security is paramount, and a critical aspect of securing MySQL involves configuring firewall rules. MySQL should only be accessible to authorized users and systems. Firewalls serve as a barrier between trusted internal networks and untrusted external networks, regulating access based on established security policies. This section explores the techniques and best practices for implementing firewall rules to protect MySQL servers effectively.

1. Understanding Firewalls and Their Role

Firewalls can be hardware-based or software-based. They monitor and control incoming and outgoing network traffic based on predetermined rules. The primary goal is to create a secure barrier that prevents unauthorized access while allowing legitimate traffic.

When setting up firewalls for MySQL, it is critical to define rules that specify which IP addresses and port numbers are allowed or denied access to the MySQL server. This minimizes the attack surface and helps mitigate the risk of unauthorized data access.

2. Configuring MySQL-Specific Firewall Rules

To configure firewall rules for MySQL, one must consider the network topology and the role of each server in the environment. The default port for MySQL is 3306, but it can be changed for security reasons.

Example Firewall Configuration with iptables

Below is an example of how to configure 'iptables', a commonly used firewall utility on Linux systems, to allow traffic on MySQL's default port (3306) only from specific IP addresses:

```
# Allow incoming MySQL connections from a specific IP address
sudo iptables -A INPUT -p tcp -s 192.168.1.100 --dport 3306 -j ACCEPT

# Allow incoming MySQL connections from a subnet
sudo iptables -A INPUT -p tcp -s 192.168.1.0/24 --dport 3306 -j ACCEPT

# Reject all other incoming MySQL connections
sudo iptables -A INPUT -p tcp --dport 3306 -j REJECT
```

These rules will allow MySQL connections only from the specified IP address (192.168.1.100) and all addresses within the subnet (192.168.1.0/24). All other connection attempts on port 3306 will be rejected.

Example Firewall Configuration with UFW

Ubuntu's Uncomplicated Firewall (UFW) offers a simpler syntax for managing firewall rules. Below is an example of how to set up UFW to allow MySQL traffic from specific IP addresses:

```
# Allow MySQL connections from a specific IP
sudo ufw allow from 192.168.1.100 to any port 3306

# Allow MySQL connections from a subnet
sudo ufw allow from 192.168.1.0/24 to any port 3306

# Deny all other MySQL connections
sudo ufw deny 3306
```

These rules accomplish the same goal as the iptables rules but are simpler to implement using UFW.

3. Advanced Firewall Configurations

For larger environments and more complex network architectures, it may be necessary to employ advanced firewall configurations. This could involve:

- **Stateful Inspection**: Ensuring that the database connections are part of an ongoing session by keeping track of active connections and allowing only those packets that are part of an established session.
- **Network Address Translation (NAT)**: Translating private IP addresses to a public IP address, and vice versa, to hide internal network structure from unauthorized users.
- **Intrusion Detection and Prevention Systems (IDPS)**: Monitoring network traffic for suspicious activity and responding to potential threats in real-time.

Example Configuration for Stateful Inspection

Below is an example of how to configure iptables to perform stateful inspection:

```
# Allow MySQL incoming connections only if they are part of an established session
sudo iptables -A INPUT -p tcp --dport 3306 -m state --state ESTABLISHED,
    RELATED -j ACCEPT
```

```
# Allow outgoing traffic to initiate a MySQL session
sudo iptables -A OUTPUT -p tcp --sport 3306 -m state --state NEW,ESTABLISHED -j
    ACCEPT

# Reject all other MySQL traffic
sudo iptables -A INPUT -p tcp --dport 3306 -j REJECT
```

This stateful inspection ensures that only packets belonging to an established session will be permitted through the firewall, adding an additional layer of security.

4. Best Practices

When implementing firewall rules for MySQL, consider the following best practices:

- **Least Privilege Principle**: Only allow IP addresses that require access to the MySQL server.
- **Port Management**: Use non-default ports for MySQL to reduce the likelihood of automated attacks.
- **Regular Audits**: Periodically review and update firewall rules to adapt to changes in the network environment.
- **Logging and Monitoring**: Enable logging of firewall events to detect and respond to unauthorized access attempts.

Implementing these best practices will help ensure that the firewall configurations remain effective over time, adapting to evolving network security requirements.

By appropriately configuring firewall rules, we can significantly enhance the security posture of MySQL databases, providing robust protection against unauthorized network access.

9.8 Auditing and Logging

Auditing and logging are critical components of a robust MySQL security strategy. They allow database administrators to track access, detect suspicious activities, and ensure compliance with organizational security policies and regulatory requirements. This section provides an in-depth examination of the tools and techniques available for auditing and logging in MySQL.

MySQL provides several mechanisms for logging and auditing, which include the general query log, slow query log, binary log, error log, and audit log. Each of these logs serves a distinct purpose and can be configured to capture specific types of information.

The General Query Log

The general query log is a general-purpose log that records all SQL statements received by the server. It can be useful for troubleshooting and monitoring purposes, as it shows what clients are sending to the MySQL server.

To enable the general query log, you can set the following parameters in your MySQL configuration file (my.cnf):

```
[mysqld]
general_log = 1
general_log_file = /var/log/mysql/mysql-general.log
```

If the MySQL server is running, you can also enable it dynamically without restarting the server:

```
SET GLOBAL general_log = 'ON';
```

To disable the general query log, you can set the option back to OFF:

```
SET GLOBAL general_log = 'OFF';
```

The Slow Query Log

The slow query log is designed to log queries that take longer than a specified time to execute. This can help identify inefficient queries that might be affecting database performance.

Configure the slow query log by adding the following settings to your my.cnf file:

```
[mysqld]
slow_query_log = 1
slow_query_log_file = /var/log/mysql/mysql-slow.log
long_query_time = 2
```

In this example, queries taking longer than 2 seconds to execute will be logged.

You can enable the slow query log dynamically as well:

```
SET GLOBAL slow_query_log = 'ON';
```

Adjust the threshold for slow queries dynamically:

```
SET GLOBAL long_query_time = 2;
```

The Binary Log

The binary log is mainly used for replication and data recovery. It logs all changes to the database (both DML and DDL statements). While its primary purpose is not auditing, it can be useful for forensics and troubleshooting.

To enable binary logging, include the following lines in the my.cnf file:

```
[mysqld]
log_bin = /var/log/mysql/mysql-bin.log
server_id = 1
binlog_format = ROW
```

It is pertinent to specify a unique server ID for each MySQL server when using binary logs, especially in a replication environment.

The Error Log

The error log contains information about server startup and shutdown, as well as critical errors that occur while the server is running. This log is crucial for diagnosing server crashes and other critical issues.

Enable and configure the error log with the following parameters:

```
[mysqld]
log_error = /var/log/mysql/mysql-error.log
```

The Audit Log

The audit log provides comprehensive tracking of database operations, including connections, disconnections, and specific SQL statements executed. Unlike the general query log, the audit log is designed to meet stringent auditing requirements and to facilitate security and compliance audits.

To use the audit logging feature, you need to install a plugin such as the

MySQL Enterprise Audit plugin. Assuming you have the appropriate MySQL edition, you can install and configure the audit plugin:

```
INSTALL PLUGIN audit_log SONAME 'audit_log.so';
SET GLOBAL audit_log_file = '/var/log/mysql/audit.log';
SET GLOBAL audit_log_format = 'JSON';
SET GLOBAL audit_log_policy = 'ALL';
```

Configuring the audit log policy to ALL ensures that all events are logged. You can also customize the policies to log specific events such as logins, logouts, or data access operations.

- **Login** and **Logout** events are critical for tracking access to the database.
- **Query** events can be filtered to capture only certain types of SQL operations.

Here is an example to log only the **Login** and **Logout** events:

```
SET GLOBAL audit_log_policy = 'LOGINS';
```

Retrieving and Analyzing Log Data

Once you have enabled and configured the relevant logs, retrieving and analyzing this data involves accessing the log files and using various tools and techniques to parse and understand the logged information.

For text-based logs like the general query log, slow query log, and error log, you can use standard command-line tools such as grep, awk, and sed, or view them with less or cat commands:

```
grep "specific_query_text" /var/log/mysql/mysql-general.log
```

For binary logs, you use the MySQL utility mysqlbinlog:

```
mysqlbinlog /var/log/mysql/mysql-bin.000001
```

Audit logs, particularly when stored in JSON format, can be processed and analyzed using tools such as jq:

```
jq '.' /var/log/mysql/audit.log
```

Implementing a robust auditing and logging strategy ensures that you can monitor your MySQL database activities effectively, respond to security incidents promptly, and comply with relevant regulatory requirements. Consistent analysis of log data can reveal patterns indicating potential security threats or system inefficiencies, allowing for proactive database management and security enhancement.

9.9 Securing Data at Rest

Securing data at rest involves implementing measures to protect stored data from unauthorized access and breaches. This section discusses various methods and practices to ensure the security of MySQL data at rest, including encryption, file permissions, and secure storage practices.

Data Encryption

A primary method of securing data at rest is encryption. MySQL provides built-in support for data encryption through various mechanisms:

File-Per-Table Tablespace Encryption

File-per-table tablespace encryption is a transparent encryption mechanism applied to individual tables. This enhances security without significant performance degradation.

To enable file-per-table tablespace encryption, ensure that your MySQL server is configured with the appropriate encryption variables:

```
SET GLOBAL innodb_file_per_table = 1;
SET GLOBAL innodb_encrypt_tables = ON;
SET GLOBAL innodb_encrypt_log = ON;
```

After setting these variables, you can create encrypted tables by specifying the ENCRYPTION option in the CREATE TABLE statement:

```
CREATE TABLE secure_table (
    id INT AUTO_INCREMENT,
    data VARCHAR(255),
    PRIMARY KEY(id)
) ENGINE=InnoDB ENCRYPTION='Y';
```

Binary Log Encryption

Binary log files can contain sensitive data and, as such, should be encrypted. Enabling binary log encryption can be achieved by configuring the –log-bin and –binlog-encryption options in your my.cnf configuration file:

```
[mysqld]
log-bin
binlog-encryption=ON
```

Restart the MySQL server to apply these changes. This ensures that all binary logs are encrypted automatically.

Encryption Key Management

Effective key management is crucial for data encryption. MySQL Enterprise Edition provides centralized key management through keyring plugins, which integrate with key management services (KMS) such as AWS KMS, Azure Key Vault, and GCP KMS.

To configure and enable a keyring plugin, add the following options to your my.cnf file:

```
[mysqld]
early-plugin-load=keyring_file.so
keyring_file_data=/var/lib/mysql-keyring/keyring
```

Restart the server, and then verify that the keyring plugin is active:

```
SHOW PLUGINS;
```

For further configuration, refer to the MySQL documentation on integrating keyring plugins with your preferred KMS.

File Permissions and Ownership

Appropriate file permissions and ownership settings are vital to preventing unauthorized access to MySQL data files. Ensure the MySQL data directory and all critical files within it are owned and readable/writable only by the MySQL user.

For example, assuming your MySQL data directory is /var/lib/mysql and the MySQL user is mysql, verify and set the permissions using the following commands:

```
sudo chown -R mysql:mysql /var/lib/mysql
sudo chmod -R 700 /var/lib/mysql
```

These commands set the ownership of the data directory to the MySQL user and restrict permissions so that only the MySQL user can access the files.

Secure Storage Practices

Implementing secure storage practices involves using appropriate hardware and software solutions to protect data physically and logically. Consider the following practices:

- Use dedicated, encrypted storage devices to store critical MySQL data.

- Employ RAID configurations for redundancy and improved durability of data.
- Regularly back up encrypted data and securely store the backups.
- Isolate the storage from general-purpose network access, limiting access only to essential MySQL server instances.

Backup Encryption

Ensure that your MySQL backups are encrypted to prevent unauthorized access to backup data. For example, when using mysqldump for logical backups, compress and encrypt the output:

```
mysqldump -u user -p database | gzip | openssl enc -aes-256-cbc -out backup.sql.gz.enc
```

Restoring the encrypted backup requires decryption, which can be done as follows:

```
openssl enc -d -aes-256-cbc -in backup.sql.gz.enc | gunzip | mysql -u user -p database
```

These commands ensure your backups are encrypted during storage and transit, adding an additional layer of security.

By implementing these techniques and measures, you can significantly enhance the security of your MySQL data at rest, aligning with best practices and regulatory requirements.

9.10 Securing Data in Transit

Securing data in transit is essential to maintain the confidentiality and integrity of data as it moves between clients and the MySQL server. During transmission, data can be susceptible to interception and unauthorized access by malicious entities. To mitigate these risks, several mechanisms can be employed to ensure secure communication channels. The following section discusses the strategies and configurations required to safeguard data as it transits across networks.

Using Secure Socket Layer (SSL)/Transport Layer Security (TLS)

SSL/TLS protocols are fundamental for encrypting data in transit. They provide a secure communication channel by encrypting data before it is transmitted, ensuring that only the intended recipient can decrypt and read the data. To configure MySQL for SSL/TLS, follow these steps:

1. Generate SSL/TLS Certificates and Keys: You need a Certificate Authority (CA) certificate, server certificate, and client certificates. OpenSSL can be utilized to generate these certificates and keys.

```
# Generate CA certificate
openssl genpkey -algorithm RSA -out ca-key.pem
openssl req -new -key ca-key.pem -x509 -days 3650 -out ca-cert.pem

# Generate server key and certificate
openssl genpkey -algorithm RSA -out server-key.pem
openssl req -new -key server-key.pem -out server-req.pem
openssl x509 -req -in server-req.pem -days 3650 -CA ca-cert.pem -CAkey ca-key.
    pem -set_serial 01 -out server-cert.pem

# Generate client key and certificate
openssl genpkey -algorithm RSA -out client-key.pem
openssl req -new -key client-key.pem -out client-req.pem
openssl x509 -req -in client-req.pem -days 3650 -CA ca-cert.pem -CAkey ca-key.
    pem -set_serial 01 -out client-cert.pem
```

2. Configure MySQL Server: Update the MySQL configuration file (my.cnf) to include the paths of the generated certificates and keys.

```
[mysqld]
ssl-ca= /path/to/ca-cert.pem
ssl-cert= /path/to/server-cert.pem
ssl-key= /path/to/server-key.pem
```

3. Restart MySQL Server: Apply the changes by restarting the MySQL server.

```
sudo systemctl restart mysql
```

4. Require SSL/TLS for User Accounts: Ensure that specific user accounts require SSL/TLS for connections.

```
CREATE USER 'secure_user'@'%' IDENTIFIED BY 'password' REQUIRE SSL
    ;
GRANT ALL PRIVILEGES ON mydb.* TO 'secure_user'@'%';
FLUSH PRIVILEGES;
```

5. Connect Using SSL/TLS: When connecting to the MySQL server using a client, specify the required certificates and keys.

```
mysql --host=server_host --ssl-ca=/path/to/ca-cert.pem --ssl-cert=/path/to/
    client-cert.pem --ssl-key=/path/to/client-key.pem --user=secure_user --
    password=my_secure_password
```

Using Secure Connections with MySQL Workbench

MySQL Workbench is a powerful tool for managing MySQL databases, and it supports SSL/TLS connections. Follow these steps to establish a secure connection:

1. Open MySQL Workbench and navigate to the "Database" menu, then select "Manage Connections."
2. Create a new connection or edit an existing one. Set the connection method to "Standard (TCP/IP) over SSH."
3. In the SSL tab, enable SSL and specify the paths to the CA certificate, client certificate, and client key files.
4. Test the connection to ensure that it is secure.

Verifying SSL/TLS Connections

Once configured, it is crucial to verify that SSL/TLS is being used for connections. This can be done by executing the following query on the MySQL server:

```
SHOW STATUS LIKE 'Ssl_cipher';
```

The output should indicate the SSL cipher being used, confirming that the connection is encrypted.

Implementing Data Encryption through Application Layer

In addition to SSL/TLS, data encryption at the application layer can further enhance security. Encrypting sensitive data before storing it in the database provides an additional layer of protection. Popular encryption libraries such as OpenSSL, PyCrypto (Python), and Node.js's crypto module can be employed for this purpose. Here is an example using Python's PyCrypto library:

```
from Crypto.Cipher import AES
import base64

# Encryption function
def encrypt_data(key, raw_data):
    cipher = AES.new(key, AES.MODE_ECB)
    return base64.b64encode(cipher.encrypt(raw_data.rjust(32)))

# Decryption function
def decrypt_data(key, enc_data):
    cipher = AES.new(key, AES.MODE_ECB)
    return cipher.decrypt(base64.b64decode(enc_data)).strip()

# Usage
key = b'mysecureencryptionkey1234' # 16, 24, or 32 bytes key
raw_data = 'Sensitive data'
```

```
encrypted_data = encrypt_data(key, raw_data)
decrypted_data = decrypt_data(key, encrypted_data)

print(f'Encrypted: {encrypted_data}')
print(f'Decrypted: {decrypted_data}')
```

```
Encrypted: b'L2c1rmLaVoY9x5StzxiLKg=='
Decrypted: b'Sensitive data'
```

These techniques ensure the secure transit of data across networks, shielding it from unauthorized access and tampering. Proper implementation of SSL/TLS and application-layer encryption fortifies your MySQL database's security posture.

9.11 Best Practices for MySQL Security

MySQL database security is fundamental to protecting sensitive data, maintaining the integrity of the database, and ensuring compliance with regulatory requirements. Implementing best practices for MySQL security involves a series of strategies and configurations designed to safeguard the database environment from unauthorized access, data breaches, and other security threats. This section outlines these best practices comprehensively, building on the knowledge acquired in the previous sections.

First and foremost, it is crucial to keep MySQL up-to-date. Regularly upgrading MySQL to the latest version ensures that you benefit from security patches, bug fixes, and new features. Upgrades should be scheduled and tested in a development environment before deployment to avoid disruptions.

Secondly, remove or disable unnecessary features and services. The default installation of MySQL includes numerous features that may not be needed for your specific use case. Disable components like the MySQL Event Scheduler or unused storage engines. This reduces the attack surface of your MySQL server.

Network security is another critical component. MySQL servers should not be accessible from the internet. Instead, restrict access using network firewalls and by configuring MySQL to listen only on localhost or a private IP address. This limits exposure to potential external threats.

Implementing robust authentication mechanisms is paramount. Avoid using default user accounts or passwords and make sure all passwords are strong and complex. For instance, to create a secure user with a strong password, execute:

```
CREATE USER 'secure_user'@'localhost' IDENTIFIED BY 'ComplexPassw0rd!';
```

Configuring the MySQL server to use encrypted connections ensures data security during transmission. Enable SSL/TLS to encrypt the session between MySQL clients and servers. Here is an example of how to require SSL for a MySQL user:

```
CREATE USER 'ssl_user'@'localhost' IDENTIFIED BY 'another_secure_password'
    REQUIRE SSL;
```

Use role-based access control to manage user privileges effectively. Create roles for different types of users and assign appropriate privileges. For example, create a read-only role and grant it the necessary permissions:

```
CREATE ROLE 'read_only';
GRANT SELECT ON my_database.* TO 'read_only';
GRANT 'read_only' TO 'secure_user'@'localhost';
```

Regularly review and audit user privileges to ensure no excessive permissions are granted. Users should only have the minimum privileges necessary for their tasks. To check granted privileges, the following query can be useful:

```
SHOW GRANTS FOR 'secure_user'@'localhost';
\end{lstisting}

Enable and configure logging and audit logs to monitor database activities. The
    MySQL Enterprise Audit plugin can be used to track login attempts, executed
    queries, and changes made to the database schema. Example configuration to
    enable the audit log:

\begin{lstlisting}
INSTALL PLUGIN audit_log SONAME 'audit_log.so';
SET GLOBAL audit_log_policy = 'ALL';
```

Data should be encrypted at rest to protect sensitive information from unauthorized access. Use MySQL's InnoDB tablespace encryption or other disk-level encryption mechanisms to ensure data stored on disk is secure.

For backups, employ encryption and secure storage practices. Ensure that backup files are encrypted using strong encryption algorithms and stored in locations with restricted access. MySQL Enterprise Backup provides built-in support for backup encryption.

Implement comprehensive monitoring systems to continuously check for unusual database activity, performance issues, and potential security incidents. The MySQL Enterprise Monitor, along with other third-party tools, can provide real-time alerts and detailed insights into your database environment.

Regularly perform security assessments and penetration testing to identify and mitigate vulnerabilities in your MySQL setup. This proactive approach helps uncover potential weaknesses and ensures that your defensive measures are effective.

Lastly, maintain detailed documentation and incident response plans. Ensure that all administrative actions are documented and that there is a clear plan in place for responding to security incidents. This includes having contact information for relevant personnel and steps to follow in case of a data breach or other security event.

9.12 Monitoring and Responding to Security Incidents

Effective monitoring and responding to security incidents in MySQL databases is vital for maintaining data integrity and system availability. This section elucidates the methodologies for setting up monitoring systems, recognizing security breaches, and the procedures for reacting to potential threats.

To begin with, establish a comprehensive monitoring framework utilizing available MySQL tools and third-party solutions. The MySQL Enterprise Monitor offers extensive capabilities for identifying potential security issues. It provides real-time alerts for various critical events, such as unsuccessful login attempts and changes to privilege structures, enabling timely responses.

Setting Up MySQL Audit Plugin:

The MySQL audit plugin is instrumental for logging database activities. By capturing SQL queries, the plugin aids in identifying unauthorized actions and understanding their context. Installation and configuration of the audit plugin involve steps demonstrated below:

```
INSTALL PLUGIN audit_log SONAME 'audit_log.so';
SET GLOBAL audit_log_format = 'JSON';
SET GLOBAL audit_log_policy = 'ALL';
```

The plugin can be customized to log specific events by altering the audit_log_policy parameter. The available policies include ALL, NONE,

LOGINS, QUERIES, or a combination. For example, to log only login attempts, use:

```
SET GLOBAL audit_log_policy = 'LOGINS';
```

Recognizing Anomalies:

A pivotal aspect of monitoring is the ability to recognize anomalies. Indicators of compromise (IoCs) can include unexpected database shutdowns, spikes in query latency, or anomalies in user activity. Employing MySQL's performance_schema and sys schema views can help in detecting such anomalies. For instance, to identify unusual login patterns, the following query can be used:

```
SELECT
  user,
  host,
  count(*) as login_attempts
FROM
  mysql.general_log
WHERE
  command_type = 'Connect'
  AND event_time > (NOW() - INTERVAL 1 DAY)
GROUP BY
  user, host;
```

Responding to Security Incidents:

Promptly responding to security incidents is as crucial as detection. The response strategy entails the following key steps:

1. **Containment:** When a security breach is detected, immediate containment is necessary to prevent further damage. Disabling the suspected user's account and isolating the compromised server are typical actions.

```
REVOKE ALL PRIVILEGES, GRANT OPTION FROM 'suspicious_user'@'localhost';
FLUSH PRIVILEGES;
```

2. **Eradication:** After containment, the root cause must be identified and removed. This could involve patching vulnerabilities, updating user passwords, or removing malicious code.

3. **Recovery:** Post-eradication, restoring the database to its normal operating state is essential. This may involve database backups and verifying data integrity. The following script shows how to restore a MySQL database from a backup file:

```
mysql -u root -p < database_backup.sql
```

4. **Documentation and Reporting:** Documenting the incident, includ-

ing all actions taken, assists in refining security policies and preventive measures. It also ensures compliance with regulatory requirements.

5. **Continuous Monitoring:** Post-incident, ensuring enhanced monitoring is pivotal to prevent recurrence. This could involve stricter user access policies, regular audits, and employing automated threat detection tools.

Automating Defensive Measures:

Automated scripts and tools can aid in real-time threat detection and response. For instance, implementing a fail2ban-like mechanism to automatically block IP addresses after a number of failed login attempts. Below is a sample shell script to ban IPs from which multiple failed logins are detected:

```
#!/bin/bash
LOGFILE="/var/log/mysql/mysql-error.log"
BANFILE="/tmp/mysql-ban.log"
THRESHOLD=5

tail -n 100 $LOGFILE | grep 'Access denied' | awk '{print $(NF-1)}' | sort | uniq -c |
    while read count ip
do
  if [ $count -gt $THRESHOLD ]
  then
    echo "Banning IP $ip with $count failed attempts" >> $BANFILE
    iptables -A INPUT -s $ip -j DROP
  fi
done
```

Conclusion:

Monitoring and responding to security incidents require a rigorous approach combining proactive monitoring, swift containment, and thorough documentation. Employing MySQL's built-in tools, combined with external automation scripts, ensures a robust defense mechanism against potential security threats.

Chapter 10

Backup and Recovery

This chapter explains the strategies for backing up and recovering MySQL data. It covers the differences between logical and physical backups, using tools like MySQLdump and MySQL Enterprise Backup, and managing binary log backups. The chapter also discusses point-in-time recovery, configuring automatic backups, and securing backup data. It addresses restoring MySQL backups, planning for disaster recovery, testing backup and recovery procedures, and outlines best practices to ensure data durability and availability.

10.1 Introduction to Backup and Recovery

In database management, the concepts of backup and recovery are critical for ensuring the integrity, availability, and longevity of data. A backup is a copy of data from your database that can be used to restore the original in case of data loss. Recovery, on the other hand, refers to the process of restoring this data from backup following an incident that results in data corruption or loss.

Database systems are susceptible to a multitude of risks including hardware failures, software bugs, human errors, and malicious attacks. These risks necessitate robust backup and recovery strategies to safeguard data. Without such mechanisms, organizations could face substantial financial and operational losses. As such, backup and recovery are integral components of a comprehensive data management strategy, aimed at ensuring data resilience and continuity.

Data backups can be broadly categorized into logical and physical backups. Logical backups involve exporting the database objects, such as tables and schemas, in a human-readable format. Tools like MySQL-dump facilitate the creation of logical backups by generating SQL statements that can recreate the database structure and populate it with data. This type of backup is suitable for smaller databases or when fine-grained control over the backup content is required.

Physical backups, however, encompass copying the actual database files at the file system level. This type of backup is typically employed for larger databases and offers a more efficient means of copying data as it avoids the overhead of SQL statement generation and parsing. MySQL Enterprise Backup is an example of a tool that allows for the creation of physical backups. It copies the data directory, including MySQL's InnoDB tablespaces, log files, and other essential components.

An essential aspect of a robust backup strategy is the concept of incremental and differential backups. Incremental backups store only the data that has changed since the last backup, which can significantly reduce the volume of data to be copied and stored. Differential backups, meanwhile, capture all changes made since the last full backup, offering a balance between backup speed and restore time.

The backup process must be meticulously planned and executed to ensure data consistency and reliability. For instance, online or hot backups are created while the database is active and serving user requests. In contrast, offline or cold backups necessitate taking the database offline. MySQL supports hot backup mechanisms and tools, such as MySQL Enterprise Backup, which can quiesce the InnoDB storage engine, ensuring a consistent state without downtime.

Recovery procedures depend heavily on the nature of the backup. Logical backups, for instance, involve replaying the SQL statements contained within the backup files to reconstruct the database. Physical backups often require copying the backup files back to their original locations and, if necessary, applying the binary logs to bring the database to a specific point in time.

Point-in-Time Recovery (PITR) is a recovery technique employed to restore the database to a specific temporal point, often just prior to an incident. This task generally involves combining backups with binary log files. Binary logs contain a record of all changes made to the database, enabling the restoration of data to a precise state. Administrators can apply these logs starting from the last backup, thereby reconstructing an accurate database state up to the specified time.

In today's fast-paced environments, configuring automatic backups is paramount. Scheduled tasks using tools such as cron jobs or MySQL Scheduler can automate backup operations, minimizing human intervention and the potential for oversight. Automated backups ensure that data is periodically backed up without manual prompts, adhering to the defined backup policy.

Securing backup data is fundamental to preventing unauthorized access, data breaches, or inadvertent leaks. Encrypting backup files, utilizing secure storage locations such as offsite data centers or cloud storage, and employing stringent access controls are best practices for securing backups. Ensuring that backup data is protected with the same rigor applied to live databases mitigates the risk of exploitation.

Understanding the basics and intricacies of backup and recovery prepares administrators to implement robust strategies capable of preserving data integrity and ensuring data availability. These processes form the bedrock of disaster recovery planning, significantly contributing to the resilience and agility of database management systems.

10.2 Types of Backups: Logical vs Physical

Comprehensive data backup strategies are crucial for ensuring data integrity, durability, and availability. MySQL supports two primary types of backups: logical and physical. Understanding the distinctions between the two, including their respective methods, use cases, and operational impacts, is essential for designing an effective backup strategy.

Logical Backups:

Logical backups involve extracting and recording the logical, human-readable structure and data from the database. This is typically accomplished via SQL statements that recreate the database's tables and insert data into them. Commonly used tools for logical backups include mysqldump and mysqlpump.

- **Process:**
  - mysqldump: This utility generates a series of SQL statements that can be executed to recreate the original database.

The utility can target specific databases, tables, or the entire server instance. A typical command to create a logical backup with mysqldump is as follows:

```
mysqldump -u root -p --databases mydatabase > mydatabase_backup.
    sql
```

- mysqlpump: An advanced tool introduced in MySQL 5.7, mysqlpump supports faster dumping using parallel processing and additional functionalities like delayed inserts. An example command looks like:

```
mysqlpump --exclude-databases=mysql,information_schema,
    performance_schema,sys --databases mydatabase >
    mydatabase_pump_backup.sql
```

- **Advantages:**
  - Readability: The backup files generated are text files containing SQL statements, thus making them human-readable and easily editable.
  - Portability: Logical backups can be restored on different versions of MySQL, even across different operating systems, facilitating data migration or replication.
  - Versatility: Logical backups allow for partial backups (specific tables or databases) and selective restores.
- **Disadvantages:**
  - Slower Performance: Logical backups generally take longer to create and restore, especially for large datasets, due to the SQL parsing and execution overhead.
  - Resource Intensive: They can consume significant CPU and memory resources, impacting server performance, particularly on a live system.
  - Inconsistencies: Without the use of –single-transaction while dumping InnoDB tables, these backups might result in inconsistencies if the data is continuously changing during the backup process.

Physical Backups:

Physical backups, also known as raw or binary backups, involve copying the actual database files (e.g., data files, redo logs, and binary logs) directly from the filesystem. This can be done using tools like mysqlbackup (part of MySQL Enterprise Backup) or traditional file system copy commands.

- **Process:**
  - mysqlbackup: A robust enterprise tool that provides hot backups, incremental backups, and point-in-time recovery capabilities. Physical backups include data stored in InnoDB (.ibd) files, binary logs, and other structure files necessary for complete restoration. A typical command to create a physical backup with mysqlbackup might be:

    ```
    mysqlbackup --user=root --password --backup-dir=/path/to/backup/
        dir --with-timestamp backup
    ```

  - File System Tools: It is also possible to use standard file system copy tools such as cp, rsync, or tar to backup MySQL database directories. Care must be taken to ensure consistency, often requiring the database to be shut down or using filesystem snapshots.
- **Advantages:**
  - Faster Backup and Restore: Physical backups are typically faster since they involve simple file copying rather than SQL statement generation and parsing.
  - Consistency: When proper methods (e.g., the use of filesystem snapshots or dedicated backup tools) are employed, physical backups can ensure consistent snapshots of the database even during operations.
  - Lower Overhead: Physical backups tend to use fewer CPU resources during the backup process compared to logical backups.
- **Disadvantages:**
  - Lack of Portability: Physical backups are often tied to the specific version and build of MySQL and underlying operating system file structures. This can make them less portable across different platforms.
  - Storage Requirements: Physical backups usually require more storage space since they include the complete raw data, indexes, and storage structures.

- Restoration Complexity: Restoring from physical backups can be more complex, especially if incremental backups need to be applied or if the backup integrity is compromised.

By understanding the benefits and limitations of logical and physical backups, database administrators can develop a hybrid strategy that leverages the strengths of both approaches, ensuring comprehensive data protection and quick recovery options.

10.3 Using MySQLdump for Logical Backups

The mysqldump utility is a versatile and reliable tool for performing logical backups of MySQL databases. This utility creates a plaintext file containing SQL statements, which can subsequently be executed to recreate the database and its objects. Employing mysqldump provides several advantages, including ease of understanding, portability, and the ability to selectively back up specific tables or databases.

To initiate a basic backup using mysqldump, execute the following command in the terminal:

```
mysqldump -u [username] -p [database_name] > [backup_file].sql
```

In this command:

- -u [username] specifies the MySQL username.
- -p prompts for the MySQL password.
- [database_name] is the name of the database to be backed up.
- The > symbol redirects the output to [backup_file].sql, the file where the backup will be stored.

Consider the sample command to back up the database company:

```
mysqldump -u admin -p company > company_backup.sql
```

Upon execution, this command will prompt for the password of the admin user and then generate an SQL dump file named company_backup.sql.

To back up multiple databases simultaneously, utilize the –databases option:

```
mysqldump -u admin -p --databases db1 db2 db3 > multi_backup.sql
```

For scenarios requiring a full backup of all databases on the MySQL server, the –all-databases option is appropriate:

```
mysqldump -u admin -p --all-databases > full_backup.sql
```

The mysqldump utility provides various options to refine and control the backup process. Notable options include:

- –single-transaction: Ensures a consistent backup by dumping all tables in a single transaction. This is particularly useful for InnoDB tables, which support transactions.
- –routines: Includes stored procedures and functions in the dump file.
- –triggers: Includes triggers associated with the tables in the dump file.
- –events: Includes scheduled events in the dump file.
- –compress: Compresses the data to reduce the dump file size during the backup process.
- –default-character-set: Specifies the character set for the dump file.

An example command utilizing several of these options to back up the sales database is shown below:

```
mysqldump -u admin -p --single-transaction --routines --triggers --events sales >
    sales_backup.sql
```

This command ensures consistency of the data and includes all routines, triggers, and events related to the sales database.

The generated SQL dump file can be examined and edited using any text editor. It typically comprises CREATE DATABASE, CREATE TABLE, INSERT, and other SQL statements necessary to recreate the database structure and contents.

To restore the backup, use the mysql command-line tool. The restoration command can be as simple as:

```
mysql -u [username] -p [database_name] < [backup_file].sql
```

For example, to restore the company database from the company_-backup.sql file:

```
mysql -u admin -p company < company_backup.sql
```

If the database does not already exist, it should be created before restoring the dump:

```
mysql -u admin -p -e "CREATE DATABASE company;"
mysql -u admin -p company < company_backup.sql
```

Logical backups with mysqldump are complemented with advanced features such as selective table backup and partial backups. To back up specific tables from a database, list the tables after the database name:

```
mysqldump -u admin -p company employees orders > tables_backup.sql
```

This command backs up only the employees and orders tables from the company database.

Logging the backup execution can provide additional oversight and is accomplished by redirecting both standard output and error output to a log file:

```
mysqldump -u admin -p company > company_backup.sql 2> backup.log
```

Using mysqldump involves considering factors such as size, performance impact, and thorough testing to ensure restore capability.

10.4 Using MySQL Enterprise Backup

MySQL Enterprise Backup (MEB) offers a comprehensive solution for backing up and restoring MySQL databases. It supports both physical and logical backups, ensuring flexibility and reliability. This section delves into the essential features and usage of MEB, guiding users through its installation, configuration, and practical applications.

MySQL Enterprise Backup is a proprietary tool provided by Oracle that addresses several limitations of open-source backup solutions like MySQLdump. It supports hot backups, which means it can back up data without shutting down the database, ensuring continuous availability of services during the backup process.

Installation and Configuration

To install MySQL Enterprise Backup, follow the steps below:

Obtain the MySQL Enterprise Backup package from the MySQL Software Downloads page, ensuring compatibility with your OS and MySQL Server version.

```
wget https://dev.mysql.com/get/Downloads/MySQL-8.0/mysql-enterprise-backup
    -8.0.17-linux-glibc2.12-x86-64bit.tar.gz
```

Extract the downloaded tarball:

```
tar -zxvf mysql-enterprise-backup-8.0.17-linux-glibc2.12-x86-64bit.tar.gz
```

Navigate to the extracted directory and move the binaries to a directory in your system PATH, typically /usr/local/bin.

```
cd mysql-enterprise-backup-8.0.17-linux-glibc2.12-x86-64bit
sudo mv bin/* /usr/local/bin/
```

MySQL Enterprise Backup uses a configuration file, typically named *my.cnf*, to define parameters like the database host, port, and user credentials. Ensure the configuration file includes necessary connection parameters:

```
[client]
user = backup_user
password = backup_password
host = localhost
port = 3306
```

Creating Backups

MySQL Enterprise Backup supports full, incremental, and partial backups. A full backup captures the entire database at a specific point in time.

To create a full backup, execute the following command:

```
mysqlbackup --defaults-file=/etc/my.cnf --backup-dir=/path/to/backup_dir/backup-
    full --with-timestamp backup
```

This command specifies the *defaults-file* for database connection parameters, sets the *backup-dir* for storing the backup, and adds a timestamp to the backup directory.

Incremental backups capture changes since the last full or incremental backup, optimizing storage by saving only the delta changes. For an incremental backup, run:

```
mysqlbackup --defaults-file=/etc/my.cnf --incremental --incremental-base=dir:/path/to/
    backup_dir/backup-full --backup-dir=/path/to/backup_dir/incremental --with-
    timestamp backup
```

Here, the *–incremental-base* option points to the previous full backup.

Partial backups enable specific tables or tablespaces to be backed up, beneficial when only a subset of the database requires frequent backups.

To back up individual tables, execute:

```
mysqlbackup --defaults-file=/etc/my.cnf --backup-dir=/path/to/backup_dir/partial --
    with-timestamp backup --include-tables='db_name.table_name'
```

Restoring Backups

Restoration may involve full or incremental backups, depending on requirements.

To restore a full backup, initiate:

```
mysqlbackup --defaults-file=/etc/my.cnf --backup-image=/path/to/backup_dir/backup-
    full/backup-image.to --backup-dir=/path/to/restore_dir/ extract
```

Prepare the database for restore by stopping the running instance:

```
systemctl stop mysqld
```

Move the extracted data to the MySQL data directory:

```
cp -r /path/to/restore_dir/* /var/lib/mysql/
chown -R mysql:mysql /var/lib/mysql/
```

Once transferred, restart the MySQL service:

```
systemctl start mysqld
```

For incremental backups, the restoration involves merging the incremental data with the full backup. Extract the full backup as shown earlier, then apply the incremental backup:

```
mysqlbackup --defaults-file=/etc/my.cnf --incremental-backup-dir=/path/to/
    backup_dir/incremental --backup-dir=/path/to/restore_dir apply-incremental-
    backup
```

Continue with database preparation and restart as outlined for the full backup.

Encryption and Compression

To enhance security and save space, MEB supports encryption and compression. Include the *–encrypt* and *–compress* flags when creating a backup:

```
mysqlbackup --defaults-file=/etc/my.cnf --backup-dir=/path/to/backup_dir --with-
    timestamp --encrypt --encrypt-key-file=/path/to/keyfile backup
```

Combine encryption with compression:

```
mysqlbackup --defaults-file=/etc/my.cnf --backup-dir=/path/to/backup_dir --with-
    timestamp --encrypt --encrypt-key-file=/path/to/keyfile --compress backup
```

MySQL Enterprise Backup's powerful capabilities make it an invaluable tool for DBAs seeking to ensure data integrity and availability. From its support for hot backups and incremental backups to its advanced features like encryption and compression, MEB provides comprehensive solutions for data protection and disaster recovery.

10.5 Creating and Managing Binary Log Backups

Binary logging is a crucial component in MySQL that records all changes to the database, such as INSERT, UPDATE, and DELETE operations. This log is indispensable for data replication and point-in-time recovery. Understanding how to create and manage binary log backups ensures resilience by enabling data recovery up to the most recent transaction before a failure.

The MySQL binary log files contain a sequential record of database operations that modify data. These logs are pivotal for replication, as they enable a slave server to replicate the changes executed on the master server. The files, typically stored with filenames of the form hostname-bin._xxxxxx, where xxxxxx is a sequential number, allow tracking and recovery of database operations.

Creating binary log backups involves systematically copying these binary logs to a secure location to ensure data integrity and allow recovery from the point of restoration up to the latest recorded transaction.

Start by enabling the binary logging feature if it is not already activated. This is done by adding or modifying the following parameters in the my.cnf configuration file:

```
[mysqld]
log-bin=mysql-bin
server-id=1
```

The log-bin parameter specifies the base name for the binary log files, while server-id provides a unique identifier for the server in a replication environment.

To create a safe and consistent binary log backup, it is crucial to lock the database momentarily during the backup process. This can be achieved using the FLUSH TABLES WITH READ LOCK command which ensures that the tables are flushed and locked allowing a consistent state for the backup.

Execute the following sequence of MySQL commands to create a binary log backup:

```
-- Lock all tables to ensure a consistent backup state
FLUSH TABLES WITH READ LOCK;

-- Get the current binary log file name and position
SHOW MASTER STATUS;
```

After this, in a separate shell session, copy the binary log files to the backup destination using the cp or rsync command. For example:

```
cp mysql-bin.000001 /backup/directory/
```

Once the backup copy is complete, release the table locks:

```
UNLOCK TABLES;
```

Consistency across backups and regular management of binary logs are crucial. Regular deletion or archiving is necessary to prevent excessive accumulation, which might consume significant disk space. The PURGE BINARY LOGS command helps in maintaining this consistency. For instance:

```
PURGE BINARY LOGS TO 'mysql-bin.000010';
```

This command deletes all binary log files up to, but not including, mysql-bin.000010. It is also possible to purge logs older than a specific period using:

```
PURGE BINARY LOGS BEFORE '2023-10-10 00:00:00';
```

Managing binary logs involves a balance between retaining sufficient log history for recovery purposes and ensuring disk usage does not escalate. Configuring automatic backup and cleanup of binary logs can be managed using the MySQL configuration options expire_logs_days or by utilizing cron jobs.

For example, to automatically purge binary logs older than seven days, add the following to the my.cnf:

```
[mysqld]
expire_logs_days = 7
```

A typical cron job for daily backup of binary logs might look like this:

```
0 2 * * * cp /var/lib/mysql/mysql-bin.* /backup/directory/; /usr/bin/mysql -e "
    PURGE BINARY LOGS BEFORE DATE_SUB(NOW(), INTERVAL 7 DAY);"
```

This job runs at 2 AM daily, backing up and purging logs older than seven days. Automating this process ensures that binary log backups are consistently maintained without manual intervention.

Monitoring the binary log ensures that the backup and replication processes are operating correctly. Query the MySQL server to check the current binary log status:

```
SHOW BINARY LOGS;
```

For enhanced data protection, consider combining binary log backups with other backup strategies such as logical or physical backups. This layered approach enhances the ability to restore the system quickly and with minimal loss of data.

10.6 Point-in-Time Recovery

Point-in-time recovery (PITR) is a crucial strategy for restoring a database to a specific state at a particular point in time. It is often employed when data corruption or accidental data loss has occurred, and it necessitates recovery to a moment just before the undesirable event. MySQL's capability for PITR leverages binary logs to replay events that occurred after the last full backup.

The fundamental process of PITR involves restoring a full backup and subsequently applying incremental changes captured in the binary logs up to the specified point in time. This method demands a thorough understanding of managing backups and binary logs, ensuring they are appropriately configured to facilitate accurate recovery.

For executing a successful point-in-time recovery, adhere to the following steps detailed below, which include restoring a full backup, capturing the binary logs, and performing the replay of logs.

Step 1: Restore the Full Backup

The initial step in point-in-time recovery is to restore the database from the most recent full backup. This can be done using physical backup tools like MySQL Enterprise Backup or logical backups created using MySQLdump.

For a logical backup restored using MySQLdump:

```
mysql -u [username] -p [database_name] < [full_backup_file].sql
```

If using MySQL Enterprise Backup, follow the restoration procedure corresponding to that tool. The full backup restoration provides the baseline from which incremental changes will be replayed.

Step 2: Identify and Locate Binary Logs

Post-restoration, you need to identify the binary logs that include the transactions to be replayed from the point of the last full backup up to the desired recovery point. Begin by listing the available binary logs using the following command inside the MySQL shell:

```
SHOW BINARY LOGS;
```

The output will display the binary log files and their sizes, ensuring you know which logs contain the necessary transactions:

```
+------------------+-----------+
| Log_name         | File_size |
+------------------+-----------+
| mysql-bin.000001 |    123456 |
| mysql-bin.000002 |    789012 |
+------------------+-----------+
```

Identify the logs corresponding to the period between your full backup and the desired point of recovery.

Step 3: Apply Binary Logs

To apply the binary logs, use the mysqlbinlog utility. This utility reads the log files and converts logged transactions into SQL statements that can be executed on the database server.

For instance, if you need to replay logs from mysql-bin.000001 and you wish to recover the state up to a specific date and time, you can use:

```
mysqlbinlog --start-datetime="YYYY-MM-DD HH:MM:SS" mysql-bin.000001 | mysql -
    u [username] -p [database_name]
```

Alternatively, if you need to replay the logs up to a specific log position:

```
mysqlbinlog --stop-position=[position] mysql-bin.000001 | mysql -u [username] -p [
    database_name]
```

This approach ensures transactions are applied only up to the desired point, preventing the replay of any unwanted changes beyond that point.

Step 4: Advanced Options and Error Handling

When performing a point-in-time recovery, there may be a need to handle errors or advanced recovery scenarios. One such scenario involves skipping specific problematic transactions using the –skip-interval option.

For example, if a certain interval of transactions in mysql-bin.000001 caused errors or issues, skip them during the replay:

```
mysqlbinlog --start-position=[start] --stop-position=[stop] --database=[database_name]
    mysql-bin.000001 | mysql -u [username] -p
```

Step 5: Verification and Validation

After the recovery process, it is vital to verify the database state to ensure consistency and correctness. Check for any discrepancies or anomalies in the data, and confirm that the database is operational as expected.

Run consistency checks and perform validations on critical tables and datasets:

```
CHECK TABLE [table_name];
ANALYZE TABLE [table_name];
```

Ensure all essential application functions depending on the database are thoroughly tested to guarantee the integrity of the recovery process.

Integrating point-in-time recovery into routine backup and disaster recovery plans is fundamental for an organization's data strategy. Proper configuration and regular maintenance of binary logs, alongside systematic testing of the PITR process, are essential practices for ensuring data resilience and availability.

10.7 Configuring Automatic Backups

Leveraging the power of automation is crucial for ensuring that database backups are consistent, timely, and reliable. Configuring automatic backups in MySQL can significantly reduce the risk of data loss and minimize manual intervention. This section delves into scripting automated logical and physical backups, scheduling these backups using cron jobs, and verifying the integrity of the automated backup processes.

Automation of backups can be achieved using simple scripts executed at defined intervals. The mysqldump utility serves as an excellent tool for logical backups, while mysqlbackup from MySQL Enterprise Backup is effective for physical backups.

To begin with, consider a shell script for automating mysqldump backups:

```
#!/bin/bash
# Define MySQL connection details
USER='your_username'
PASSWORD='your_password'
DATABASE='your_database'
BACKUP_DIR='/path/to/backup/directory'
DATE=$(date +%Y%m%d%H%M%S)

# Create the backup directory if it doesn't exist
mkdir -p ${BACKUP_DIR}

# Perform the backup using mysqldump
mysqldump -u${USER} -p${PASSWORD} ${DATABASE} > ${BACKUP_DIR}/${
    DATABASE}_${DATE}.sql

# Optionally, compress the backup file to save space
gzip ${BACKUP_DIR}/${DATABASE}_${DATE}.sql

# Print confirmation message
echo "Backup of ${DATABASE} completed at ${DATE}"
```

This script establishes the necessary details for the MySQL connection, including username, password, and database name. The backup location is specified by BACKUP_DIR, and a timestamp is utilized to ensure backups are unique and easily traceable. The script then runs mysqldump to create a backup and optionally compresses the output file to conserve storage space.

For automated execution, scheduling this script using cron is necessary. Edit the crontab file using the command:

```
crontab -e
```

Add a cron job definition that schedules the script to run at a preferred frequency. For example, to run the backup script daily at 2 AM:

```
0 2 * * * /path/to/backup/script.sh
```

This cron job entry specifies that the script located at /path/to/backup/script.sh will be executed at 2:00 AM every day.

For physical backups using mysqlbackup, consider a script like the following:

```
#!/bin/bash
# Define MySQL connection details
USER='your_username'
PASSWORD='your_password'
BACKUP_DIR='/path/to/backup/directory'
DATE=$(date +%Y%m%d%H%M%S)

# Create the backup directory if it doesn't exist
mkdir -p ${BACKUP_DIR}

# Perform the physical backup using mysqlbackup
mysqlbackup --user=${USER} --password=${PASSWORD} --backup-dir=${
    BACKUP_DIR}/backup_${DATE} backup-and-apply-log

# Print confirmation message
echo "Physical backup completed at ${DATE}"
```

This script utilizes the mysqlbackup command to create a physical backup, storing the backup files in a timestamped directory within the specified BACKUP_DIR. As with the mysqldump script, this script can be scheduled using a similar cron job definition.

A crucial part of the automation process is ensuring the integrity and reliability of the backup data. Regularly testing the backup restoration process is essential. Schedule separate cron jobs for verification, where a subset of the backups is periodically restored to a test environment to confirm the backups are functional.

To schedule a verification script that runs weekly on Sundays at 3 AM:

```
0 3 * * 0 /path/to/verification/script.sh
```

Automation scripts should also handle error logging and notifications. Incorporate error-checking mechanisms within the scripts to capture any failures during the backup process and send alerts via email or other notification systems.

An example segment in the mysqldump script for error handling could be:

```
if [ $? -ne 0 ]; then
    echo "Backup failed at ${DATE}" | mail -s "MySQL Backup Failed"
        your_email@example.com
else
    echo "Backup of ${DATABASE} completed at ${DATE}"
fi
```

This code segment checks the exit status of the mysqldump command.

If the command fails (non-zero exit status), it sends an email notification indicating the failure. If successful, it prints the confirmation message.

Establishing automatic backups ensures data durability, minimizes manual errors, and keeps administrators informed of the backup status. Implementing these scripts and scheduling them effectively create a robust backup regimen for MySQL databases.

10.8 Storing and Securing Backups

Storing and securing backups is a crucial aspect of ensuring data integrity and availability in MySQL database management. Proper storage and secure handling of backup files can prevent data loss due to corruption, unauthorized access, or physical damage. This section delves into strategies for effective storage and security measures for MySQL backups.

1. Backup Storage Locations

The choice of backup storage locations is pivotal. Storing backups locally on the same server as the database may offer convenience, but it poses risks. Any hardware failure or catastrophic event affecting the server can result in the loss of both the primary data and the backups. Therefore, consider the following best practices for selecting backup storage locations:

- **Offsite Storage:** Store backups at a different physical location from the database server. This can be achieved through external data centers or cloud storage solutions.
- **Remote Servers:** Utilize remote servers dedicated to backup storage; ensuring redundancy across different physical infrastructures.
- **Network-Attached Storage (NAS):** Use NAS devices, which can be situated geographically apart from the primary server, to store backups.
- **Cloud Backup Services:** Employ cloud backup services, such as Amazon S3, Google Cloud Storage, or Microsoft Azure, which provide scalable and resilient storage options.

2. Redundancy and Replication

Implementing redundancy and replication in backup storage ensures that data remains accessible even if one copy of the backup is lost or corrupted. Consider these methods to enhance redundancy:

- **Multiple Copies:** Maintain multiple copies of backups in different locations.
- **Geographical Distribution:** Distribute copies across various regions to protect against regional disasters.
- **Versioning:** Keep multiple versions of backups to guard against corruption or data integrity issues.

For databases of significant size or critical importance, combining local and remote storage solutions can offer a balanced approach to performance and security.

3. Encryption

Encryption is vital to securing backups, especially when transmitting over networks or storing in third-party locations. Encrypting backups ensures that data cannot be easily accessed by unauthorized individuals. Implement encryption with the following methods:

- **At Rest:** Apply encryption to backups stored on disk using tools or scripts that support AES (Advanced Encryption Standard) encryption.
- **In Transit:** Secure backups during transmission over networks using encryption protocols such as SSL/TLS.
- **Database-Level Encryption:** Utilize MySQL's built-in encryption features if available.

Consider using tools like openssl to encrypt backup files. For example:

```
openssl aes-256-cbc -in backup.sql -out backup.sql.enc
```

To decrypt the file:

```
openssl aes-256-cbc -d -in backup.sql.enc -out backup.sql
```

4. Access Control

Restrict access to backups to minimize the risk of unauthorized access. Use principle of least privilege to manage user access, ensuring that only necessary personnel have permissions related to backup handling. Apply the following practices for access control:

- **Restricted Permissions:** Limit access permissions on the filesystem level using ACLs (Access Control Lists) and directory permissions.
- **Audit Logs:** Implement audit logs to monitor and record access to backup files.
- **Role-Based Access Control (RBAC):** Define roles and permissions within the backup management systems to control who can read, write, or delete backups.

5. Backup Rotation and Retention Policies

Establish clear rotation and retention policies to manage the lifecycle of backup files. Properly defining these policies helps in maintaining a balance between storage cost and data availability:

- **Backup Rotation:** Regularly cycle through backups, ensuring that older backups are appropriately archived or discarded based on retention policies.
- **Retention Periods:** Define retention periods according to organizational needs and compliance requirements, ensuring that backups are kept long enough to provide recovery options.
- **Automated Cleanup:** Automate the cleanup of old backups to manage storage efficiently, using scripts or backup management tools.

A practical example of implementing a simple rotation policy in a Unix-based system using a shell script might look like this:

```
#!/bin/bash
BACKUP_DIR=/path/to/backup
RETENTION_DAYS=30

# Remove backups older than the retention period
find $BACKUP_DIR -type f -mtime +$RETENTION_DAYS -exec rm -f {} \;

# Create a new backup
mysqldump -u user -p password --all-databases > $BACKUP_DIR/backup_$(date +%
    F).sql
```

6. Compression

Compressing backup files saves storage space and can also accelerate the transmission of backups to remote locations. Use compression tools that integrate well with MySQL backups, such as gzip or bzip2. Commands to compress backups might look like:

```
# Compressing using gzip
mysqldump -u user -p password --all-databases | gzip > backup.sql.gz

# Compressing using bzip2
mysqldump -u user -p password --all-databases | bzip2 > backup.sql.bz2
```

These compressions can be subsequently decompressed with:

```
# Decompressing using gzip
gunzip backup.sql.gz

# Decompressing using bzip2
bunzip2 backup.sql.bz2
```

Combining multiple strategies for storing and securing backups is recommended to ensure comprehensive protection. By adhering to structured storage protocols and robust security measures, the resilience of MySQL databases against data loss can be profoundly enhanced.

10.9 Restoring MySQL Backups

Restoring MySQL backups is a critical aspect of maintaining database integrity and ensuring data availability. This section focuses on different methods and tools for restoring MySQL backups depending on the type of backup used: logical, physical, or binary log backups.

Restoring a logical backup created with mysqldump involves a straightforward process. The mysql client is often utilized for importing the data from a dumped file. Here is a step-by-step approach to restoring a logical backup:

1. First, ensure the target database exists. If it does not, create the database:

```
CREATE DATABASE target_database;
```

2. Next, import the dump file into the database:

```
mysql -u root -p target_database < backup.sql
```

This command connects to the MySQL server using the root user and restores the contents of backup.sql into target_database.

The mysql command processes the SQL statements in the dump file, recreating tables and populating them with data. Errors during this process should be corrected by reviewing the backup.sql file and ensuring it is compatible with the target database schema and MySQL version.

Restoring from a physical backup, such as one created by MySQL Enterprise Backup (mysqlbackup), typically involves different steps. Physical backups include data files, configuration files, and the necessary binary log files. Here is an example process:

1. Stop the MySQL server:

```
sudo systemctl stop mysql
```

2. Ensure the data directory is prepared for the restoration. This might involve deleting the current contents of the data directory:

```
sudo rm -rf /var/lib/mysql/*
```

3. Download and extract the backup files to the MySQL data directory:

```
sudo mysqlbackup --backup-dir=/backup/ --datadir=/var/lib/mysql/ --apply
    -log
```

4. Restart the MySQL server:

```
sudo systemctl start mysql
```

Using binary log backups allows you to perform point-in-time recovery. Suppose a logical or physical backup has been restored, but you need the database to reflect the state it was in at a specific moment. You can replay binary logs from the point of the backup until the desired point in time.

1. Identify the binary log files and positions. This information is typically obtained from the backup file that contains a snapshot of the binary log position.

2. Use the mysqlbinlog utility to apply these log files. Here is an example:

```
mysqlbinlog binlog.000001 binlog.000002 | mysql -u root -p
```

This command processes the binary log files binlog.000001 and binlog.000002, applying them to the MySQL server to replay transactions.

It is essential to understand that different restoration tools and methodologies require rigorous testing to ensure they perform as expected in various scenarios. Testing should be part of routine database administration practices.

For complex recovery situations such as those involving corrupted data files or incomplete backups, tools like innochecksum, mysqlcheck, and myisamchk may be required to diagnose and repair database inconsistencies:

```
# Check a MyISAM table for errors
myisamchk -c /var/lib/mysql/data/table.MYI

# Repair a MyISAM table
myisamchk -r /var/lib/mysql/data/table.MYI

# Check and repair InnoDB tables
mysqlcheck -u root -p --auto-repair --check --optimize database_name
```

While logical backups offer ease of restoration, they require more time for larger datasets. Physical backups provide a faster restore time but typically demand more storage space. Binary logs enable point-in-time recovery but require precise management and alignment with full backups.

By aligning the chosen backup and recovery strategy with the organizational needs, data latency tolerance, and the desired recovery time objective (RTO), database administrators can ensure data durability and business continuity. A comprehensive disaster recovery plan incorporating periodic testing of restore procedures will help anticipate issues and streamline the recovery process when needed.

10.10 Disaster Recovery Planning

Disaster recovery planning (DRP) is a critical component of maintaining MySQL database systems. It involves the strategic preparation for responding to catastrophic events that may interrupt normal operations. Effective DRP ensures minimal data loss and downtime, enhancing the overall resilience of database infrastructures. The following principles, methodologies, and tools detail the essential aspects of disaster recovery planning.

Risk Assessment and Business Impact Analysis (BIA): Risk assessment identifies potential threats to the database system, including hardware failures, software bugs, natural disasters, and cyber-attacks. Business impact analysis evaluates the consequences of these disruptions. By quantifying the impact, organizations can prioritize recovery efforts and allocate resources effectively.

Recovery Objectives: Two key objectives in DRP are the Recovery Point Objective (RPO) and Recovery Time Objective (RTO).

- **RPO** defines the maximum acceptable age of data that can be lost in the event of a failure. For example, an RPO of four hours means that backups must be taken at least every four hours. - **RTO** specifies the maximum acceptable duration to restore the database to operational status. For instance, an RTO of two hours indicates that the database needs to be functional within two hours of a failure.

Backup Strategies: A robust backup strategy is foundational for disaster recovery. Implementing a combination of full, incremental, and differential backups ensures data security and quick restoration.

- *Full Backups*: A complete snapshot of the database. - *Incremental Backups*: Only changes since the last backup. - *Differential Backups*: Changes since the last full backup.

Automating backup processes helps in maintaining consistency and reduces the risk of human error. Schedule backups during off-peak hours to minimize performance impact.

Redundancy and Replication: Redundancy involves having multiple copies of data. Replication can be synchronous or asynchronous. - *Synchronous Replication*: Ensures data consistency but may affect performance. - *Asynchronous Replication*: Better performance but risks data loss.

MySQL supports replication configurations such as master-slave and multi-source replication. The choice of replication setup depends on factors such as RPO, RTO, and network latency.

Failover Mechanisms: Failover is the process of switching to a standby database server upon failure of the primary server. Automated failover mechanisms enable seamless transition without significant downtime. MySQL Group Replication and MySQL InnoDB Cluster are tools that facilitate automatic failover and high availability.

Network Considerations: Reliable network infrastructure is vital for disaster recovery, especially for remote data centers and cloud environments. Network redundancy and bandwidth capabilities should align with the RPO and RTO requirements.

Testing and Validation: Regular testing of disaster recovery plans ensures their effectiveness. Simulating different disaster scenarios helps identify weaknesses in the plan. Documenting and refining procedures based on test outcomes enhances preparedness.

```
#!/bin/bash
CURRENT_DATE=$(date +%Y-%m-%d)
BACKUP_DIR="/backups/$CURRENT_DATE"
MYSQLDUMP=/usr/bin/mysqldump
MYSQL_USER="backup_user"
MYSQL_PASSWORD="password"
MYSQL_HOST="localhost"
DATABASE="mydatabase"

mkdir -p ${BACKUP_DIR}

${MYSQLDUMP} --user=${MYSQL_USER} --password=${MYSQL_PASSWORD} --
    host=${MYSQL_HOST} ${DATABASE} > ${BACKUP_DIR}/${DATABASE}.
    sql

# Verify the backup
if [ $? -eq 0 ]; then
  echo "Backup successful"
else
  echo "Backup failed"
fi
```

The output from the above script, when executed successfully, will be:

```
Backup successful
```

In case of failure:

```
Backup failed
```

Data Center and Cloud Strategies: Hybrid strategies combining on-premises data centers and cloud-based solutions provide enhanced flexibility and reliability. Cloud services such as AWS, Google Cloud, and Azure offer integrated backup and recovery options. Offsite backups safeguard against local disasters, while cloud-based recovery can expedite the restoration process.

Documentation and Training: Comprehensive documentation of all DRP procedures ensures clarity and consistency. Training personnel on disaster recovery processes fosters a culture of preparedness. Mock drills and regular briefings can enhance team readiness.

Integrating these elements into a cohesive disaster recovery plan helps safeguard MySQL databases against unforeseen events. Prioritizing resilience, redundancy, and proactive testing will contribute to robust continuity and data integrity.

10.11 Testing Backup and Recovery Procedures

Effective backup and recovery procedures are critical to ensure the data durability and availability of MySQL databases. Testing these procedures regularly verifies that backups are valid, complete, and restorable within acceptable time frames. This section details the steps and best practices for testing backup and recovery methodologies.

To begin testing, one must have an existing backup that adheres to the organization's backup policy. The backup can be either logical or physical. For logical backups, tools such as mysqldump are typically employed, whereas physical backups may involve tools like mysqlbackup from MySQL Enterprise Backup.

Step-by-Step Guide to Testing Backups

1. Retrieve the Backup: To test a backup, first retrieve a copy of the backup file from your storage location. Ensure that this process does not alter the original backup file.

```
# Copy backup file from storage to test environment
cp /path/to/backup/mysql-backup.sql /test-environment/mysql-backup.sql
```

2. Prepare a Test Environment: Utilize a separate testing environment reflective of your production environment. This avoids any disruptions to the actual operational database. Ensure the MySQL server in the test environment is configured similarly to the production server.

```
# Start MySQL server in test environment
systemctl start mysqld
```

3. Restore the Backup: Use the appropriate tools to restore the backup. For logical backups created using mysqldump, the mysql command-line tool is typically used.

```
# Restore the logical backup
mysql -u root -p < /test-environment/mysql-backup.sql
```

For physical backups taken with MySQL Enterprise Backup, the mysqlbackup tool will be used differently.

```
# Restore the physical backup
mysqlbackup --backup-dir=/backup-folder copy-back
```

Validate that no errors occur during the restore process. Log files should be closely examined for any discrepancies or warnings.

4. Verify Data Integrity: Once the backup is restored, perform a series of checks to verify data integrity. Compare data statistics, checksum values, and other consistency checks between the restored database and the production data.

```
-- Example SQL query to get row count
SELECT COUNT(*) FROM my_table;

-- Example command to compare checksums if available
mysqlcheck --checksum my_database
```

5. Functional Tests: Execute a batch of predefined functional tests to ensure that the restored database operates correctly. This includes running queries, transactions, and stored procedures that the application typically executes.

```
# Sample batch script running crucial application queries
./run-functional-tests.sh
```

Automating Backup and Recovery Tests

Automating the backup and recovery procedure tests improves efficiency and ensures regularity in testing. Below is an example of a shell script to automate the testing for logical backups:

```
#!/bin/bash

# Script to automate backup and recovery testing

BACKUP_FILE="/path/to/backup/mysql-backup.sql"
TEST_ENV_DIR="/test-environment"
MYSQL_USER="root"
MYSQL_PASS="your_password"

# Copy the backup file to the test environment
echo "Copying backup file to test environment..."
cp $BACKUP_FILE $TEST_ENV_DIR

# Start MySQL server in test environment
echo "Starting MySQL server..."
systemctl start mysqld

# Restoring the backup
echo "Restoring the backup..."
mysql -u $MYSQL_USER -p$MYSQL_PASS < $TEST_ENV_DIR/mysql-backup.sql
```

```
# Running data integrity checks
echo "Running data integrity checks..."
mysql -u $MYSQL_USER -p$MYSQL_PASS -e "SELECT COUNT(*) FROM
      my_database.my_table;"

# Running functional tests
echo "Running functional tests..."
./run-functional-tests.sh
```

By incorporating logging mechanisms, notifications, and error checking routines, the script can be extended to provide more functionality and resilience.

Validation and Documentation

After running tests, the results should be thoroughly reviewed and documented. This documentation must detail the tests performed, the observed outcomes, any errors encountered, and the corrective actions taken.

Documentation serves several purposes:

- Provides a reference point for evaluating backup and recovery reliability.
- Aids in identifying recurring issues or patterns.
- Offers a historical log for audit purposes.

Regularly scheduled testing, coupled with thorough documentation, ensures that your MySQL backup and recovery procedures remain effective and reliable under various conditions. Authentication of the testing procedures also builds confidence in handling real-world disaster recovery scenarios.

10.12 Best Practices for Backup and Recovery

Effective backup and recovery strategies are essential to ensure data integrity and availability in MySQL. This section outlines best practices that combine configuration, operations, and planning to maintain a robust data protection regime.

Regularly Scheduled Backups: Regularly scheduled backups reduce the risk of data loss. Daily, weekly, and monthly schedules can be established using *cron* jobs on Unix-like systems or *Task Scheduler* on Windows. Automating backups eliminates dependency on manual interventions, ensuring consistency.

```
0 2 * * * /usr/bin/mysqldump -u root -pYourPassword mydatabase > /backups/
    mydatabase-$(date +\%F).sql
```

Regular backup testing is essential. Ensure that backups are consistently verified for integrity and completeness. Additionally, periodically perform test restorations to verify the backup and recovery process. These tests confirm that backups are valid and protocols are effective.

Retention Policies: Implement retention policies that define the duration for which backups are stored. Common practice involves retaining daily backups for a week, weekly backups for a month, and monthly backups for a year. A proper retention policy ensures efficient use of storage space without compromising the availability of historical data for recovery.

```
0 3 * * * find /backups -type f -name '*.sql' -mtime +30 -exec rm {} \;
```

Encryption and Security: Backup data must be encrypted to protect against unauthorized access. Utilize **OpenSSL** or other encryption tools to encrypt backup files. Secure transmission of backups using protocols such as **SFTP** or **HTTPS** ensures data safety during transfer.

```
openssl enc -aes-256-cbc -salt -in mydatabase.sql -out mydatabase.sql.enc -k
    MySecretPassword
```

Limit access to backup files and scripts to authorized personnel only. Implement strict access controls and regularly review privileges to minimize the risk of data breaches.

Geographical Redundancy: Store copies of backups in geographically diverse locations. This practice ensures data availability even if one site is compromised due to natural disasters or other catastrophic events. Cloud storage options like Amazon S3, Google Cloud Storage, or Microsoft Azure provide scalable and reliable solutions for offsite backups.

Consistent Backup Processes: Utilize consistent backup methods to avoid discrepancies. Programmatic tools should use identical procedures for daily operations, maintaining uniformity. Documentation of backup scripts and schedules in a centralized repository helps ensure adherence and facilitates troubleshooting.

Point-in-Time Recovery (PITR): Implementing point-in-time recovery capabilities requires configuring and managing binary logs. Proper management of binary logs enables recovery of data to an exact moment, reducing potential data loss due to system failures.

Monitoring and Alerts: Set up monitoring tools to track backup processes and storage utilization. Integrate alerts for backup failures, storage thresholds, and other critical events. Monitoring solutions such as Nagios, and Prometheus can provide real-time insights and ensure timely responses to issues.

```
# Nagios command to check backup status
define command{
    command_name check_backup_status
    command_line /usr/local/nagios/libexec/check_file_exists.sh /backups/
        mydatabase-$(date +\%F).sql
}
# Service definition
define service{
    use generic-service
    host_name localhost
    service_description MySQL Backup
    check_command check_backup_status
}
```

Documentation and Training: Thorough documentation of backup and recovery procedures helps streamline operations. Training DBA teams to understand and execute these procedures is vital. Regularly updated documentation ensures all team members are aligned with the current processes and tools.

Document details on:

- Backup schedules and retention policies
- Software and scripts used in backup processes
- Encryption and security measures
- Recovery procedures including test plans
- Contact information for support and escalation

Compliance and Auditing: Ensure backup processes align with relevant regulatory requirements, such as GDPR, HIPAA, or industry standards. Conduct periodic audits to verify adherence and update processes as necessary to remain compliant.

Implementing these practices will lead to reliable data protection, minimizing risks associated with data loss and ensuring quick resumption of operations post-recovery.

Made in the USA
Monee, IL
14 September 2026

63117178R00184